T0375517

Japanese
Management
Accounting Today

Monden Institute of Management: Japanese Management and International Studies (ISSN: 1793-2874)

Editor-in-Chief: Yasuhiro Monden *(Mejiro University, Japan)*

Published

Vol. 1 Value-Based Management of the Rising Sun
edited by Yasuhiro Monden, Kanji Miyamoto, Kazuki Hamada, Gunyung Lee & Takayuki Asada

Vol. 2 Japanese Management Accounting Today
edited by Yasuhiro Monden, Masanobu Kosuga, Yoshiyuki Nagasaka, Shufuku Hiraoka & Noriko Hoshi

Monden Institute of Management
Japanese Management and International Studies – Vol. 2

Japanese Management Accounting Today

editors

Yasuhiro Monden
Mejiro University, Japan

Masanobu Kosuga
Kwansei Gakuin University, Japan

Yoshiyuki Nagasaka
Konan University, Japan

Shufuku Hiraoka
Soka University, Japan

Noriko Hoshi
Hakuoh University, Japan

 World Scientific

NEW JERSEY · LONDON · SINGAPORE · BEIJING · SHANGHAI · HONG KONG · TAIPEI · CHENNAI

Published by

World Scientific Publishing Co. Pte. Ltd.

5 Toh Tuck Link, Singapore 596224

USA office: 27 Warren Street, Suite 401-402, Hackensack, NJ 07601

UK office: 57 Shelton Street, Covent Garden, London WC2H 9HE

Library of Congress Cataloging-in-Publication Data
Japanese management accounting today / edited by Yasuhiro Monden ... [et al.].
    p. cm. -- (Monden Institute of Management : Japanese management and international
studies, ISSN 1793-2874 ; v. 2)
    Includes bibliographical references and index.
    ISBN-13 978-981-270-081-0 -- ISBN-10 981-270-081-1
    1. Managerial accounting--Japan. 2. Industrial management--Japan. 3. Corporations--
Japan--Accounting. I. Monden, Yasuhiro, 1940–   II. Monden Institute of Management
and Accounting.

HF5657.4.J373 2007
658.15'110952--dc22

                                                                                2007015313

British Library Cataloguing-in-Publication Data
A catalogue record for this book is available from the British Library.

Copyright © 2007 by World Scientific Publishing Co. Pte. Ltd.

All rights reserved. This book, or parts thereof, may not be reproduced in any form or by any means, electronic or mechanical, including photocopying, recording or any information storage and retrieval system now known or to be invented, without written permission from the Publisher.

For photocopying of material in this volume, please pay a copying fee through the Copyright Clearance Center, Inc., 222 Rosewood Drive, Danvers, MA 01923, USA. In this case permission to photocopy is not required from the publisher.

Typeset by Stallion Press
Email: enquiries@stallionpress.com

Printed in Singapore.

Monden Institute of Management

President: **Yasuhiro Monden**, Mejiro University, Japan
Vice President: **Kazuki Hamada**, Kwansei Gakuin University, Japan
Vice President: **Gunyung Lee**, Niigata University, Japan

Directors:
Henry Aigbedo, Oakland University, USA
Shufuku Hiraoka, Soka University, Japan
Mahfuzul Hoque, University of Dhaka, Bangladesh
Noriko Hoshi, Hakuoh University, Japan
Tomonori Inooka, Kokushikan University, Japan
Chao Hsiung Lee, National Chung Cheng University, Taiwan
Yoshiyuki Nagasaka, Konan University, Japan

The Mission of the Institute and Editorial Information

For the purpose of making a contribution to the business and academic communities, Monden Institute of Management is committed to publishing the book series coherently entitled *Japanese Management and International Studies*, a kind of book-length journal with a referee system.

Focusing on Japan and Japan-related issues, the series is designed to inform the world about research outcomes of the new "Japanese-style management system" developed in Japan. It includes the Japanese version of management systems developed abroad. In addition, it publishes research by overseas scholars and concerning overseas systems that constitute significant points of comparison with the Japanese system.

Research topics included in this series are management of organization in a broad sense (including the business group) and the accounting that supports the organization. More specifically, topics include business strategy, organizational restructuring, corporate finance, M&A, environmental management, business models, operations management, managerial accounting, financial accounting for organizational restructuring, manager performance evaluation, remuneration systems, and management of revenues and costs. The research approach is interdisciplinary, which includes case studies, theoretical studies, normative studies, and empirical studies.

Each volume contains the series title and a book title which reflects the volume's special theme.

Our institute's board of directors has established an editorial board of international standing. In each volume, guest editors who are experts on the volume's special theme will serve as the volume editors.

Editorial Board of
Japanese Management and International Studies

Editor-in Chief

Yasuhiro Monden, Mejiro University, Japan

Managing Editors

Henry Aigbedo, Oakland University, USA
Kazuki Hamada, Kwansei Gakuin University, Japan
Shufuku Hiraoka, Soka University, Japan
Mahfuzul Hoque, University of Dhaka, Bangladesh
Noriko Hoshi, Hakuoh University, Japan
Tomonori Inooka, Kokushikan University, Japan
Chao Hsiung Lee, National Chung Cheng University, Taiwan
Gunyung Lee, Niigata University, Japan
Yoshiyuki Nagasaka, Konan University, Japan

Editorial Advisory Board

Mohammad Aghdassi, Tarbiat Modarres University, Iran
Mahmuda Akter, University of Dhaka, Bangladesh
Takayuki Asada, Osaka University, Japan
Takahiro Fujimoto, University of Tokyo, Japan
Péter Horváth, University Stuttgart, Germany
Arnd Huchzermeier, WHU Koblenz, Germany
Christer Karlsson, Copenhagen Business School, Denmark
Masanobu Kosuga, Kwansei Gakuin University, Japan
Bruce Henry Lambert, Stockholm School of Entrepreneurship, Sweden
Rolf G. Larsson, Växjö University, Sweden
John Y. Lee, Pace University, USA

Jose Antonio Dominguez Machuca, University of Sevilla, Spain
Kenneth A. Merchant, University of Southern California, USA
Yoshiteru Minagawa, Nagoya Gakuin University, Japan
Kanji Miyamoto, Osaka Gakuin University, Japan
Tengku Akbar Tengku Abdullah, Universiti Kebangsaan Malaysia,
     Malaysia
Jimmy Y.T. Tsay, National Taiwan University, Taiwan
Susumu Ueno, Konan University, Japan
Eri Yokota, Keio University, Japan
Walid Zaramdini, UAE University, United Arab Emirates

Preface

Japanese companies have, in recent times, been greatly affected by market-oriented management and stockholder-oriented management concepts disseminated by US companies. Some view this phenomenon as alignment to global standard.

In Japan, however, in contrast to the US market-oriented transactions, organization-based transactions within a business group including *keiretsu* and alliances or partnership are still widely used. Further, contrary to the stockholder-oriented management, employee-based management together with shareholder-driven management is also still popular. Such organization-based transactions and employee-based management are well integrated with the American ways of thinking in contemporary Japanese management.

Thus this volume will investigate how organizational transactions within a business group or *keiretsu* or alliances are useful and how supply and demand are adjusted through business process management within the organization in a broad sense.

Additionally, the volume will also explore how Japanese management systems can motivate various stakeholders, including not only stockholders but also employees, top management, customers and transaction partners, etc., to willingly participate in organizational behavior. In particular, management accounting where top management effectively motivates employees to improve business performance seems to be generally sought after in Japan.

Therefore, integrating organization-based and employee-based management with market-based and stockholder-based management seems to be more balanced.

Investigating such a hybrid approach will be the characteristics of this volume, *Japanese Management Accounting Today*.

Let us now briefly consider how such intentions are specifically presented in each part of this volume.

Part 1: Strategy and Business Restructuring to Enhance Business Value

This part considers strategies, including M&A for business and organizational restructurings, that intend to enhance the stockholder's value. However, the main topic here will be to investigate how such M&A will be used to make organizational restructures in the consolidated business group and how it will affect the interests of top management and employees.

Part 2: Management Control Systems and Budgeting

This part especially emphasizes that the performance-based merit system is closely linked to the performance measurement system in the Japanese management control system, which encourages a change in the thinking of employees. The next topic is the global cash management system adopted by many Japanese multi-national companies. This system also influences a change in the thinking of managers regarding cash management.

Part 3: Cost Management

The first topic deals with opportunity costs, that can help motivate managers to examine new alternatives or combinations of scares resources which will not be specified under conditions of uncertainty. Next, target costing is discussed. If target costing is continuously used, product development knowledge called "information capital readiness" is accumulated. This is an intelligence asset or a human asset yielding a human capacity surplus for product development. The final topic is employees' activities for *kaizen* or continuous improvement. This is supported by *kaizen* costing which measures the efforts of *kaizen*. A new approach to measure *kaizen* activity will be proposed here.

Part 4: Management Accounting for Supply Chain and Shared Services

The first topic introduces the Japanese method of assigning various objectives to employees in a hierarchical organization in the supply chain. Next, a new concept to allocate joint profit of the whole supply chain is proposed. This is to motivate the manager of each company to be willing to participate in the chain. The risk reduction method in the supply chain in the following paper also has a similar aim. These issues deal with how to motivate stakeholders, also called transacting partners. Finally, various types of "shared service centers" in Japan are examined from the viewpoint of responsibility accounting, which identifies differences in the goals of each center. The manager's thinking will differ depending on whether the center is a profit center or a cost center.

Part 5: Process Management
The first topic deals with Japanese MBO (Management By Objectives), which has a vertical chain effect among objectives and is also a system that enhances the acceptance level of the employee affecting performance evaluation. The next topic considers case studies of the process management of Dell Computer that stresses customer satisfaction through a quick response by cross-functional process management, and of Toyota that promotes human collaboration through cross-functional projects. These are of course not an automatic market-based adjustment of supply and demand, but a quick adjustment of supply to the final customer order.

The editors are very grateful to Ms. Juliet Lee Ley Chin, the Social Sciences commissioning editor of World Scientific Publishing Company for her various invaluable efforts to make this volume a reality. Further, Ms. Chean Chian Cheong, the book editor, is also much appreciated for her handling of our manuscripts. Finally, the co-editors and authors of this volume will be amply rewarded if it contributes new ideas or knowledge to the literature on business management and managerial accounting, thereby being of some use to people around the world.

Editor-in-chief
Yasuhiro Monden
April 7, 2007

Contents

Part 3 COST MANAGEMENT

Part 4 MANAGEMENT ACCOUNTING FOR SUPPLY CHAIN AND SHARED SERVICES

Part 5 PROCESS MANAGEMENT

Part 1

Strategy and Business Restructuring to Enhance Business Value

How Japanese Legal and Accounting Rules Can Facilitate Business Group Restructuring

Yasuhiro Monden

Professor, Faculty of Business Administration
Mejiro University

Yasuto Monden

Director, Investment Banking Division
UBS Investment Bank

1 Introduction

During 1991–2004, Japan suffered from long-term economic depression. In order to overcome this problem Japan eagerly and quickly introduced legal rules and accounting standards to facilitate mergers and acquisitions (M&A). M&A in this paper implies *business combinations* in a broad sense; that is, the combination of a company or a business unit with another company or business unit such that a single reporting unit is formed.

This paper explores the kinds of legal and accounting rules that were introduced in Japan and how they facilitate M&A for Japanese corporate restructuring. Japanese characteristics of these institutional supports seem to be conducive to the *restructuring of a business group*, as group behavior is one of the strengths of Japanese corporations. Such a group restructuring scheme is examined in this paper.

The authors also wish to explain that there is a consistent logic or theory among Japanese corporate law, tax law, and accounting standards that can process various types of business combination and splitting.

Especially important is the effect of new corporate tax laws on organizational restructuring. To undertake M&A by considering the earnings per share affected by the depreciation of goodwill and tax payment is a managerial accounting way of thinking.

2　Corporate Law for M&A

In order to simplify business group restructuring, Japan has created various laws for "deregulation," benefiting the group reforms that began in 1997, as shown in Figure 1.

Stock swap is to establish a complete (fully owned) subsidiary company and is effective during business group restructuring between a parent company and a partially owned subsidiary company.

On the other hand, *stock transfer* is to establish a complete parent holding company, which will control various fully owned subsidiaries. This system is used to allow for the efficient management of a business group as well as industry comprehensive reforms that can even cover multiple consolidated business groups. A common governing company as a stock holding company can control many companies in the same business group as its subsidiaries.

Year*	Corporate law	Accounting standards	Tax laws
1997	Pure holding company		
1999	Stock swap and stock transfer	Revised consolidated financial statements	Tax law for stock swap and stock transfer
2001	Company splitting, purchase of treasury stock		Tax law for business organizational reforms
2002			Tax payment based on consolidated financial statements
2003			Revised tax law for business organizational reforms
2006	Comprehensive revision of corporate law: (a) various payment means of merger (b) simplified procedures of organizational reforms	Business combination accounting, and business splitting accounting	

* The year stands for the introductory or application beginning year.
Also note that there is other new introduction of laws for business restructurings such as the industry revitalization law, etc.
Source: Maekawa *et al.* (2005, p. 17).

Fig. 1　New laws for M&A

Company splitting is the procedure to separate a business out of a company and to make such split business a separate company. Japanese characteristics of this method can be seen in the following three applications:

(1) establishing a new joint venture company by separating a certain business from a few companies of the same industry;
(2) absorbing part of a business from company A into company B;
(3) splitting a business within a consolidated business group.

In the above three cases, the first two methods are called "formation of a jointly governed company." The third is called "a commonly governed transaction," though this may not be considered a kind of M&A. It is noteworthy that in all these cases, neither a transfer of governance right to the absorbing company in terms of the ownership of majority vote stocks nor any effective governance relationship is observed.

3 Japanese Accounting Standards for Business Combination and Splitting

There are four types of business combinations in Japan from the viewpoint of accounting procedures (see Figure 2). These are as follows:

(1) transaction under common governance;
(2) formation of a joint venture company;
(3) uniting of interests;
(4) acquisition.

The first two types are original classifications of combinations unique to Japan and do not exist in the international accounting standard. They are also identified in the Japanese tax law as cases that facilitate group business restructuring from the viewpoint of tax postponement.

3.1 *Concepts and identification of acquisition and uniting of interests*

First, let us review how acquisition and uniting of interests differ. Difference is determined by whether the transferred assets are governed by the shareholders of the assets succeeding company or not.

In other words, *acquisition or purchase* essentially is when the majority of voting rights in the after-combination company Y is owned by the group

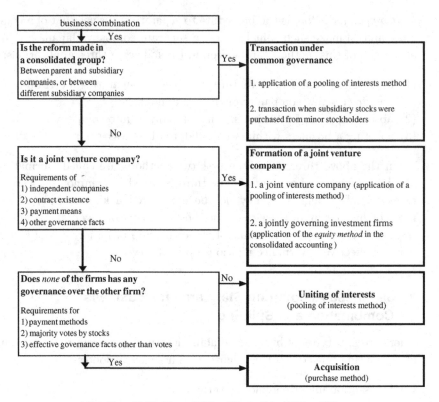

Adapted from FASF of Japan (2006, p. 33); also Saito (2006, p. 296).

Fig. 2   Four types of business combinations and their accounting processing

of *original* stockholders of the combining company Y, rather than the *original* stockholders group of the to-be combined company X. If the combination is an acquisition, then the top management of the acquiring company Y has *purchased* the assets transferred from the acquired company X. Thus company Y will pay for the transferred assets at *current price*. This is called the "purchase method," by which the transferred assets and liabilities from the to-be combined company X will be valued by the current price of stock Y or both the cash and current prices of the stock paid by the combining company Y.

On the other hand, *uniting of interests* implies a situation where both groups of the original stockholders and both companies participate in the merger, taking almost the same number of vote stocks in the after-combination company Y, and where neither participating company X or Y has any other effective governance power over the after-combination company. This is also called a *merger of equals*. In this situation, the assets transferred will be succeeded to the after-combination company at the *book value* of the assets of the companies before-combination. This accounting method is called the "pooling of interests method."

Identification of acquisition and uniting of interests is summarized in Figure 3.

Most combinations in the real world are acquisitions, and pooling of interests is rare. Note that requirement (3) in Figure 3 is similar to the governance criteria that determine the scope of subsidiary companies to be included in the consolidated financial statements. This requirement includes the following four facts:

(1) Directors or employees of either company participating in the combination have joined the board of directors of the after-combination company as its majority members.

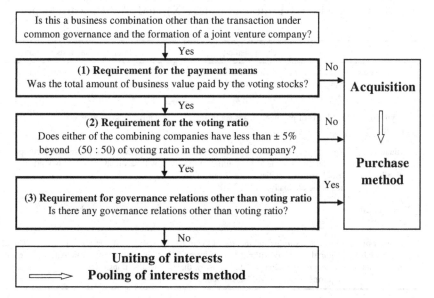

Adapted from Accounting Standards Board of Japan (2005), No. 10 Guideline, p. 112.

Fig. 3   Identification of acquisition and uniting of interests

(2) Based on the contract that controls important financial and operational policy-making, the group of the original stockholders of either company participating in the combination is in a stronger position.

(3) The sale of most of the businesses of either company participating in the combination within two years is scheduled.

(4) The exchange ratio of the stock paid for the transferred assets has deviated from the exchange ratio calculated by the current prices of the stocks of both companies, and a large premium has accrued.

The comparison between the purchase method and the pooling of interests method is summarized in Figure 4 below.

3.1.1 *Valuation of goodwill*

When the purchase method is applied, the goodwill that reflects the earning power of the to-be combined company will be measured by valuing the total amount of net assets or the "business value" of the to-be combined company. Suppose that A = the amount of comprehensive business value of the to-be combined company X measured by the current price of stocks or cash paid by the acquiring company Y (in other terms, the investment amount or the cost of purchase for the acquired business X), and B = the current price of

	Purchase method	Pooling of interests method
Difference in transactions	One of the combination-participating companies gains control right over the other participating company	All of the combination-participating companies continue to have their interests on equity
Types of payment means	All kinds of payment means applicable	Only stock applicable
Valuation of assets and liabilities	Current price is used only for the assets transferred from the to-be acquired company. (Book value is applied to the assets of the acquiring company)	The assets of all participating companies will be valuated by the book prices
Measurement of goodwill	Yes	No
Transfer of the earned surplus and income	The earned surplus and income of the to-be acquired company will not be transferred to the acquiring company. (Only those of the acquiring company will be succeeded)	The earned surplus and income of all of the combination participating companies will be transferred

Adapted from Maekawa *et al.* (2005, p. 93).

Fig. 4   Comparison of the purchase and the pooling of interests methods

the *identifiable* assets and liabilities acquired. Then,

$$\text{Goodwill} = A - B \text{ when } A \geq B, \text{ and}$$
$$\text{a negative goodwill} = B - A \text{ when } A < B.$$

Under the Japanese accounting standard for business combination the goodwill should be constantly amortized within 20 years as well as impairment written off. Also the Japanese tax law regulates constant depreciation for a fixed five years as of year 2006. These rules play a negative role in the amount of EPS (earnings per share), so shareholders may be inclined to say "No" to an M&A that would be accepted by Western stockholders. On the other hand, for the case of "negative" goodwill, the response of Japanese shareholders may be opposite, because depreciation of negative goodwill contributes to an increase of non-operating profit.

3.2   *Formation of a joint venture company*

Japanese business combination accounting specifies accounting rules for the joint venture company and the joint-controlling investment companies of the joint venture. A joint-controlling investment company looks similar to uniting of interests, but they are not identical.

Uniting of interests is the merger of equals, with the original merger participating companies ceasing to exist after the merger is complete. However, to establish a new joint venture, the joint-control companies split off some business. The original combination participating companies continue to exist and receive stocks of the new joint venture company as payment for their transferred business, which are recorded on the balance sheet as an investment account. Therefore the joint venture is an *associated* company of the joint-control investment firms, which satisfies all of the requirements given in Figure 5.

Regarding accounting procedures, the newly built joint venture will apply the pooling of interests method, while the joint-controlling investment firms will value the transferred net assets by book value and hold the investment account (stocks of the joint venture) as stated above.

Because the joint-control companies do not cease to exist, they may prepare consolidated financial statements that include the said joint venture. In this case they handle the "investment account" by the *equity method*.

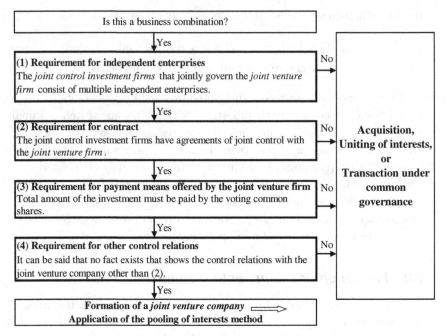

Adapted from Accounting Standards Board of Japan (2005), No. 10 Guideline, p. 113.

Fig. 5   Formation of the jointly controlling investment companies

3.3   *Transaction under common governance*

This combination is the merger between parent and subsidiary companies, or the merger between subsidiaries, etc.

All of the merger-participating companies are eventually controlled by the same company (i.e., a parent company as the majority shareholder) before and after the merger in question. As such, this combination is an internal transaction within a business group, and thus the transferred assets and liabilities are evaluated by the book value. However, in the consolidated financial statement of a parent company that is the common controller, the investment of the parent and the equity of subsidiary must be offset (Figure 6).

Another item included in the transaction under common governance is the transaction when the parent company additionally purchases the stocks of the subsidiary company from minor stockholders. This is an external transaction outside the group and is not a merger. The additionally acquired

	Variety of mergers	Classification of business combinations	Accounting procedures	
			Single company financial statements	Consolidated financial statements
Type 1	Merger between parent company and subsidiary company	Transaction under common control	Book value	Off setting
Type 2	Merger between parent company and the less than 100% owned subsidiary	Transaction under common control	Book value	Off setting
Type 2'	Among the merger type 2, the parent company offers its treasury stocks to the minor shareholders of the subsidiary	Transaction under common control (transaction with minor shareholders)	Valuation of the additionally acquired subsidiary stocks by the current price	Idem as above. Goodwill or negative goodwill on the balance sheet
Type 3	Merger between subsidiary companies	Transaction under common control	Book value	Off setting
Type 4	Merger between investment firm and associated firm	Acquisition, uniting of interests, or formation of a joint venture company	Methods based on each category of business combinations as left	

Adapted from FASF of Japan (2006, p. 43); also from Saito (2006, p. 305).

Fig. 6   Transaction under common governance

subsidiary stock of the parent company must be valued on a balance sheet at current price. On the consolidated balance sheet of the parent company, however, the goodwill is measured as the difference between the current price value of the additional stock acquired and the minority share equity recorded on the consolidated B/S before the said additional acquisition.

4   Japanese Corporate Tax Law Facilitating M&A

Ordinary M&A are processed by evaluating the transferred assets with their current prices so that the *asset transfer income* accrues in the asset transferring company whenever the current price is greater than the book value (except when there is a big deficit in the company). As a result, the asset transferring company will suffer from cash-outlay due to the tax subtraction from the asset transfer income. Thus, through this merger, organizational restructuring is discouraged.

Therefore the tax authority has introduced the *competent* taxation system that allows the asset transferring company to be exempt from immediate taxation of the asset transfer income of certain types of mergers and business splittings, etc. Such competent M&A can transfer assets by applying *book value.*

4.1   *Incompetent taxation system*

Business combinations that are *incompetent* to the taxation postponement system are summarized in Figure 7. There are two kinds of incomes:

First, taxation on "asset transfer income" is applied to the asset transferring merged company so long as the merger is, in effect, an "acquisition" made by the merging company. In this case, the transferred asset is actually sold to the stockholders of the merging company with the new stock paid at the current price. This is same as the *purchase* method in the accounting standard.

Second, there are two categories of the stockholder income of the merged company. The first type is "stock transfer income" gained by the stockholders who rendered their stock and other assets to the acquiring company. If only the stock is rendered as a stock swap, then the stock transfer income is not recognized. But if cash is also paid, then the stock transfer income is recognized, since this gain is realized by a cash reception. The second type is "delivery of the earned surplus regarded as dividend" (abbreviated as "regarded dividend") to the stockholder. This is due to the understanding that the earned surplus of the merged company will not be succeeded to the acquirer because the earned surplus is retained as a result of operating activities of company X and should be redeemed to company X stockholders.

Taxation objects	Procedures		
	Incompetent taxation system		Competent taxation system
Merged company	The asset transfer income will be recognized by the current price transfer		The book value transfer will not recognize the asset transfer income
Merging company (acquirer)	Earned surplus of the merged company will not be succeeded to the acquirer		Earned surplus of the merged company will be succeeded to the acquirer
	Delivery of the earned surplus regarded as dividend will be recognized		Delivery of the earned surplus regarded as dividend will not be recognized
Stockholders of merged company	(When cash is also offered)	(When only stock is offered)	(Only stock will be offered)
	Stock transfer income is recognized	Stock transfer income is not recognized	Stock transfer income will not be recognized

Adapted from TAC Corporation tax law section (2004, p. 13 and 24).

Fig. 7   Incompetent taxation system and competent taxation system

4.2   Competent taxation system

Business combinations that are *competent* to the taxation postponement system are summarized in Figure 7. Suppose that both of the merger participating companies X and Y send their directors of the board to the merging company Y as directors with effective control rights in company Y. In such case, the merged company X also continues to keep control of the financial and operation policy-making in the new merging company Y. The *pooling of interests method* is then applied, and thus none of the *assets transfer income*, *regarded dividend*, and *stock transfer income* are recognized.

It is important to note the effect of taxation postponement on organizational restructuring. To select the form of M&A by considering the earnings per share as affected by the tax payment system is a managerial accounting way of thinking.

4.2.1   Merger within a consolidated business group

The following cases are similar to *transactions of common governance* in the Japanese accounting standard for combinations:

(1) a merger between companies with 100% ownership;
(2) a merger between companies with more than 50%, but less than 100%, ownership.

These cases are seen in the mergers between parent and subsidiary companies or between the brother and sister subsidiary companies. The following two requirements must also be satisfied:

(a) More than 80% of employees of the merged company are succeeded to the merging company.
(b) The main business of the merged company is succeeded to the acquirer.

4.2.2   Merger as a joint venture

This is similar for a company of *joint control* and *uniting of interests* in the Japanese accounting standard of combinations. In order for a joint venture to be competent to the taxation postponement, the following four conditions must be satisfied. Although the terminology *uniting of interests* is not used in the Japanese corporate tax law, this type of business combination can be included as the uniting of interests, by considering the requirements below:

(1) **Requirement of mutually related businesses:** The merger participating companies have a mutually related business.
(2) **Requirement of similar scale of business or the joint participation in the new company by the existing directors:** The business
of the acquirer must not exceed more than five times the business transferred from the merged company.
(3) **Requirement of employee transfer** (the same as a merger within a
consolidated business group).
(4) **Requirement of main business succession** (the same as a merger
within a consolidated business group).
(5) **Requirement of successive holding of stocks:** The majority of
shareholders before the merger continue to be stockholders after the
merger.

4.3 *Numerical examples of mergers handled by the tax law*

Incompetent and competent taxation systems are examined using the
numerical example in Figure 8.

4.3.1 *Numerical example of an incompetent taxation system*

Based on the example given in Figure 8, first let us assume that *acquisition*
of assets of the merged company X is carried out by the merging company Y,
in consideration of the *smaller* number of voting common stocks given to the
current shareholders of company X and the *greater* number of stocks held
by the current stockholders of company Y. Therefore this is an incompetent
merger.

4.3.1.1 Handling of the merged company X

(Step 1) Company X sells its assets for a total amount of 32,000 at the
current price of the company Y stock. Thus,

(Dr.) company Y stock 32,000 / (Cr.) assets   24,000
                                   / **assets transfer income**   8,000

Tax is charged to this assets transfer income, which is added to the earned
surplus of company X (strictly speaking after deduction of tax):

(Dr.) assets transfer income 8,000 / (Cr.) **earned surplus**   8,000

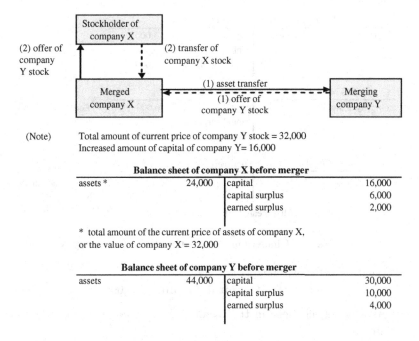

(Note)   Total amount of current price of company Y stock = 32,000
Increased amount of capital of company Y= 16,000

Balance sheet of company X before merger

assets *	24,000	capital	16,000
		capital surplus	6,000
		earned surplus	2,000

* total amount of the current price of assets of company X,
or the value of company X = 32,000

Balance sheet of company Y before merger

assets	44,000	capital	30,000
		capital surplus	10,000
		earned surplus	4,000

Fig. 8   Numerical example of a taxation system

(Step 2) The company Y stock is immediately given to company X share-holders in exchange for their company X stock, which disappears at the same time.

(Dr.) capital	16,000	/	(Cr.) company Y stock	32,000
capital surplus	6,000	/		
earned surplus	10,000	/		

(Step 3) Changes in the balance sheet of company X are shown in Figure 9.

4.3.1.2   Handling of merging company Y

Company Y receives the assets provided by company X stockholders at the current price of 32,000 and as a result increases its capital and capital surplus as follows:

The predetermined incremental amount of capital = 16,000

The incremental amount of capital surplus = 16,000

= incremental assets 32,000 – incremental capital 16,000

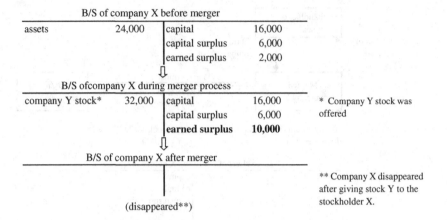

B/S of company X before merger

assets	24,000	capital	16,000
		capital surplus	6,000
		earned surplus	2,000

⇩

B/S ofcompany X during merger process

company Y stock*	32,000	capital	16,000
		capital surplus	6,000
		earned surplus	**10,000**

* Company Y stock was offered

⇩

B/S of company X after merger

(disappeared**)

** Company X disappeared after giving stock Y to the stockholder X.

Fig. 9   Changes in the balance sheet of company X

(Dr.)   assets   32,000 / (Cr.)   capital   16,000
                              / **capital surplus**   16,000

As a result, changes in the balance sheet of company Y are shown in Figure 10.

B/S of company Y during merger

assets	44,000	capital	30,000	
		capital surplus	10,000	original assets, etc.
		earned surplus	4,000	of company Y
assets	32,000	capital	16,000	purchase from company X
		capital surplus	16,000	by capital increase
sum	76,000	sum	76,000	

⇩

B/S of company Y after merger

assets	76,000	capital	46,000
		capital surplus	26,000
		earned surplus	4,000
sum	76,000	sum	76,000

Fig. 10   Changes in the balance sheet of company Y

4.3.1.3   Handling of company X stockholders

(1) Regarded Dividend

Company X shareholders receive the amount of the net assets valued at the current price of the company Y stock; this amount includes *earned surplus as a regarded dividend*. As in this numerical example only the stock of Y was given to the shareholders of X, it follows that

Procurement amount of company Y stock
= book value of company X stock + regarded dividend.

(Dr.) company Y stock 36,000 / (Cr.) company X stock   26,000
/ **regarded dividend   10,000**

In this example, the total amount of *regarded dividend* is equivalent to the total amount of earned surplus of company X. However, if the merging company Y also had a part of the company X stock, the regarded dividend should be allocated to both stockholders X and Y in proportion to their share of the holding stock numbers.

(2) Stock Transfer Income
So long as the stockholders of company X are given the cash (excluding the regarded dividend) as well as the stock of company Y, it means they have gained stock transfer income when they rendered their own stock as a stock exchange.

In the above numerical example, suppose stockholders of company X receive 2,000 cash and the stock of company Y equals 30,000 at current price. Then, stock transfer income = total amount of payment from company Y (30,000 + 2,000) – regarded dividend (10,000) – book value cost of the stock rendered (26,000).

(Dr.) stock of company Y   30,000 / (Cr.) stock of company X 26,000
   cash   2,000 / **regarded dividend   10,000**
   stock transfer income 4,000 /

Here, the amount of the company Y stock (30,000) is measured as the amount considered necessary for acquisition. When only stock is offered by company Y as payment, it means latent profit is included in the amount of stock of company Y, although not recognized.

4.3.2   *Numerical example of the competent taxation system*

In the above numerical example, suppose that both companies X and Y send their board of directors to the merging company Y as directors with effective control rights in company Y. In such a case, neither the assets transfer income, the regarded dividend, nor the stock transfer income will be recognized.

4.3.2.1 Handling of merged company X

(Step 1) The stock of company Y is offered as a payment to the transferred net asset 22,000 (= book value 24,000 – transferred earned surplus 2,000).

(Dr.)   stock of company Y   22,000 / (Cr.)   assets   24,000
       earned surplus*   2,000 /

    *In the case of the competent taxation, the earned surplus is transferred to merging company Y.

(Step 2) Company X offers stock of company Y, which is equivalent to the total amount of owner's capital minus the transferred earned surplus, to their stockholders X.

(Dr.)   capital   16,000 / (Cr.)   company Y stock   22,000
      capital surplus   6,000 /

(Step 3) Changes in the balance sheet of company X are as follows (see Figure 11).

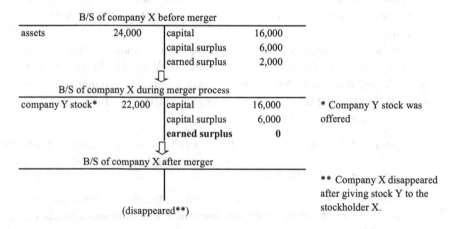

Fig. 11   Changes in the balance sheet of company X

4.3.2.2 Handling for merging company Y

Merging company Y receives the assets from company X at book value 24,000, as well as succeeding its earned surplus 2000.

(Dr.)   assets 24,000 / (Cr.) capital   16,000
              /   capital surplus   6,000
              /   **earned surplus   2,000**

B/S of company Y during merger				
assets	44,000	capital	30,000	original assets, etc. of company Y
		capital surplus	10,000	
		earned surplus	4,000	
assets	24,000	capital	16,000	succeeded from company X by capital increase
		capital surplus	6,000	
		earned surplus	2,000	
sum	68,000	sum	68,000	

⇩

B/S of company Y after merger			
Company Y Stock	68,000	capital	46,000
		capital surplus	16,000
		earned surplus	6,000
sum	68,000	sum	68,000

Fig. 12 Changes in the balance sheet of company Y

where the capital surplus 6,000 = (assets 24,000 − earned surplus 2,000) − capital 16,000.

Thus, changes in the balance sheet of company Y are shown in Figure 12.

4.3.2.3 Handling for the company X stockholders

Because this is a taxation *competent* case, neither regarded dividend nor stock transfer income is recognized. Therefore, the cost of acquiring company Y stock is equivalent to the book value of the original stock of company X:

(Dr.) company Y stock 26,000 / (Cr.) company X stock 26,000

5 Conclusion

Among the various types of business combinations, the rules for *transaction under common governance* and *formation of a joint venture company* are unique to Japan and do not exist in international and US accounting standards.

A transaction under common governance is a merger between a parent and subsidiary companies or a merger between subsidiaries. These combinations are made within a certain consolidated business group and are implemented in order to *restructure* the business group. To facilitate such group restructuring, these types of combinations are handled by *the pooling of interests method* in the Japanese accounting standards and tax law.

Formation of a joint venture company is divided into two types: In the first type, the original merger-participating companies cease to exist after the merger, while in the second type, the original companies continue to exist and merely split off part of their businesses and establish a new joint ventures.

The pooling of interests method is applied to such a joint venture company if certain requirements are satisfied. This handling also vitalizes Japanese group reorganization through the achievement of quick decision-making by the managers of such joint ventures.

Furthermore, the authors would like to emphasize that there is a consistent logic among the Japanese corporate law, accounting standards, and tax law. During the past 10 years the Japanese corporate law has been deregulated to encourage business group restructuring by allowing a holding company, stock swap and stock transfer, company splitting, various payment means for transferred assets in the merger, etc. While Japanese accounting standards recognize the pooling of interests method for combinations of group restructuring, as stated above, the Japanese tax law has also eased conditions for similar combinations such as group restructuring or a joint venture through the postponement of immediate taxation on *asset transfer income* and *stock transfer income* by allowing the *pooling of interests method.*

The various applications of the pooling of interests method mentioned above can enhance the value of an after-merger company since EPS can be more increased than the purchase method due to no effect of goodwill-depreciation under the book value, thereby encouraging and boosting group restructuring and formation of a joint venture in the Japanese business world. However, the situation is reversed when a "negative" goodwill occurs through the purchase method.

Another character of Japanese business combinations lies in the handling of goodwill that appears when the purchase method is applied. Japanese accounting standards and tax law are both stricter in terms of the depreciation method for the "positive" goodwill, and more relaxed in the depreciation method for the "negative" goodwill than Western countries, because the Japanese accounting standard forces constant depreciation for 20 years or less and the Japanese tax law for fixed five years, respectively. The western purchase method is similar to the

Japanese pooling of interests method when seen from the income statement since their purchase method allows no periodical depreciation of goodwill.

References

Accounting Standards Board of Japan (2005). *Accounting Standard No. 7. Accounting Standard for Business Separations, etc.*, December 27, 2005 (in Japanese).

Accounting Standards Board of Japan (2005). *No. 10 Guideline of the Accounting Standard, Guideline for the Application of the Accounting Standards for Business Combinations and Business Separations, etc.*, December 27, 2005 (in Japanese).

Business Accounting Council of Japan (2003). *Opinion on the Accounting Standard for Business Combinations*, October 31, 2003 (in Japanese).

Business Accounting Council of Japan (2003). *Accounting Standard for Business Combinations*, October 31, 2003 (in Japanese).

Financial Accounting Standard Foundation (FASF) of Japan (2006), Seminar résumé of FASF, Lecture on the recently proclaimed accounting standards, etc., February 8 (in Japanese).

Maekawa, N., Nodera, D., and Matsushita, M. (2005). *Basics of M&A*, Nihon Keizai Shinbun Sha (in Japanese).

Nobuhira, M. (2001). *Basics of Business Reorganization Tax Law*, Supplement to *Zeikei-Seminar* 45(17), published by Zeimu Keiri Kyoukai, December (in Japanese).

Oshima, T. and Kojima, N. (eds.) (2002). *Tax Law of Business Organizational Reforms*, Chuo Keizai Sha (in Japanese).

Saito, M. (2006). Business combinations and business separations, in *Financial Statements*, edited by Hiramatsu, K., Tokyo Keizai-Joho Shuppan, pp. 293–310, Chapter 23 (in Japanese).

Saito, S. (ed.) (2004). *Clause by Clause Lecture: Accounting Standard for Business Combinations*, Chuo Keizai Sha (in Japanese).

TAC Corporation tax law section (2004). *Tax Law of Business Reorganization*, Supplement to *Zeikei-Seminar* 49(9), published by Zeimu Keiri Kyoukai, January (in Japanese).

Changes in the Concept of Capital and Their Effects on Economic Profit in Japan

Shufuku Hiraoka

Professor, Faculty of Business Administration
Soka University

1 Introduction

So far, the valuation of firms and businesses has been widely applied in Japanese companies, but the concept of capital to be utilized for measuring economic profit varies and is now changing, being influenced by the new financial accounting standard and the new corporate law. Thus, this paper will explore how the recent institutional changes in the accounting standard and legal rules have influenced economic profit in the field of management accounting. The author will finally propose the concept of capital that he believes can contribute to the enhancement of the value of a business group.

2 The Concept of Capital in Relation to Economic Profit

At present, there are three main types of economic profit that Japanese companies work with. The first type of profit is "abnormal earnings" included in Ohlson model (Ohlson, 1995). The second type of profit is "residual income" traditionally used for management accounting (Horngren *et al.*, 1996; Aoki, 1998). The third type of profit is "EVA®" (Economic Value Added) developed by Stern Stewart & Co. (Stewart, 1991). They are calculated as follows:

Abnormal earnings = net income − equity × risk-free rate.

Residual income = profit before interest − imputed interest.

EVA® = NOPAT − Capital × weighted average cost of capital.

First, when Japanese companies use the economic profits that are similar to the abnormal earnings in Ohlson model, it is important for them to clarify the contents of equity. The concept of equity has been interpreted widely in the present Japanese accounting standard, which acknowledges three types of equity: net assets, equity, and stockholder's equity. The differences between these three types of equity are explained in Section 6.

Second, "imputed interest" in residual income is the cost amount of capital. When residual income is used for management accounting, even if it is difficult or impossible to divide the overall stockholder's equity and interest-bearing liability among the business units, the total assets invested in each business unit are substituted for the capital from the viewpoint of capital recovery (Hiraoka, 2006). However, we should pay attention to the frequent changes in the accounting standard in Japan because they affect both the capital and the assets of the business units.

Third, regarding the capital in EVA®, many special adjustments are made in calculating it. One of these adjustments resembles a procedure once admitted by the Japanese accounting standard. However, several adjustments aim for strategic effects as in management accounting, in order to supplement certain insufficiencies of the current accounting standard in Japan. Additionally, many concepts of capital are involved in the three types of equity described above.

The author will explain all of these in detail in Sections 3 to 6.

3   The Impact of Lease Accounting upon Capital in Japan

With regard to lease accounting, the Japanese accounting standard has allowed Japanese companies to regard part of the financial leases as off-balance on an exception basis. It is a lease without ownership transfer. The lease expense appears in income statement in the off-balanced lease. However, all financial leases will be unified into on-balanced leases in Japan. It has not been an issue in the international accounting standard whether or not a lease has ownership transfer, because all financial leases are on-balanced. In contrast, many Japanese companies have adopted off-balanced leases on an exception basis. In such cases, the total assets and the total liabilities directly displayed in the financial statements are smaller even if they must disclose the information needed for on-balance. Needless to say, the differences affect the capital in calculating some types of economic profit. However, not all types of economic profit are affected in this way, because all leases, including operating leases, are always on-balanced in calculating the EVA®, even if the leases are operating leases. So far, most Japanese companies have not adequately considered on-balancing in calculating economic profit. Unifying all finance leases into on-balance affects the capital and the economic profit even in the companies that never use the EVA®. The following model makes this influence clear. The survival price is presumed to be zero and the straight-line method is adopted for the depreciation:

$$V_i = (P/U - L)(1 - T) + [P - (i - 1)P/U]k,$$

where

P: acquisition cost of lease appliance,
U: useful life of lease appliance,
L: lease expense during one year,
i: period i $(i = 1, 2, 3, \ldots, U)$,
k: the cost of capital,
V_i: the profit variance between the off-balanced lease and the on-balanced lease over period i,
T: the rate of corporation taxes.

If V_i is larger than zero, the profit based on the application of off-balanced lease profit is larger than the profit based on the application of on-balanced lease. In other words, the company's on-balanced lease decreases the economic profit. Conversely, if V_i is less than zero, the company's on-balanced lease increases the economic profit.

Let us explain this case by means of an example using concrete numerical values. Substituting the following numerical values for each variable, V_1, V_2, and V_3 are calculated as follows:
If
    $P = \$120{,}003$
    $U = 3$ years
    $L = \$44{,}066$
    $i = 1, 2, 3$
    $k = 0.05$
    $T = 0.5$,
then
    $V_1 = \$3{,}967.65$
    $V_2 = \$1967.6$
    $V_3 = -\$32.45$.

In other words, in this case, the influence of the capital changed by the on-balance decreases the economic profit at the first stage and increases it at the last stage. It is important that the economic profit is sometimes increased by the on-balance. So, whenever the economic profit of a business unit is calculated for management accounting, we should use the capital that reflects the on-balance rather than the off-balance.

4 The Procedure for Research & Development Expenditures in Japan

The past Japanese commercial code allowed Japanese companies to defer examination & research expenses and development expenses as assets. This procedure is similar to the capitalization of research & development expenditures, which is one of the adjustments in calculating the EVA®. Japanese accounting standard allowed this in the past. In short, even if there were expenditures and services offered in the current term, it was possible to defer them as assets when the effect reached into the next term. In this case, research & development are not revenue expenditures (expense) but capital expenditures (investment). Examination & research expenses in the past Japanese commercial code were expenditures disbursed specially for new products or new technologies. Development expenses in the past Japanese commercial code were expenditures disbursed specially for adopting new technologies and management organization, developing resources or opening up new markets. All examination & research expenses belong to research & development expenses. The expenditures for adopting new technologies as part of the development expenses belonged to research & development expenses.

In contrast, the current accounting standard does not allow Japanese companies to capitalize research & development expenses after these expenses are implemented. In harmony with the international accounting standard, these expenses are, in principle, attributed to the period when they are disbursed. The reasons are as follows:

1. It is not clear whether there will be any profit in the future.
2. It is difficult to formulate a basis on which to appropriate them as assets objectively.

The Japanese accounting standard does not allow the deferment of research & development expenses, even if Japanese companies routinely adopt their deferment as a strategic measure in the practices of Japanese management accounting and financing. Only when the ordinal research & development expenses of production activities get mixed with the final inventory assets in the procedure of cost accounting, is the capitalization of research & development expenses admitted as an institutional accounting procedure, except in cases where research & development expenses are not recognized as an investment which has an effect in the future. This rule is contrary to the strategic measure involving the EVA®. It is meant to strategically deal with research & development expenses as capital expenditures when calculating economic profit. However, it is impossible to accomplish this goal using the procedure allowed by the current financial accounting standard in Japan.

On the other hand, there is one view according to which even marketing costs should be capitalized strategically in calculating economic profit (Biddle, 1997). The author has already asserted in a different paper that it is important for the management accounting practice in Japan to deal with strategic expenditures as investment (Hiraoka, 2003). It is especially effective to change the procedures so that they correspond to the differences in the characteristics of the business life cycle and research & development expenses. In this way, Japanese companies can use economic profits both to support the business portfolio strategy and to evaluate the performance of their business units. For example, some businesses called "cash cows" in PPM (Product Portfolio Management) may be evaluated after all research & development expenses are dealt with as costs in the period in which they are disbursed. Some businesses called "stars" or prospective "question marks" in PPM may be evaluated after research & development expenses are deferred in accordance with the present stage of the life cycle.

If research & development expenses are capitalized, the cost amount of the capital is larger than before because the capital increases. However, the economic profit increases more than before because the amount of expenses converted into capital exceeds the cost amount of the capital.

5   Business Combination Accounting and Capital in Japan

5.1   *Influence of goodwill on the capital in M&A*

The regulation of M&A has been mitigated by the new corporate law in Japan. Starting with May 2007, it will be possible to use not only the stocks of one's own company but also the cash and stocks of the parent company when one's company merges with a future parent company. When foreign companies have a high stock price, it is easy for them to merge with Japanese companies through their subsidiaries in Japan.

As for the general meeting of stockholders, when the assets of the disappearing company are less than 20% of those of the surviving company, the surviving company can omit the general meeting of stockholders. Also, a subsidiary can omit the general meeting of stockholders when the parent company merges with it. These legal revisions will accelerate M&A in Japan.

Incidentally, Japanese business combination accounting prescribes in principle the adoption of the purchase method. The pooling of interests method is admitted only when the merger corresponds almost entirely to an equal merger in the current standard. There are two main differences between the latter and the former:

1. Whether or not goodwill accompanies the merger.
2. Whether or not the merger takes over the contents of the capital as it is.

For instance, EVA® supports the purchase method in calculating the economic capital. Therefore, the pooling of interests method must be transformed into the purchase method when Japanese companies adopt the pooling of interests method to calculate the EVA®.

Also, goodwill is not periodically depreciated in the international accounting standard and the US accounting standard. In contrast, the Japanese accounting standard does not allow goodwill to keep appearing on the balance sheets as assets without depreciation. It forces Japanese companies to use both periodical depreciation and impairment loss. However, if the effects of positive goodwill continue after the current term contrary to the periodical depreciation, Japanese companies had better added the accumulated depreciation to the capital in calculating the economic profit and impose the cost of capital on the accumulated depreciation. Even if the goodwill is negative, they need to include the accumulated depreciation in the economic capital, because it belongs to the fixed liabilities. In other words, they had better added depreciated goodwill to their accounting profits in calculating the NOPAT when they deal with it as an expense item in the current term. Otherwise, the accounting basis might disturb the measurement of the economic profit of a business or a firm. When the M&A ends up with goodwill, it should be considered capital utilized by the business. This seems to be the reason why the procedure of goodwill is one of the adjustment items in EVA®.

Thus, it is very important that differences in processing goodwill lead to differences in capital when calculating economic profit. Moreover, we should understand the peculiar characteristics of the Japanese accounting conventions, so that we can grasp the effects of goodwill on Japanese companies. For example, stockholders tend to make their decision based on accounting profit. However, we hope that Japanese companies adopt not only accounting profit but also economic profit when valuating and evaluating their businesses. They should still try it, if they want to pursue corporate value more actively and promote M&A strategy, aiming at the effective utilization of substantial capital by management accounting.

5.2　*Goodwill and minority equity in consolidated financial statements*

Consolidated statements are already frequently used as the main source of accounting information. For the purpose of management accounting, some subgroups are reorganized by linking business units (divisions or subsidiaries) to the foreign and functional subsidiaries associated with them (Hiraoka, 1998, 2003). Some corporate groups adopt a "management approach" which uses segment information in financial accounting. One of them has been disclosing the information on its business segments including minority equity and goodwill in its management accounting information (Hiraoka, 2005a,b). Therefore, we cannot disregard the effects of minority equity and goodwill on the capital when not only the whole business group, but also each business unit, calculates economic profit.

Now, let us explain this using an easy example of capital consolidation.

Company X acquires 80% of the outstanding capital stock of company Y for $5,000,000 at the beginning of the current period and makes company Y its subsidiary. The book value of the total assets that company Y possessed is $10,000,000 and the market value is $12,000,000. The book value of the liabilities that company Y owed is $5,000,000 and the market value is $6,000,000. The common stock of company Y is $4,000,000, and the surplus is $1,000,000. In this case, the tax effect is disregarded. The differences in minority equity and goodwill derived from the differences in the capital consolidation method used under these conditions are shown in Figure 1. The Japanese accounting standard has admitted only the goodwill-buying method. Under such conditions, the variance between the capital amount of the partial valuation at market price and that of the overall valuation at market price is $200,000 in the example shown above. In this case, the capital amount in the overall valuation method is clearly larger than that in the partial valuation method. The total goodwill method is not admitted

Capital consolidation methods	Balances of consolidation accounts (ten thousand dollars)	
	Minority equity	Goodwill
Partial valuation at market price — Buying goodwill	100	20
Partial valuation at market price — Total goodwill	125	45
Overall valuation at market price — Buying goodwill	120	20
Overall valuation at market price — Total goodwill	145	45

Fig. 1 Difference between capital consolidation methods

in the current Japanese accounting standard. However, if minority stockholders expect the same return on investment at the time when the parent company–subsidiary relationship materializes, the minority equity should be calculated using the total goodwill method. In this case, the capital amount in the "overall valuation — total goodwill" method increases by $450,000 from that of the "partial valuation at market price — goodwill-buying" method. When the WACC (weighted average cost of capital) is 8%, the variance of the capital charge reaches $36,000. The minority equity includes the market premium in the "overall valuation — total goodwill" method. For example, when the parent company needs to buy back the treasury stocks from the minority stockholders of the subsidiary for restructuring its business, it might find the real value created by calculating the economic profit on the minority equity using the "overall valuation — total goodwill" method.

6 Three Types of Equity and Economic Capital in Japan

The fifth corporate accounting standard in Japan, "Standard for the Lists of Net Assets on the Balance Sheet," or simply the "Net Assets Accounting Standard," was announced on December 9, 2005. It transformed equity into net assets on Japanese balance sheets. There had been only one type of equity in the past. However, now there are three types of equity: net assets, equity, and shareholder's equity. The relationship among these three types of equity is as follows:

Net assets = total assets − total liability.

Equity = net assets − stock subscription right − minority equity.

Shareholder's equity = equity − revaluation variance of assets
− deferred hedge profit and loss
− adjustment of foreign exchange balance.

When looking at these three types of equity, we have to decide which one to adopt when we calculate economic profit in harmony with the Ohlson model. If we hold the Ohlson model in high regard, it might be a good idea to adopt the shareholder's equity, which seems to be closest to it. The Ohlson model supposes that the variance between the initial equity book value and the final one is equal to the variance between the net income and the dividend. This is why we recommend the adoption of shareholder's equity. Also, economic capital combines any type of equity above with interest-bearing floating liabilities and fixed liabilities into total liabilities. Moreover, this capital is adjusted by many items, including some of those used in calculating the EVA® as discussed above.

Let us examine some important elements involved in the three types of equity. First, regarding the stock subscription right, some Japanese companies tried to make use of it as a defense against TOB (take over bids, tender offer), although there are only a few examples of this as yet in Japan. This right used to be considered as one of the liabilities. However, it now becomes a type of capital if it is exercised. Even if the deadline comes without it being exercised, it becomes an extraordinary profit. That is to say, it is part of the economic capital because it has the nature of capital. When funds are procured for a particular business with the stock subscription right exercised, they are obviously part of the economic capital of the business.

Second, the minority equity used to be somewhere between liability and equity. However, it now belongs to the net assets, after the lists of equity were transformed into lists of net assets. In any case, the economic capital includes the minority equity. Once the minority equity is entered into the net assets, it means that the economic profit is calculated under the overall valuation in the "market price — total goodwill" method. Even if the minority equity is included in the capital multiplied by the WACC when calculating the capital charge, there is a case in which using the capital in calculating the WACC does not include the minority equity. However, as long as the minority stockholders are part of the people investing in corporate groups, the minority equity should be included in the process of calculating the WACC by multiplying it by the capital cost of the subsidiary. As the ratio of cost to equity capital is generally higher than the ratio of interest to liability, the WACC increases because of the minority equity included in calculating it.

Third, let us explain the difference between equity and shareholder's equity. The main elements in the revaluation variance of assets are cross-holding stock and land in Japan. The tax effects are eliminated from each of those. Although cross-holding stock seemed to be canceled much of the time in the past, some Japanese companies are now returning to cross-holding because their stock prices have gone up on stock markets and they have been thinking about ways to defend themselves against TOBs from foreign companies. When a parent company makes a financial decision to cross-hold, cross-holding stocks in unrelated business should be excluded from the economic capital. However, if the business subsidiaries are authorized to cross-hold in defense against a TOB, the revaluation variance of the cross-holding stock composes the economic capital of the business. The revaluation variance of land used to be accrued by implementing the land revaluation law as a capital reinforcement plan in Japan before impairment loss accounting was institutionalized. Before that time, the revaluation variance of land had been calculated not only by the corporate group but also by the single company as entity, because the Japanese commercial code and the Japanese tax law had been applied mainly to single companies. Therefore, the revaluation variance of land in a business subsidiary should be included when calculating economic capital, because it is only used for the business. Also, the economic capital should include the revaluation variance of land in functional subsidiaries linked to business units for the purpose of management accounting.

Next, we have to judge whether or not the deferred hedge profit and loss should be included in the economic capital. As the Japanese financial accounting standard admits only the deferred hedge, it appears on the balance sheets of the companies that make use of hedge accounting. If foreign claimable assets from operating activities as hedge objects and exchange contracts as hedge measures in deferred hedge profit and loss result in the process of periodical correspondence, they should be included in the economic capital. Deferred hedge profit and loss in business units should be included for performance management in the economic capital if they are authorized to hedge.

Finally, the adjustment of the foreign exchange balance is the variance result of the differences in the exchange rates among assets, liabilities and capital when the balance sheets of foreign subsidiaries are linked to that of the parent company. Therefore, it should be included in the economic capital when foreign subsidiaries are tied to a particular business unit (division or subsidiary) in terms of decision-making at the head office. Also, the adjustment of the foreign exchange balance should be included in the economic capital for evaluating the performances of business units if the business units are authorized to invest in foreign subsidiaries.

7 Summary

Japanese companies have fully realized that it is necessary to valuate and evaluate their businesses based on economic profit. For example, the Hitachi group has adopted an original type of economic profit called FIV since February, 2002 (Hiraoka, 2006). Hitachi has decided or is planning to resign from those businesses (divisions and subsidiaries) which continue to show a FIV deficit. In this paper, the author has indicated and explained the effects of the new accounting standards and regulations that top Japanese companies should pay attention to in calculating economic profit on economic capital. Surely, the changes in lease accounting, R&D accounting, business combination accounting, and capital accounting have affected capital-based management accounting in Japanese companies. We will not be able to avert our eyes from the effects of these accounting standard revisions on Japanese management accounting from now on.

References

Aoki, S. (1998). The nature of EVA (economic value added) and various problems in it, *JICPA Journal* 512-March, pp. 60–64 (in Japanese).

Biddle, G. C., Bowen, R. M., and Wallance, J. S. (1997). Does EVA beat earning? Evidence on association with stock returns and firm values, *Journal of Accounting and Economics* 24, pp. 301–336.

Hiraoka, S. (1998). How to use business segment reporting for strategic decision, *The Japan Industrial Management & Accounting* 58(2), pp. 81–94 (in Japanese).

Hiraoka, S. (2003). Business valuation based on EVA for management accounting, in *Organization Structure and Management Accounting*, edited by Monden, Y., Zeim-keiri-kyokai, pp. 19–37 (in Japanese).

Hiraoka, S. (2005a). Valuation and goal growth rate of business segments: the case study of Matsushita Electric Works, Ltd., in *Organization Design and Management Accounting for Corporate Value*, edited by Monden, Y., Zeim-keiri-kyokai, pp. 89–99 (in Japanese).

Hiraoka, S. (2005b). *Contemporary Accounting and Financial Statements Analysis*, Sou-sei-sya (in Japanese).

Hiraoka, S. (2006). Valuation of business based on EVA-type metrics in Japanese companies, in *Value-Based Management of the Rising Sun*, edited by Monden, Y., Miyamoto, K., Hamada, K., Lee, G., and Asada, T., World Scientific, pp. 75–87.

Horngren, C. T., Sundem, G. L., and Stratton, W. O. (1996). *Introduction to Management Accounting*, 10th ed., Prentice Hall.

Ohlson, J. A. (1995). Earning, book values, dividends in equity valuation, *Contemporary Accounting Research* 11(2), pp. 661–687.

Stewart, G. B. III (1991). *The Quest for Value: The EVA^{TM} Management Guide*, Harper Business.

The Relationship between Strategies, Organizational Design, and Management Control Systems at Matsushita

Masanobu Kosuga

Professor, School of Business Administration
Kwansei Gakuin University

1   Introduction

Japanese corporations are confronted with opportunities and obstacles in their quest for creating corporate value. One way of benefiting from opportunities and fending off obstacles is to achieve the appropriate fit among strategies, organizations, and management control systems.

The purposes of this study are to examine the relationship between strategies, organization, and management control systems, using the case study of Matsushita Electric Industrial Co., Ltd., and to get some insights to extract some characteristics of Japanese management [for the reason to focus on Matsushita, see Pascale and Athos (1982) and Monden (1985)]. Which type of organizational structures, and what management control systems have been supporting and implementing the strategies adopted by the top management of Matsushita in the past and the present are explored in this chapter. Based on the survey of several publications, the semi-structured interview method was used in this study. Interviewees were senior financial director, chief operating officers, and managers of planning department in its head office in Osaka, Japan (for the details of the company, see Appendix).

2   The Management Philosophy and Traditional Patterns of Strategic Behaviors at Matsushita

2.1   *Basic management objectives and business creed*

The founder of Matsushita, Mr. Konosuke Matsushita formulated its basic management objective in 1929, around 10 years after the establishment of

Matsushita Electric Devices Manufacturing Works. The objective, to sum up, was stated as follows: "To devote all Matsushita group to the progress and development of the human society and the well-being of people through their business activities, thereby enhancing the quality of all the people throughout the world."

This objective was in line with Mr. Konosuke's firm belief and/or strong desire that was known as the business creed; "water-supply" philosophy. As Kono and Clegg (2001, p. 80) explained, the intent of "water-supply" philosophy is as follows: "Matsushita continues making efforts to improve and enrich people's lifestyles with electrical appliances that are as cheap and plentiful as water." This philosophy embodies the next five creeds:

(a) Growth through mutual benefits to Matsushita and its customers.
(b) Profit as a result of Matsushita's contribution to the society.
(c) Fair competition in the market.
(d) Mutual benefits between Matsushita and the suppliers, dealers, and shareholders.
(e) Participation by all employees.

Since 1918, Matsushita has provided customers with high-quality, high-performance products and services. The company keeps making efforts to contribute to the progress and development of the world.

2.2   *Traditional patterns of strategic behaviors*

According to some prior survey results on Matsushita (Pascale and Athos, 1982, pp. 30–31; Kono and Clegg, 2001), there were clear patterns Matsushita did behave strategically till the end of the 20th century. They were as follows:

(a) "National" brand strategy.
(b) Distribution strategy: creating own distributing channels and going directly to the retailers.
(c) Aggressive "market share" oriented management.
(d) "Not pioneer, but follower" strategy.

In 1925, "National" brand name was registered. Matsushita promoted *National* brand vigorously through advertising. The founder, Mr. Konosuke Matsushita decided to use *National* as the trademark focusing importance on the meaning of the word, i.e., "relating to or characteristics of the people of a nation." Matsushita did not play as a pioneer of new technologies and/or new products, but persisted in acting as a follower. Until the potentiality of the new products was confirmed, Matsushita allowed its competitors to make several experimental efforts in introducing new products into the market. And, once Matsushita decided to enter the market, the company tried to make itself the volume leader with large investments and high level of sales targets strongly supported by "high quality and low price" sales promotion and its own distribution channels.

Needless to say, the founder's management objective and business creeds were embodied in these behaviors.

2.3   *Philosophy of organizational design*

In addition to management objective and business creed, Mr. Konosuke Matsushita had a firm belief concerning organizational design. His belief was as follows: "There should be an optimal scale of business for a manager to be able to control it effectively and efficiently."

Based on this simple notion of the optimally scaled business, he decided to launch the *Divisional System* in 1933. According to the founder's thought, as a company grows and expands into new product market and/or new business domain, it is necessary to empower the person to manage all operations in this new area.

The underlying philosophy of the *Divisional System* at Matsushita was established as "one product for one division" in line with the founder's belief. This basic principle let the divisions specialize in each product area and enhanced their agility to the market.

In the following sections, we would investigate which type of organizational structures Matsushita established and what management control systems Matsushita used in order to support and implement the corporate strategies. The *Divisional System*, the *Business Group System* (that is, the *Division-Group System*), the *Bunsha System*, and the *Business Domain System* are organizational structures that top management up to now have established historically one by one.

3   Organizational Design during the Great Founder, *Konosuke* Era: 1918–1960

3.1   *Period 1: 1918–1943*

Matsushita Electric Devices Manufacturing Works was founded in 1918. The function-based organization was introduced there to implement the centralized management through the direct control from Mr. Konosuke Matsushita. And then, following the philosophy of organizational design, the *Divisional System* was launched in May 1933 to cope with the Great Depression all over the world.

In December 1935, Matsushita was incorporated as Matsushita Electric Industrial Co., Ltd. This new Matsushita was a holding company that had the *Bunsha System*. Matsushita set up nine legally separated companies (what is called, *Bunsha*), based on and developed from the *Divisional System*, in order to enhance the autonomy and to make a quick response to the market.

At the same time, *Monthly Accounting Settlement System* was started in 1935. In this system, monthly performance is calculated in almost the same way as an annual base. As the top management must have some tool for coordinating decentralized decision-making and control in each division, President Konosuke established the *Accounting Staff System* in 1940, in addition to the *Monthly Accounting Settlement System*. In the *Accounting Staff System*, accountants at both the head office and each division support the divisional managers make their divisional plans and measure their monthly performance.

From the late 1930s to the mid-1940s, several practical rules and guidelines for cost accounting, budgetary control, and internal controls were set by Japanese Army and Navy. Matsushita had to comply with those regulations.

3.2   *Period 2: 1944–1949*

After World War II broke out, Matsushita merged all *Bunsha* into the head office to abolish the *Bunsha System*, dismantled the *Divisional System*, and introduced the *Factory System* in November 1944. The aim of this strongly centralized system was to adapt all Matsushita groups to the severe wartime regime.

After World War II ended in 1945, Matsushita started the new *Factory System* in July 1949 to strengthen the president's direct supervision. In this system, 19 factories were treated as profit centers. The aim of introducing this centralized system into the company was to bear and cope with the economic confusion and recession in Postwar Japan.

3.3 *Period 3: 1950–1960*

During March 1950, Matsushita reestablished the *Divisional System* (that is, *Multi-Division Based System*) to adapt all Matsushita groups to the rapid economic reconstruction, and designed the organization to build up the *Business Group System* (that is, the *Division-Group System*) by grouping its divisions into some product-based groups and adding separate marketing, administrative, and R&D functions to them.

In November 1959, Matsushita consisted of 11 business groups and 20 product divisions. The aim of this reestablishment was to institute independent and decentralized organizations in order to enhance the responsiveness and flexibility of Matsushita toward the increasing competition in the product markets.

In those days, President Konosuke actively introduced management control systems into Matsushita for group-wide coordination (that is, toward centralization). They are as follows [for the details of these systems, see Monden (1985) and Fushimi (1989)]:

(a) *Divisional Planning System* in 1952.
(b) *Internal Capital System* in 1954.
(c) *Middle-range* (five-years) *Business Planning System* in 1956.
(d) *Budget System* for cost control in 1957.

According to Monden (1985), these management control systems at Matsushita are classified into two ways: (1) for the top management to control divisional managers by *Divisional Planning System, Internal Capital System,* and *Monthly Accounting Settlement System,* and (2) for divisional managers to control departmental managers by *Budget System (Departmental Budget* and *Standard Cost System)* and *Monthly Accounting Settlement System.*

4 Organizational Design during the Successors' Struggles: 1961–1999

4.1 *Period 4: 1961–1976*

In 1961, Mr. Masaharu Matsushita was appointed the 2nd president. Matsushita expanded its operating areas on a worldwide level again in those days. For example, National Thai Co. was established as the first postwar overseas manufacturing company in 1961, and National Panasonic GmbH as the first sales company in Europe was established in 1962. As a result of this enlargement, Matsushita reorganized its sales and distribution mechanisms both at home and abroad from 1964 to 1965. This organizational reform resulted in more empowerment to the field. Each business group was given more initiatives and full responsibility for its marketing and sales activities. In 1970, Matsushita began to publish the consolidated financial statements and Matsushita Electric shares began to be traded on NYSE in 1971.

In the 1970s, Japanese economy entered into the period of low growth. During the period of Nixon Dollar Shock in 1971 and First Oil Crisis in 1973, Matsushita had been struggling to cope with the economic crisis and stagnation. In December 1972, Matsushita decided to abolish the *Business Group System* in order to reactivate its organizations, and established 12 product divisions which were intra-companies by products under the direct supervision of chief executives (including Executive Adviser, Kono-suke Matsushita). This organizational reform meant that the trend moved back again toward centralized control.

As the economic confusion calmed down, Matsushita acquired Motorola TV division and established Quasar Company in 1974, and then reformed the organizational design of Matsushita into the new *Business Group System* (*Division-Group System*) which consisted of three business groups in January 1975.

4.2   *Period 5: 1977–1985*

In February 1977, Mr. Konosuke Matsushita appointed Mr. Toshihiko Yamashita as the 3rd president of Matsushita. President Yamashita began to transform Matsushita from a manufacturer of strictly home appliances to an all-round manufacturer of electric and electronics-related products. He passionately advocated the needs to change management awareness, to bring up human resources, to restructure and reactivate the organization, and to modify the management control systems.

First, in February 1978, President Yamashita decided to abolish the *Business Group System* and did it. All divisions (41 in total) were placed under the president's direct supervision. And then, he announced the organization policy, and started promoting interdivisional personnel rotation. Besides these organizational reforms, Matsushita had been going ahead with the new *Bunsha System* by the spin-off of some divisions during 1976–1979.

Second, in November 1982, President Yamashita notified all division managers to write off their corporate account deposits (that is, the accumulated surplus of net cash flow) and their earned surplus corresponding to the deposits. The aims of this change were to reactivate divisions, to make management more aggressive, and to strengthen the competitiveness and profitability.

Third, in May 1983, President Yamashita announced *Action-61 Plan* and started it in November 1983. The meanings of *Action-61* were as follows: *A* for action, *C* for cost reduction, *T* for topical products, *I* for initiative marketing, *O* for organizational reactivation, *N* for new managing strength, and 61 means fiscal year 1986.

In 1984, Matsushita began merging and reforming the divisions, and reconstructed *the Business Group System* again. Top management recognized that it was necessary to re-examine its organizational philosophy of "one product for one division." This new *Business Group System* was revised partly by the next president Tanii, but it lasted till 1994.

4.3 *Period 6: 1986–1992*

Mr. Akio Tanii was appointed as the 4th president in 1986. He stated that "small head office" and "autonomous management based on independent divisional organizations" were the most important matters.

In July 1987, he announced six areas to be emphasized, promoting, and poured their resources.

In 1989, the great founder, Konosuke Matsushita, passed away, and "bubble economy" in Japan burst. From that period, his successors' struggles began. In 1990, Matsushita acquired MCA, and in 1991, introduced the *Section System* into the *Business Group System*. This organizational reform resulted in a kind of the virtual matrix system, that is, a matrix with a "business group axis" for really existing divisions, *Bunsha*, subsidiary and affiliated companies, and a "sector axis" for three areas to be emphasized. In this *Section System*, each division still belonged to a business group and was delegated two kinds of responsibilities: profit and cash.

4.4 *Period 7: 1993–1999*

In 1993, Mr. Yoichi Morishita became the 5th president. He tried to accomplish a middle-range business plan, *Innovation Plan* (Innovation of Business

Structure Plan) which was formulated in September 1992, at the end of former president, Tanii Era.

New president Morishita encouraged "Creation and Challenge" spirits. And then, in January 1994, Matsushita announced *Regeneration Plan* and abolished the *Business Group System*. The *Divisional System* was revived to promote the agile decision-making, quick response, and its speedy implementation under the direct supervision of the president.

In April 1997, *Progress 2000 Plan* was launched. At the same time, *Internal Division Company System* (what is called, *Company System* in Japan) was launched. Four internal *Bunsha* (intra-companies as previous *Business Groups*) were established.

By implementing these strategies, Matsushita had been trying to work in order to enhance capital efficiency through the utilization of *Capital Cost Management* (CCM) which was introduced in 1999. CCM is a Matsushita's own yardstick for internal divisional management control, and it is a kind of a residual income. CCM is calculated as follows:

$$\text{CCM} = (\text{Income before tax} - \text{interest earned} + \text{interest expense})$$
$$- \text{cost of assets invested.}$$

The balance of operating assets multiplied by cost of capital set at 8.4% is cost of assets invested.

5   Organizational Design during the *Nakamura* Era: 2000–2006

5.1   *From the progress 2000 plan to the value creation 21*

In 2000, Mr. Kunio Nakamura was appointed as the 6th president. He announced *Value Creation 21* that was the next mid-term plan, and started from April 2001. *Value Creation 21* was designed to take full advantage of the opportunities created by evolving digital networking society. The goal of this plan was to transform Matsushita into a Super Manufacturing Company, which would provide truly customer-oriented services as its principal mission through the development and supply of systems, equipment, and devices (*Annual Report 2001*, p. 3).

Value Creation 21 initiated a new corporate model based on the concept of a Super Manufacturing Company. The attributes of a Super

Manufacturing Company are as follows (*Annual Report 2001*, p. 4):

(a) Outstanding strength in components and devices, backed by leading-edge technologies.
(b) Manufacturing products at speed with astute responsiveness to market needs.
(c) A firm commitment to providing truly customer-oriented services.

Figure 1 shows the core concepts of *Value Creation 21*. The most important concept is the shifting of all focus to "creation" for a "lean and agile" Matsushita through *Deconstruction* (*Annual Report 2003*, p. 6).

5.2 *Business and organizational restructuring*

To maximize corporate value, *Value Creation 21* called for the re-engineering of traditional business structures based on Matsushita's successful experience in the 20th century. The core elements of the plan were (1) structural reforms with an emphasis on profitability and efficiency improvements, and (2) the creation of a new growth strategy.

In January 2003, Matsushita reorganized their group structure to maximize corporate value of the entire Matsushita Group. This system is called the *Business Domain System* (*Multi-Business Domain System*). As a result of this reform, 14 new business domains were established. The business domain means a strategic large business unit.

The aims of this business restructuring were to provide the most effective solution services from a customer's point of view, to eliminate counter-productive overlapping of businesses among group companies, to concentrate and make optimum use of group-wide R&D resources, and to establish an integrated operational structure that covers everything from

From: "Lean and Agile" (Structural reform)	To: "Creation" (Growth strategies)
IT innovation	Business domain-based structure
Headquarter reforms	Management focusing on cash flows
Closure/integration of manufacturing bases	Management quality innovation
Employment structure reforms	More efficient organization
R&D and design reform	Increased brand value
Reform of sales/distribution structure in Japan	Global strategy
Manufacturing innovation	Black-box technologies
Corporate culture reform	V-products

Fig. 1   Core concepts of *Value Creation 21* plan

	"Deconstruction"	**"Creation"**
Fiscal 2002	Domestic consumer sales and distribution restructuring Employment restructuring Closure/integration of manufacturing locations	Manufacturing process innovation More efficient organization
Fiscal 2003	Transformation of five group companies into wholly owned subsidiaries	Management focusing on capital cost management (CCM) and cash flows
Fiscal 2004	Organizational restructuring by business domain	Business domain-based organizational structure and new management system

Fig. 2   Results of implementing *Value Creation 21* plan

product development and manufacturing to sales, thereby ensuring a pertinent autonomous management structure (*Annual Report 2002*, p. 5). Indeed, this structural reformation was designed to "deconstruct" management structures of the 20th century and "create" business and products that would lead to future growth. Figure 2 shows the results how Matsushita restructured its business and organizations from 2002 to 2004 based on *Value Creation 21* (*Annual Report 2004*, p. 7).

5.3   *Roles of business domain companies and headquarters*

The key features of this new structure were empowerment (delegation of authority) and capital governance. Under this new organizational structure, all business domain companies were established as the customer-oriented, autonomous organizations.

The business domain companies have complete authority over, and must take responsibility for, all aspects of business activities in their respective domain, including not only domestic but also overseas operations, from R&D and manufacturing to sales. By delegating such responsibilities, Matsushita tried to promote autonomous management by each business domain company, thus accelerating decision-making, and facilitating efficient allocation of management resources. The role of the Headquarters is to oversee these operations from a shareholder's perspective.

5.4   *New group management system*

In 2004, Matsushita implemented further reform to establish an optimum management and governance structure tailored to the Group's new business and organizational structure. Under the new structure, the Headquarters empower each of the business domain companies by delegating authority in order to expedite autonomous management (*Annual Report 2003*, p. 10). The aims of this restructuring were to eliminate business duplications, to integrate R&D manufacturing and sales, and to concentrate R&D resources. Figure 3 shows the outline of the *New Group Management System Annual Report 2003*, p. 10).

To increase the effectiveness of these reforms, Matsushita created a framework for capital governance in a new management system. The Company revised the fundamental components of the previous internal divisional management system: Headquarters Fee Structure, Internal Share Investment/Dividend System, and Business Performance Evaluation Standards (*Annual Report 2003*, p. 9).

First, charges paid to the Headquarters were treated as variable under the previous system, because they were calculated based on sales amount. This treatment has been changed. They are now fixed in accordance with services provided by the Headquarters.

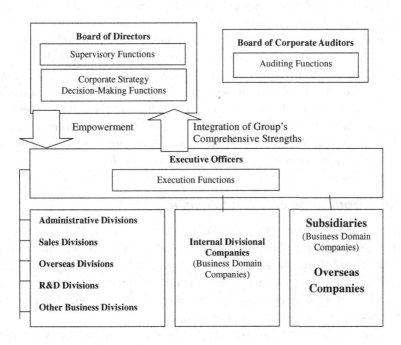

Fig. 3 New group management system

Second, a new standard regarding internal dividends was started, in which each business domain company pays dividends to the Headquarters at a fixed rate, based on the domain company's consolidated shareholder's equity. Under this system, business domain companies are required to pay dividends whether or not they are profitable, thereby providing an incentive for closure/integration of unprofitable business. Furthermore, Matsushita introduced a new overseas share investment system, where business domain companies deposit funds with the Headquarters in an amount equivalent to the share investment in the relevant overseas subsidiaries under their control, and in turn, the Headquarters, through regional headquarter companies, invests 100% in shares of such overseas subsidiaries. With this new system, business domain companies are effectively responsible for not only investment but also management of overseas subsidiaries in their domain (*Annual Report 2003*, p. 9).

Finally, Matsushita revised the performance evaluation measures for business domain companies to promote autonomous management and allow for effective delegation of authority. Their performance is evaluated based on two results-based measurements. They are CCM for evaluating capital efficiency and cash flows for evaluating a company's ability to generate cash. Both of these measures are applied to each business domain company's performance on a global consolidated basis (*Annual Report 2003*, p. 9). Through these management system reforms, business domain companies are shifting from the parent-alone, domestic focus of the past, to an autonomous management style that emphasizes cash flow on a global consolidated basis (*Annual Report 2003*, p. 9). Furthermore, compensation for members of the Board of Directors and Executive Officers is linked to these new performance evaluation measures to pursue management based on shareholder interests and enhance corporate value.

5.5   *From value creation to leap ahead*

After *Value Creation 21* plan ended in March 31, 2004, Matsushita started the next mid-term plan called *Leap Ahead 21*. The aim of this plan is to achieve global excellence by the fiscal year 2010 to fulfill its mission of creating value for customers. Overseas initiative within the *Leap Ahead 21* plan is a vital role of overseas operations as a "growth engine" in expanding business and enhancing overall earnings.

The key strategies for future growth were (1) a unified global brand, (2) matrix management, (3) superior products, (4) creating a "lean and agile" structure. Matsushita has expanded the responsibilities of regional headquarter companies to include corporate governance functions regarding overseas operations. These operations are managed according to a matrix with a "business axis" for the global strategies of business domains, and a "region axis" for the comprehensive growth strategies of regional headquarter companies.

In 2006, Mr. Fumio Ohtsubo was appointed as the 7th president of Matsushita. He now continues efforts to implement *Leap Ahead 21*.

6 Conclusion

In this chapter, we correlated organizational structures with their guiding strategies and supporting management control systems. The major findings are as follows:

(a) As Lawrence and Lorsch (1967) previously stated, centralization *vs.* decentralization is an irresolvable conflict and the excellent company must have both.
(b) Matsushita continuously carries out an organizational reform to ensure its organizational vitality.
(c) Matsushita continuously tries to adapt its organizational structure to the changing environment.
(d) Centralized organization and decentralized organization have been swinging from side to side like a pendulum in a clock.
(e) The founder's philosophy of management and organization has strong influences upon management decisions with regard to the organizational design and management control systems.
(f) Mr. Konosuke Matsushita and other headquarters staff were the key persons to balance the tensions between centralization and decentralization in Matsushita.
(g) Matsushita uses quite simple performance measures: CCM and cash flows to manage its business domain companies.

Appendix: Corporate Profile of Matsushita

Company name: Matsushita Electric Industrial Co., Ltd.
Head office location: Kadoma City, Osaka, Japan
Net sales in fiscal year 2005: ¥8,894.3 billion
Net income in fiscal year 2005: ¥154.4 billion

Number of employees as of March 31, 2006: 334,402

Number of consolidated companies in fiscal year 2005: 638

Brand name: *Panasonic* (global brand), *National* (region-specific brand for Japan), *Technics* (product-specific brand), and *Quasar* (region-specific brand for North America)

References

Abegglen, J. C. and Stalk, G. (1985). *Kaisha: The Japanese Corporation*, New York: Harper & Row.

Fushimi, T. (1989). Corporate strategies and divisionalized management control at Matsushita, in *Japanese Management Accounting: A World Class Approach to Profit Management*, edited by Monden, Y. and Sakurai, M., Portland, Oregon: Productivity Press.

Kono, T. and Clegg, S. (2001). *Trends in Japanese Management: Continuing Strengths, Current Problems and Changing Priorities*, Hampshire, UK: Palgrave Publishers Ltd.

Lawrence, P. and Lorsch, J. (1967). *Organization and Environment*, Boston, MA.: Division of Research, Harvard Business School.

Miyamoto, K. and Kosuga, M. (2006). Management accounting in Japanese multinational corporations: lessons from Matsushita and Sanyo, in *Value-Based Management of the Rising Sun*, edited by Monden, Y. *et al.*, Singapore: World Scientific Publishing Co., Pte. Ltd.

Monden, Y. (1985). Japanese management control systems, in *Innovations in Management: The Japanese Corporation*, edited by Monden, Y. *et al.*, Atlanta, Georgia: Industrial Engineering and Management Press.

Pascale, R. T. and Athos, A. G. (1982). *The Art of Japanese Management: Applications for American Executives*, London, UK: Penguin Books Ltd.

Valuations in Business Combinations: Focusing on the Resource Supply & Demand and the Ownership Structure

Yasuhiro Monden

Professor, Faculty of Business Administration
Mejiro University

1 Introduction

In this paper, the author uses a mathematical programming model to analyze the accounting measurement in business combinations.

Since a merger is a transaction that transfers assets or business from company X to company Y, which are involved in the combination, the problem of giving value to the transferred assets or business is similar to the so-called "transfer pricing" problem that handles valuation of goods or services transferred between divisional units. Since transfer pricing problems are often handled by mathematical programming models (Böhm and Wille, 1960, 1965; Churchill and Stedry, 1966; Manes, 1970; Onsi, 1970; Monden, 1982, 1989, 1992; etc.), measurement problems of transferred assets in a business combination should also be able to be analyzed by a similar model.

As a model to be applied to the asset transfer from one company to another, the author sought to apply the inventory valuation model developed by Wright (1970), because inventory is an asset transferred from the previous period to the current period (See also Carsberg (1969), Wright (1968, 1969) and Manes *et al.* (1982), etc.).

While this paper uses a conventional model, it is the first one to handle accounting measurements in business combinations by using dual prices up to now. The author will explore the relationship between supply & demand of the resources and the ownership structure.

2 Situations before and after the Merger of Companies Involved in the Combination of Capital Relationships

Some assumptions regarding the relationship between transferred assets and the capital ownership structure of a combined company X and a combining company Y must be made. As such, the related parameters before and after the merger are as shown in Figures 1 and 2, respectively. Important points in these figures are:

Before the merger, the stockholders of company X give the funds necessary for capacities $(a+c)$ to company X, and accordingly, company X offers the total number of its stocks $(a' + c')$ to stockholders X. Then company X gives the funds necessary for capacity c to company Y, and accordingly, company Y offers its stocks by the number of c' to company X. Company X installs facility a into its company, and company Y introduces facility c

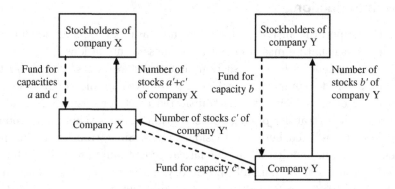

Fig. 1   Capital relationship between company X and company Y before merger

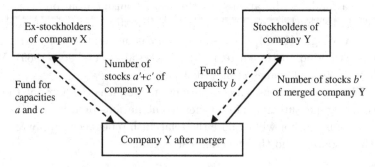

Fig. 2   Capital relationship between the ex-stockholders of company X and the stockholders of company Y after merger

into its company. The facilities a and c are for procurement (production or purchasing) of assets. On the other hand, company Y introduces selling capacity b by receiving funds from stockholders Y, to whom company Y offers its stocks by the number of b'.

When company X is merged, company Y gives its stock by the number of $(a' + c')$ to stockholders X. The number of stocks c' of company Y which was previously given to company X is offset by the owner's capital of company Y. In other words company X sells only asset a to company Y. Of course, stocks of company X previously given to company X stockholders are diminished through this merger after stockholders X render the stocks to company Y.

It should be noted that there is an assumed corresponding relationship between the resources (a, b, c) including transferred assets and the stock-ownership structure (a', b', c'); that is, $(a : b : c) = (a' : b' : c')$ in the above description.

3 Mathematical Programming Model of the Merger

A linear programming model of the merger can be formulated as follows: The primal problem:

$$\text{Max} : sx - py \tag{1}$$
$$\text{s.t. } x - y \leq a, \tag{2}$$
$$x \leq b, \tag{3}$$
$$y \leq c, \tag{4}$$
$$x, y \geq 0, \tag{5}$$

where
  $s =$ selling price of assets (after deducting selling costs),
  $p =$ procurement cost of assets,
  $x =$ sales quantity of assets during a period,
  $y =$ procured quantity of assets during a period.
For simplicity, an asset is assumed to be usable in "a period," which implies a year. Thus, the value of the objective function is an income and at the same time a cash flow. The objective function shows the income of the combined firms as a total, and thus this function omits $(-pa)$, which is the amount of the original procurement cost by company X.

The dual problem:

$$\text{Min} : au + bv + cw \tag{6}$$

$$\text{s.t. } u + v \geq s, \tag{7}$$

$$u - w \leq p, \tag{8}$$

$$u, v, w \geq 0, \tag{9}$$

where dual variable u is related to constraint (2) of additional asset a, which is transferred from company X to company Y. Variable u stands for the increased value of objective function (1) when one unit of capacity a is added to the present number of a. Since objective function (1) expresses the future net cash inflow in the next period, u also implies the increased amount of net cash inflow when capacity a increases by one unit. This future net cash inflow is either (i) the amount of savings of future cash-outlay "p" or (ii) the amount of future revenue increase "s."

4 Values of the Transferred Asset under Various Conditions

In this section, the value of a dual variable u under various realistic environments (Case 1-1, 1-2, and 1-3, Case 2, and Case 3) of the parameters is examined.

4.1 *Case 1: s > p and b > c*

When $s > p$ and $b > c$, the values of transferred assets behave as shown in Figure 3, depending on the parameter value of a. Below, the author describes what values of the transfer assets are taken for each segment of value a.

4.1.1 *Case 1-1: s > p, b > c, and a < b < a + c*

Since $s > p$ and $b > c$, both x and y will take positive values in the optimal solution. As a result, both of the dual constraints (7) and (8) hold equality based on the *complementary slackness theorem*. However, since $b < a + c$, constraint (4) is not binding, and thus dual variable w of this constraint will be zero due to the complementary slackness theorem. Therefore, constraint (8) is $u = p$. In other words, the unit value of transferred asset a will be equivalent to its replacement cost p.

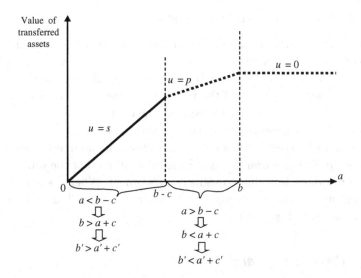

Fig. 3   Segmental valuations of transferred assets under $s > p$ and $b > c$

Here, when $b < a+c$, $b' < a'+c'$. This means the number of stocks held by the stockholders of company X is larger than the number of stocks held by the stockholders of company Y. Therefore, the situation of "ACQUISITION" by the merging company Y does not occur, and governance of company X for the transferred assets is still held by the original stockholders X. Thus, the pooling of interests method will be applied to the transferred assets, and procurement cost p or the original book value of the assets is used.

4.1.2   Case 1-2: s > p, b > c, and b > a + c

In this case, since selling capacity b exceeds supplying capacity $a + c$, constraint (3) is unbinding, and thus its dual variable v is zero. Therefore, constraint (7) simplifies to $u = s$. In other words, the unit value of transferred asset a is equivalent to s or the net realizable value.

Again when $b > a+c$, $b' > a'+c'$. This means the number of stocks held by the stockholders of company Y is larger than the number of stocks held by the stockholders of company X. Therefore, the ACQUISITION is valid, and thus the purchasing method is applied to the transferred assets, and in turn, net realizable value s of the assets is used.

4.1.3   *Case 1-3: s > p, b > c, and a > b*

Since $a > b$ in this situation, the number of units, a, of transferred assets exceeds the sales capacity of company Y. Therefore, y is zero, and constraint (2) of transferred asset a is unbinding. As a result, $u = 0$. However, it is not reasonable to give all of the transferred assets a zero value. Because, if only number $(a-b-1)$ is negated from the transferred assets, the situation is equivalent to Case 1-1, where $a < b$, and thus $u = p$.

In order to handle such an abnormal situation, parametric programming can be applied to parameter a of constraint (2) so that the total number of assets of value a is evaluated segment by segment. When a segment changes, the optimal basis also changes, and the dual value will also change at the same time (see Figure 3).

4.2   *Case 2: s > p and b < c*

In this case when $a < b$, or when $a < b < c$, in order to satisfy sales capacity b, procurement capacity c can be utilized by the number of b, but if a is used, it is simpler to use c by the number of $b - a$. Thus by using one unit of a you can save the cost of using one unit of procuring capacity c, which is the amount of p. Therefore, in this case $u = p$. However, when $a > b$, the number of $a - b$ is not used at all, such that the final unit of a will not contribute to the enhancement of the value of the objective function, and thus $u = 0$. In this way, when the value of a changes parametrically, the value of the transferred assets behaves as in Figure 4.

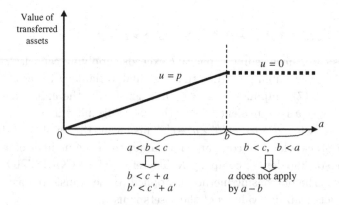

Fig. 4   Segmental valuations of transferred assets under $s > p$ and $b < c$

When $b < c$ and $a < b$, $b < c + a$. Therefore, $b' < c' + a'$ can hold, and thus again the number of stocks held by the stockholders of company X is larger than the number of stocks held by the stockholders of company Y. Therefore, "ACQUISITION" by merging company Y does not occur, and governance of company X for the transferred asset is retained by company X. Thus, the pooling of interests method is applied to the transferred assets, and procurement cost p or the original book value of the assets is used.

4.3   *Case 3: s < p*

Where $s < p$, the values of the transferred asset are evaluated as in Figure 5 when the parameter value of asset a is changed continuously.

When $s < p$, $y = 0$ and constraint (4) is unbinding. If $y = 0$ and $a < b$, then constraint (3) is also unbinding since sale capacity b cannot be satisfied by transferred asset a alone. Therefore, $w = v = 0$, and only u has a positive value. That means the optimal policy is to sell only transferred asset a without using in-house capacity c. Therefore, because x is positive, constraint (7) takes equality, and thus $u = s$.

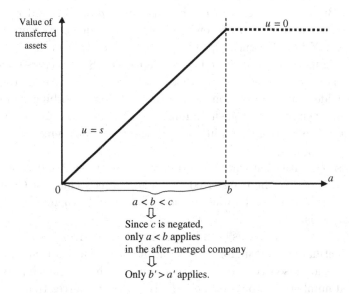

Fig. 5   Segmental valuations of transferred assets under $s < p$ and $b < c$

In this case, since $y = 0$, in-house capacity c is not used at all; this is equivalent to the removal of the total amount of c. When c is negated, only a and b exist in the after-merger company and only the resource relation of $a < b$ is valid in the after-merger company. Therefore $a' < b'$ is valid by removing fund c' in the initial setting of the capital relationship of Figure 2. And thus the number of stocks held by the original stockholders X is less than the number of stocks held by the original stockholders Y. Hence, the *purchase method* is applied to the transfer of assets.

The case of $u = s$ under the situation of $s < p$ is that the net realizable value of *fair value s* of the transferred assets is less than procurement cost or original *book value p*, and thus a *negative value of goodwill* will occur.

5   Conclusion: A Practical Consideration

An accountant would never accept the above parametric or multiple segmental valuations of transferred assets saying that it varies too much and is confusing. However, when viewing the actual situation in the real world, such multiple segmental valuations are not necessary.

First under Case 1 of $s > p$ and $b > c$, the situation of $u = s$ occurs often. But $u = p$ rarely occurs, because, $u = p$ applies under $b > c$ and $a < b < a + c$. In view of the ownership structure of the merger, if merging company Y has an ownership structure of $b' > c'$, that means it has governance rights over company Y before the merger. Such ownership structure rarely is upset as $b' < a' + c'$, where the governance power of the original stockholders of merging company Y is lost after absorbing merged company X. Such reverse acquisition implies that absorbed company X actually acquired the control rights in terms of the vote stock number of the after merger company Y.

Also the situation where $u = 0$ in the above Case 2 and Case 3 will be avoided if part of the transferred assets is negated. Thus, for Case 2 where $s > p$ and $b < c$, dual variable u is p. For Case 3 where $s < p$, the dual variable u is s.

Up to this point it has been assumed that transferred assets a are merely the identifiable and tangible assets and further regarded that the relationship of such resources $(a : b : c)$ conforms to the relationship among the offered numbers of stocks $(a' : b' : c')$. However, resources that are actually transferred in a merger in the real world are not confined to identifiable and tangible assets, but may include intangible assets of both identifiable and unidentifiable ones, including corporate brand assets.

When such comprehensive assets are referred to as "business" as a whole, the value of such business is made by *fair value*, the valuation of the business value or enterprise value, which corresponds to the number of stocks of merging company Y offered as payment for the merged business or company. Thus the application of the model and analysis in this chapter can be extended to such business as a whole, including goodwill assets, etc.

In addition, the model in this paper determining valuation of transferred assets is based on the supply and demand relationship of the "resources" in the after-merged company. This is basically an examination from the viewpoint of economics. On the other hand, from the viewpoint of corporate law, tax law, and financial accounting standards, the valuation of transferred assets in a merger is based on the source of the funds used to procure such resources. In other words, it is the ownership structure or the holding ratio between the original stockholders of merged company X and the original shareholders of merging company Y. Then what kind of reasonable correspondence can be found between the supply and demand relationship of "resources" and the ownership structure or the holding ratio?

As stated in Section 2, it has been assumed that a corresponding relationship of $(a : b : c) = (a' : b' : c')$ exists. In turn, this applies:

(A) If $b > a+c$, then the number of stocks held by the stockholders of company Y is greater than the number of stocks held by the stockholders of company X.

(B) If $b \leq a + c$, then the number of stocks held by the stockholders of company Y $\leq$ the number of stocks held by the stockholders of company X.

Then how can the rationale of the above assumption regarding the corresponding relationship be maintained? For Case (A), the benefit to the merging company Y is very large since the transferred assets are scarce; so, company Y would wish to *purchase* the transferred assets to maintain the control rights in the after-merger company and does not wish company X to keep control of rights over the transferred assets after the merger. On the other hand, for Case (B), the benefit to the merging company Y is rather small because the transferred assets are not scarce but are instead too much in the after-merger company; so, company Y itself would wish to be *purchased* by company X and thus its control rights in the after-merger company would be smaller.

References

Böhm, H.-H. und Wille, F. (1960). *Direct Costing und Programmplanung*, München: Verlag Moderne Industrie.

Böhm, H.-H. und Wille, F. (1965). *Deckungsbeitragsrechnung und Programmoptimierung*, München: Verlag Moderne Industrie.

Carsberg, B. (1969). On the linear programming approach to asset valuation, *Journal of Accounting Research*, Autumn, pp. 165–182.

Churchill, N. C. and Stedry, A. C. (1966). Some development of management science and information systems with respect to measurement in accounting, in *Research in Accounting Measurement*, edited by Jaedicke, R. K., Ijiri, Y., and Nielsen, O., American Accounting Association, pp. 28–48.

Manes, R. P. (1970). Birch paper company revisited: an exercise in transfer pricing, *The Accounting Review*, July, pp. 565–572.

Manes, R. P., Park, S. H., and Jensen, R. (1982). Relevant costs of intermediate goods and services, *The Accounting Review*, July, pp. 594–606.

Monden, Y. (1982). The transfer price based on a shadow price for resource transfers among departments, in *A Compendium of Research on Information and Accounting for Managerial Decision and Control in Japan*, edited by Sato, Skate, Mueller, and Radebaugh, American Accounting Association, pp. 51–71.

Monden, Y. (1989). *Foundations of Transfer Pricing and Profit Allocation*, Tokyo: Dobunkan Pub. Co. (in Japanese).

Monden, Y. (1992). *Development of Transfer Pricing and Profit Allocation*, Tokyo: Dobunkan Pub. Co. (in Japanese).

Onsi, M. (1970). A transfer pricing based on opportunity costs, *The Accounting Review*, July.

Samuels, J. W. (1965). Opportunity costing: an application of mathematical programming, *Journal of Accounting Research* 3(2), pp. 182–191.

Strum, J. E. (1969). Note on "two-sided shadow prices," *Journal of Accounting Research*, Spring, pp. 160–163.

Wright, F. K. (1968). Measuring asset services: a linear programming approach, *Journal of Accounting Research*, Autumn, pp. 222–236.

Wright, F. K. (1969). A reply, *Journal of Accounting Research*, Autumn, pp. 182–187.

Wright, F. K. (1970). Dual variable in inventory measurement, *The Accounting Review*, January, pp. 129–133.

Part 2

Management Control Systems and Budgeting

Analysis of the Influence of Performance-Based Systems on Japanese Management Control

Eri Yokota

Professor, Faculty of Business and Commerce
Keio University

1 Introduction: Issues

The reward system, along with measuring and assessing business performance, is a crucial part of the management control process. Since the latter half of the 1990s, the Japanese corporate reward system has been changing.

Previously, in most cases there was no direct connection between business performance from a managerial accounting perspective and an increase or decrease in reward, largely because the reward system had been built around the characteristically Japanese seniority-based wage system premised on long-term employment. In the past few years, however, an increasing number of companies have unexpectedly scrapped the seniority-based wages system and introduced a performance-based system in its place. At the same time, accounting on a cash-flow basis has come under the managerial accounting spotlight, and some companies have begun introducing new criteria for measuring and assessing business performance.

What then does this shift to performance-based systems mean to Japanese management control? And how does this relate to the almost simultaneously implemented change in criteria for measuring and assessing business performance?

In response to these questions, this paper aims to first examine the characteristics and objectives of the US reward system, which is said to be performance-based. Next, we will explore the Japanese corporate trends toward performance-based systems and the implications of these trends from within a management control framework. This paper aims to explain, in concrete terms, the underlying concepts, using case studies of companies that have led the way in introducing performance-based systems and new performance measurement and assessment criteria. In this paper, we present an examination of the essential impact on management control resulting from Japanese companies' shift toward performance-based systems, and the implications.

2   The US Reward System: Position and Changes in Management Control

Studies of US managerial accounting systems underscore the importance of the reward system (Bruns and McKinnon, 1992; Anthony and Govindarajan, 1998) which functions as a critical mechanism for motivating managers to achieve organizational objectives (Anthony and Govindarajan, 1998).

Management control studies indicate that managers' monetary rewards consist of salary, benefits, and incentives (Merchant, 1997, Anthony and Govindarajan, 1998). Of these, incentives (including bonuses) are closely linked to management control (Anthony and Govindarajan, 1998). Short-term incentives based on short-term performance and long-term incentives corresponding to a longer term viewpoint (e.g. stock prices) are used as a tool for motivating managers toward the short- and long-term objectives of the company. Stock options are fairly representative of the array of long-term incentives offered to managers by companies (Merchant, 1997).

According to Merchant, in many companies, reward and performance are defined in a linear sense. However, Merchant also highlights the importance of rewards that have value, have an impact, are understood, and are timely. It has also been said that monetary rewards do not easily satisfy all of these requirements (Merchant, 1997), thus non-monetary rewards, in both the positive and negative sense, are used in conjunction with monetary rewards.

Morishima (1996) states that the tendency to link salary with individual achievements in the US — especially in white-collar managerial positions — took strong root in the 1970s and gained further momentum in the 1980s. Takahashi (1999) also states that the performance principle appeared in the US in the 1980s. Because the job grading system widely applied in the 1960s had a number of inherent problems, the performance principle was introduced with the aim of heightening performance orientation while retaining the existing system. The system of linking individual wages to company profits was also applied to general workers beginning in the 1980s.

During the 1990s, the number of job layers was reduced in a shift toward a broader approach; job evaluations were abolished, and more emphasis was placed on the wage market. Personnel departments were scaled down, and the system of central management by personnel staff came to an end as companies began moving toward a more linear focus (Takahashi, 1999). These days, white-collar employment and the wage system in the US are being even more rigidly linked to market values as the reform process continues (Morishima, 1996).

US companies are also increasing the proportion of long-term incentives (Takahashi *et al.*, 1997). Many of these incentives are linked to stock prices, and are targeted at periods of 2 to 10 years. There are various long-term incentives other than stock options, which lately have attracted a great deal of attention in Japan (Takahashi *et al.*, 1997).

Economic theory (or "agency theory") maintains that CEO and/or upper management rewards should be closely correlated with the performance of the company or division, but reports indicate there is no clear evidence that this is actually happening (Barkema and Gomez-Mejia, 1998). Corroborative research also shows that CEO/management rewards in the US or UK are connected to other factors, such as strategies or corporate scale (Murthy, 1997; Merchant, 1997; Barkema and Gomez-Mejia, 1998; Conyon and Peck, 1998; Sanders and Carpenter, 1998; Finkelstein and Boyd, 1998). On the other hand, there are also studies showing that offering profit-center rewards to directors or managers correlates to corporate performance, the scale of the profit center, and residual profit (Fisher and Govindarajan, 1992; Wallace, 1997).

From the references mentioned, it can be seen that even in the US, which is generally regarded as a symbol of the performance principle, moves toward such a system really only became distinctive from the 1980s onwards. And even at the CEO or manager reward level, the performance of their overseen division is not necessarily the sole reward determinant.

However, in terms of monetary reward (which is closely linked with the management control framework) there is a tendency to make the relationship between performance and short-term incentives much stronger, and also to strengthen the link between performance and stockholder profit through long-term incentives. This entails providing short-term incentives linked to performance in line with company goals (e.g., ROE), while building long-term motivation through various incentives to achieve long-term goals based on stock-price criteria (which is bound together with stockholder profit). Although distinct, both short-term and long-term incentives

Fig. 1   Management control process in the US

aim to motivate by binding the setting, measurement, and evaluation of clear numerical goals.

Figure 1 shows the US framework. The flow of goal-setting, planning, evaluation, and reward is firmly linked to the clear goal of maximizing stockholders' profits. Stockholders demand that CEOs maximize their profits, and this demand is passed on to subordinate managers by way of their respective goals. The connection between long- and short-term goals and their evaluation and incentives are quite clear in each case. Naturally, there are other forms of rewards, but it is conjectured that the connection between goals, evaluation, and incentives are clearly indicated.

3   Changes in the Reward System in Japanese Companies

3.1   *Shift to a performance-based system*

In the recent years, the term "performance principle" has been used to express the distinctive features of future reward systems. As for "performance principle," it seems that even human resource management researchers are not always clear about what exactly is meant by this term. Morishima (1999, p. 3) states that:

> Despite the excessive use of the term "performance principle," there is no widely accepted understanding of what it in fact means. Nor is the kind of shift in thinking that

forms the basis for the trend toward performance-based systems always adequately understood in human resources management.

Nonetheless, the use of the term does signify a concept distinct from the traditional Japanese wage system based on length of service. In this study, the performance principle reflects a move toward wages determination according to performance, rather than according to age and the number of years served.

According to a survey conducted by the Japan Institute for Labor Policy and Training (January 2004, $N = 1066$), as many as 60.5% of respondent companies said their systems over the past three years are "more or less in line with" the "performance principle" of employee evaluation criteria that places greater emphasis on performance than age or length of service. In response to the question whether they have introduced a system under which business performance is reflected by wages, 55.8% of respondents said they have already introduced such a system (Japan Institute for Labor Policy and Training, 2004). In a separate 2002 survey by the Institute of Labor Administration covering a total of 3927 companies — 3575 firms listed on stock exchanges across Japan and 352 unlisted firms paralleling listed firms, the weight of "performance evaluation" was an average 80.8% for bonuses and an average 35.6% for salaries for section chief-level employees at 220 responding companies. In another survey conducted in May–July 2003 covering a total of 2912 companies, 77.7% of 112 respondents said they have introduced performance-based personnel systems. The "performance principle" in this survey means less orientation toward the length of service, clarification of performance, roles and business achievements of individual employees, fairness, and transparency of evaluation (Rome Gyosei Kenkyujyo, 2003).

These days, many Japanese companies are linking bonuses or salary to the company's or individual's results/performance. Reasons highlighted for such changes include an aging company workforce, bloated personnel costs due to the business downturn, and cost cutting to cope with the shortage of posts.

Somewhat more positive reasons were also given, including a greater emphasis on creativity over experience, and the need for adaptable employees to cope with the rapidly changing corporate environment. In other words, the "autonomy of the individual" is touted as the reason for the shift to a performance-based system. Companies are seeking to clarify not just the results of the group, but the achievements of the individual as well. Companies are aiming to link performance with rewards commensurate with the skills and capabilities displayed by the individual.

Next, what impact does this reorientation of the reward system have on management control in Japanese companies?

3.2   *The role of reward systems in management control in Japanese companies*

Management control is a framework for ensuring that strategies are executed with certainty to achieve organizational goals. It applies to managers responsible for implementing strategies, and the mechanism for coordinating the achievement of their respective sectional goals and the achievement of the overall goal is the management control system. In the management control process described in management control studies, feedback through goals, assessment, and reward has a single flow as a mechanism for achieving the goals of the responsible manager and the goals of the organization (Anthony, 1988).

As for the characteristics of business management systems at Japanese companies, Monden cites places of work organized as small groups, horizontal division of job duties, and career development programs based on lifetime employment, generalizing them as group-oriented. In other words, they are characterized by solidarity mechanisms for collective goal-setting, execution, and evaluation conducted by workplace groups (Monden, 1985, p. 28; Monden, 1989, pp. 416 and 417).

With their reward systems premised on long-term employment, large companies to date have not linked reward directly to business results measured through managerial accounting systems. Rather, they have used their reward systems to give employees long-term motivation to achieve company goals. To these companies, long-serving employees are important assets, as they have a depth of experience and are able to firmly grasp the range of circumstances facing the company when making a decision.

The characteristics of management control at Japanese companies (where reward is premised on long-term employment and is not directly linked to the fluctuations of quarterly business results) can be described as the "two-part structure of management control at Japanese companies" (Yokota, 1998; Figure 2). In this framework, the reward system contributes to the formation of a psychological contract between employees and

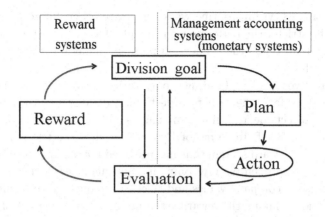

Fig. 2   Two-part structure of management control within Japanese companies

the company, while the managerial accounting systems — including business performance measurements and assessments — functioned to motivate managers to short-term improvements in business performance (Yokota, 1998). Under this structure, managers at Japanese companies have been able to view company objectives as personal goals, and have therefore focused entirely on short-term business performance.

The reward system at Japanese companies is, however, undergoing a change. Though not the same in all cases, the system is shifting to a framework in which the performance of the organization or the overseeing organizational unit is directly reflected in the monetary reward given to the employees responsible and/or to the employees as a whole.

The move to a performance-based system tends to be either misunderstood or mistaken for a results-based system (Takahashi, 1999). Takahashi states that a results-based system basically disregards process or interim outcomes, and looks only at the final business results. A performance-based system, on the other hand, looks at business performance from a much broader perspective, such as the processes that gave rise to the performance as well as concrete interim outcomes. In reality, though, if one uses such terms as "assessment and reward according to business performance and outcomes," and if the business performance is centered on short-term performance criteria, it is only natural that attention would be directed toward short-term outcomes. To look at the processes from which performance is derived, companies will also have to conduct capability assessments, which many companies had previously been carrying out, or assessments within routine work, or devise other different methods. In short, the stricter the performance principle that is applied, the greater the focus tends to be on the connection between monetary reward and assessment results.

While eyes tend to be drawn only to its effects (i.e., short-term performance), in fact, the shift to a performance-based system does not seek simply to direct the attention of managers and employees to "business performance" in itself. In terms of Figure 2, within the two-part structure, changing the reward system that has provided for the long-term psychological contract between mainly companies and managers will enable changes in the sense of company values and rules to be conveyed to members of the organization. Making the reward structure built on tacit rules of long-term employment that existed between companies and employees performance-oriented shows to managers that the company now has different rules and expectations from those of the past. This will result in a heightened interest in measuring and assessing business performance among members of the organization. Therefore, even though this results in a focus on business performance, its significance is not just the focus on business performance, but that it is also a means of conveying that what the company expects from its managers is changing.

At the same time, there are moves to introduce new business performance measurement criteria. This is generally taking place concurrently with the shift to performance-based reward systems. This would seem to indicate that the two-part structure of the management control process in Japanese companies is taking on the characteristics of a single cycle. Is management control about to shift toward a single process system, comprising dual long-term and short-term incentives? Or is it morphing into an integration of the previous two systems? If the latter is the case, it represents the coexistence of a new process of goal setting, evaluation, and reward on a short-term premise and a reward system premised on long-term employment. And unless the premise of long-term employment is abolished, the latter case will always apply. Today, Japanese companies are searching for new management systems.

In the past, Japanese companies have not had to clearly spell out reward or assessment standards within personnel management systems premised on a long-term employment relationship. But, with a performance-based system, what has to be done, how it has to be done, and the level of reward for doing it should be set out clearly. So, even if the premise of long-term employment were to remain the same, at least the rules of the reward system and what the company assesses as important should be clearly stated. Clarifying the link between results from measuring performance and individual reward will also clarify the goals expected of the individual, and further raise worker interest in how the company is performing. If a company pushes ahead with a performance-based system without adequately delegating authority to managers, it really is only focusing on performance or on the goals resulting from that performance. If, however, it properly delegates authority to managers, then specifies the rules clearly, managers will know the exact parameters of the decisions they are required to make, and assessments of their performance will be reflected in their reward. In the latter case, managers will accept their reward as an assessment that expresses the results of their own decision-making. Therefore, managers will start to consider how their decision-making can produce effective outcomes, rather than producing outcomes to raise their reward.

A heightened interest in company performance by managers is not the only benefit arising from a change in business performance assessment criteria and a shift to a performance-based reward system; a change in the management control process signifies a major change in what a company expects from its managers. So, what is needed is not just a change in the reward system, but a transformation of the general management system, in aspects such as business performance assessment criteria, and the delegation of authority.

In the following section, the author introduces some findings and examines this transition to a performance-based system, and discusses how specific changes in measuring and assessing business performance will affect management control.

4 Discussions with Examples

The change from a reward system to a performance-based system was a signal from the companies that there would be a shift in company awareness (Yokota, 2000, 2004). The change in the reward system and performance measuring criteria were, as processes leading to this end, carried out virtually simultaneously.

It goes without saying that performance has always been important, especially for divisional directors. But with reward linked to performance through changes to the reward system, and the previous two management control processes combined, companies made it known that they were changing the rules between company and managers and seeking to bring about a new awareness within the company. All of the observed companies revealed new management concepts and changes in strategies through changes to their reward systems and performance measurement (Yokota, 2000).

All these companies have embarked on a course toward performance-based systems. Through this, they are opening up the corporate reward system, and seeking to clarify the previously tacit rules between the company and the individual. It can be said that extending the performance principle to general employees and not just to responsible executives — and having improvements in performance through new performance criteria reach not just executives and managers but general employees as well — is one way of having the idea of "management" shared among all employees.

Of course, if this change takes root, interest among the members of the organization for outcomes that are linked to reward will become much stronger. But as pointed out by Pfeffer (1998) not all such effects are positive; for example, dealing with the overemphasis on short-term outcomes will be the next issue.

5 Consideration and Conclusions

Previously, management control at Japanese companies was characterized by its two-part structure. With the spread of the performance principle, however, some or most of these parts are beginning to be linked. At first glance, management control at Japanese companies seems to be getting closer to the management control process as described in American management control texts. But the objective of the linkage was rather to change the awareness of employees through changes in management control. The change was to raise awareness about short-term business performance, but at the base of it, the long-term relationship between an organization and its members remains intact. The change is not directed as much toward the control of organizational goals with a strong awareness of the maximization of shareholder interests. In other words, what Japanese companies have chosen is the change of awareness on the part of employees using the term "performance principle."

The two-part structure of management control at Japanese companies appears to be gradually turning into a single system. The conventional

systems were based on the two-part structure of the "psychological contract premised on long-term employment through reward systems" and the
"promotion of decision-making largely based on management accounting,"
which performed their respective and separate roles. In contrast, present
developments, while retaining approaches based on corporate philosophy or
visions of top corporate executives and long-term employment as long-term
goals of companies, have been moving toward building mechanisms under
which the degree of contribution to corporate profits as the concretization
of corporate philosophy is measured and evaluated each term and the performance is rewarded accordingly. In other words, the two-part structure of
the management control process that previously characterized management
control at Japanese companies is beginning to take on a new structure with
the rise of the performance principle. The performance evaluation system
characterized by the performance principle is beginning to link the two
structures. However, rather than viewing it as a single cycle of management control, it would fit in with the reality to think that some parts of
the two structures are being linked by the performance evaluation system.
It is the system under which goals, plans, and evaluation are to be shared
explicitly, with the performance evaluation system of both short-term and
long-term orientation linking between the personnel management system
with long-term orientation and the short-term system revolving around
financial information (Figure 3).

The systemic structure of management-control influences members of
organizations through psychological contracts between organizations and
their members. Thus, regarding how to build psychological contracts

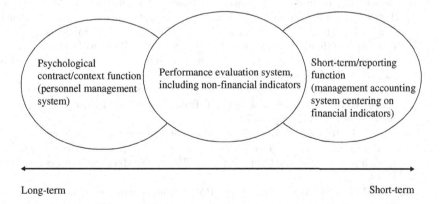

Fig. 3   Management control structure at Japanese companies

between organizations and their members, it should be possible to change the organizational context underlying it by consciously demonstrating the linkage between them by performance evaluation systems. It would be desirable to build management systems by taking this into account.

At present, employees of Japanese companies are required to understand that the new mechanism that sheds light on the evaluation of their performance is something that does not necessarily emphasize performance alone, but rather makes clear the proof of the fulfillment of their responsibilities. In seeking to conclude new psychological contracts with employees, it is important for companies to clearly demonstrate to their employees that the recent series of developments related to management control are not designed to simply get tough on business performance and reduce costs, but rather to pursue a change in corporate awareness and to show a change of business model. Furthermore, it is necessary to understand that the change sought is a change in companies' and managers' awareness without altering the long-term relationship between them.

Acknowledgment

The author would like to thank people at the companies he visited for their cooperation in interview surveys on case examples. This paper is a product of additions to and alterations of Yokota (2000) and Yokota (2004).

References

An editorial department of the Institute of Labor Administration (2003). Introduction and a definition of performance-based personal systems (Seika Syugi Jinji noDonyu to Teigi), *Rosei Jihou*, No. 359, pp. 3–6 (in Japanese).

Anthony, R. N. (1988). *Management Control Function*, Harvard Business Press.

Anthony, R. N. and Govindarajan, V. (1998) *Management Control Systems*, 9th ed., Irwin/McGraw-Hill.

Barkema, H. G. and Gomez-Mejia, L. R. (1998). Managerial compensation and firm performance: a general research framework, *The Academy of Management Journal*, 41(2), pp. 135–145.

Bruns, W. J. Jr. and McKinnon, S. M. (1992). Performance evaluation and description of tasks and activities, in *Performance, Measurement, Evaluation, and Incentives*, edited by Bruns, W. J. Jr, Harvard Business School Press.

Canyon, M. J. and Peck, S. I. (1998). Board control remuneration committees, and top management compensation, *The Academy of Management Journal*, 41(2), pp. 146–157.

Ezzamel, M. and Watson, R. (1998). Market comparison earnings and the bidding-up of executive cash compensation: evidence the united kingdom, *The Academy of Management Journal*, 41(2), pp. 221–231.

Finkelstein, S. and Boyd, B. K. (1998). How much does the CEO matter? the role of managerial discretion in the setting of CEO compensation, *The Academy of Management Journal*, 41(2), pp. 179–199.

Fisher, J. and Govindarajan, V. (1992). Profit center manager compensation: An examination of market, political and human capital factors, *Strategic Management Journal*, 13, pp. 205–217.

Fuji Sogo Kenkyujyo (1998). A report about treatment of "pay-per-performance systems"/"Based on ability" (Jitsuryoku-syugi, Seika-syugi' teki shigu ni kansuru jittai tyousa houkokusyo), Fuji Sogo Kenkyujyo (in Japanese).

Japan Institute for Labor Policy and Training (2004). Motivation and the investigation of workers and methods of employment management (Roudousya no hataraku iyokuto koyoukannri no arikata ni kansuru chosa), *Chosa shirizu*, No. 1 (in Japanese).

Keizai Doyukai (1998). A white paper of companies (Kigyo Hakusyo), No. 14 (in Japanese).

Merchant, K. (1989). *Rewarding Results*, Harvard Business School Press.

Merchant, K. A. (1997). *Modern Management Control Systems: Text and Cases*, Prentice-Hall.

Monden, Y. (1985). Characteristics of performance control systems in Japan (Wagakuni no Gyoseki Kanri Seido no Tokucho), *Keiei Jitsumu*, No. 374, pp. 26–28, 35.

Monden, Y. (1989). Characteristics of performance control systems in Japanese corporations, *Japanese Management Accounting*, Productivity Press, pp. 413–423.

Morishima, M. (1996). A recent trend over a reward system of an American white-collar (White–Color no chingin-Shogu–Seido wo meguru Saikin no Doukou: Koyou no Gaibuka to Kyuyo Kettei no Junansei Zoudai), *Rodo Horitsu Junpo*, No. 1391, 1996.9.10, pp. 32–42 (in Japanese).

Morishima, M. (1999). The influence that penetration of the principle of result gives a place of work (Seika Syugi no Shinto ga Syokuba ni Ataeru Eikyo), *Japan Labor Review*, No. 474, pp. 2–13 (in Japanese).

Murthy, K. R. S. (1997). *Corporate Strategy and Top Executive Compensation*, Harvard University Press.

Nikkeiren Shokumu Bunseki Center (ed.) (1997). *A Design and Operation of "Japanese Annual Wage plan"* (*Japanese Nenpouse no Sekkei to Unyo*), Nikeiren Syuppanbu (in Japanese).

Ogata, H. (1996). Takeda Chemical Industory ni okeru Kanpani sei to Honsya bumon kaikaku no jissai, *Business Research*, September, pp. 62–67 (in Japanese).

Pfeffer, J. (1998). Six dangerous myths about pay, *Harvard Business Review*, May–June, pp. 109–119.

Takahashi, K., Hara, N. and Maeda, T. (1997). *Reward System Management (Hoshu Management)*, President sha (in Japanese).

Takahashi, S. (1999). *Pay for Performance Systems (Seika Shugi)*, Toyo Keizai Shinpo sya (in Japanese).

Wallace, J. M. (1997). Adopting residual income-based compensation plans: do you get you pay for? *Journal of Accounting and Economics*, 24, pp. 275–300.

Yokota, E. (1998). *Clinical Aspects between Management and Psychology of Flat Organizations: The New Age Needs the New Management Control Systems*, Keio University Press (in Japanese).

Yokota, E. (2000). The effect of the introduction of paying for performance and new performance measurement on Japanese management control systems, *Journal of Management Accounting, Japan*, 1/2(8), pp. 51–68 (in Japanese).

Yokota, E. (2004). An examination into the management base that affects the performance evaluation systems of Japanese companies, *Journal of Management Accounting, Japan*, 1/2(13), pp. 55–66 (in Japanese).

An Example of Japanese "Beyond Budgeting" Philosophy

Katsuhiro Ito

Professor, Faculty of Economics
Seikei University

1 Introduction

This paper shall pick up two recent developments in the budgetary control theory, and discuss what they mean to Japanese corporations. Recent research on budgetary control may be classified into the following two streams[1]: One is a "better budgeting" approach that pursues refinement of corporate budgeting, a typical example of which is the so-called Activity-Based Budgeting (ABB). The other is a so-called "beyond budgeting" approach that is critical about the traditional style of budgeting and thus seeks to either remove or improve it. This paper discusses the latter and its implication for the Japanese corporate management system.

One of the characteristics of Japanese corporations is that they are typically *autonomous organizations* that adapt to their environment by means of group dynamics. To cut it short, the Beyond Budgeting model that is about to be explored in this paper is, as it were, a counterproposal by the organizations seeking *group dynamics*, against the traditional budgetary control system that has been compatible with *bureaucratic dynamics* (the concepts of which shall be explained later). Hope and Fraser (2003) propose to change the organizational operation itself through the reform of the budgetary control system (which they call "implementation of the adaptation process"). From this point of view, it is not surprising that some elements observed in the Beyond Budgeting model can be identified in the budgeting practices of Japanese corporations, of which two points, namely (1) separation of budgetary control from performance evaluation and (2) the rolling budgeting, shall be discussed here as the most remarkable ones.

---

[1]This classification is also employed in other works such as those by Horngren (2004) and Otley (2006).

To start, let us review how the traditional budgetary control system is criticized from the Beyond Budgeting point of view, and what methodologies are proposed in the Beyond Budgeting model.

2 Changing Corporate Environment and the Beyond Budgeting Model

2.1 *Criticism of the traditional budgetary control system by BBRT*

The Beyond Budgeting Round Table (BBRT) was established in January 1998, by CAM-I (Europe). According to the BBRT, Beyond Budgeting refers to a set of principles that enables an organization to adequately manage its performance without relying on a budgetary control system, while promoting decentralization of its various decision-making processes to the frontline.

The Beyond Budgeting concept assumes the following procedures in the operational process of the traditional budgetary control: (i) A certain vision is materialized into a strategic plan, (ii) a mid-term operational plan and annual budgets are prepared on the basis of such strategic plan, (iii) such budgets are used as criteria (targets) for measuring performance, and (iv) incentives are paid based on the performance measured against the budget targets. The BBRT claims that while such a traditional budgetary control system was quite useful, in an industrialized society meant to secure a stable supply of industrial goods in a less variable environment, this system no longer works effectively in an advanced information-intensive society in which intangibles (intellectual capital) largely determine competitiveness. Hope and Fraser (2003) point the following critical comments as the basis of the above claim.

First, too much time and resources are devoted to budget preparation and the budgetary control process, resulting in unjustifiably large excess costs. Second, where compensation is calculated relative to budget performance, management under the budgetary control is less encouraged to disclose genuine information, creating a situation in which false/deceitful management information tends to be distributed within the organization (and people start to play games over budget figures).[2] Third, since the

---

[2]Similar remarks are found in Jensen (2001).

allocation of resources is fixed beforehand at the stage of budget preparation, the organization is no longer capable of adaptive actions vital to cope with changes in environment, which means the organization can no longer flexibly respond to the changing environment, because of the fixed allocation of internal resources given by the prior budgeting. At the same time, managers are motivated to claim more than necessary expense budgets, just to cope with possible contingencies that require additional resources. Fourth, emphasis on the control based on financial performance undermines the accumulation of intellectual capital crucial to the long-term survival of a corporation. This is a harmful effect of the management attitude in pursuit of apparent financial performance on a short-term basis, without working hard to build up organizational competence under a long-term perspective.

The traditional budgetary control system is not only incapable of performing its originally assumed role any more but likely to preclude, in various aspects, a corporation from adopting an organization structure compatible with the information-oriented age. The traditional budgetary control system is highly compatible with a management style by "command and control," thus restraining unconfined and autonomous activities at the frontline and discouraging challenge. Specifically, the system shifts the attention of too many managers toward the attainment of short-term financial targets, undermining the potential for longer-term growth.

2.2 *Propositions by the beyond budgeting model*

Now, let us review how the BBRT proposes to reform the traditional budgetary control system associated with many ill effects. Hope and Fraser (2003) position our age as the information-oriented age subsequent to the industrialized age, and point out increasing uncertainty as this age's greatest characteristic. They further point out such preconditions for success in the information-oriented age, such as processes promptly adapting to changes, timely procurement of information, and the delegation of authority by thorough decentralization. In other words, what the BBRT pursues is the adoption of a corporate structure compatible with a highly uncertain environment, in which the traditional budgetary control system is simply perceived as an obstruction.

The traditional budgetary control system has been deployed in close association with the traditional framework of organizations. In a highly uncertain environment, however, such frameworks are no longer adaptive enough, as they preclude the formulation of emergent strategies, and thus have been criticized. The essential contribution of the Beyond Budgeting model is that it extended the theories of the budgetary control system that have been built on the traditional organizational frameworks to an unexplored realm. The model's purposes are deemed to be directed toward a budgetary control system that activates adaptive behavior without obstructing organizational learning. What the Beyond Budgeting theorists criticize is not the specific calculation structure in a budgetary control system but its actual operation method. A considerable portion of the criticism toward the traditional budgetary control system is directed at the traditional organization model associated with the budgetary control system. Thus we need to appreciate the fact that the same management accounting tool is expected to operate in completely different ways, depending on the type of organizational framework on which the tool is based. The Beyond Budgeting theory has been pursuing a budgetary control system that fits the adaptive organization model, based on the appreciation of the flaws in the traditional budgetary control system such as an obstructive element against organizational learning.

3   Comparison of Management between the US and Japanese Corporations

3.1   *Difference in organizational structure and operational principles*

Japanese corporate management attracted considerable attention since the 1980s, because of their (particularly some of the Japanese manufacturers') strengthened international competitiveness compared with their American counterparts. At the same time, the management accounting system used by American corporations was alleged by Johnson and Kaplan (1987) to have lost its relevance (*relevance lost*), which was regarded by many researchers as a serious issue, giving rise to the massive attention toward the cost management methods practiced by Japanese corporations, such as target costing and kaizen costing. It is appropriate to assume that this was the period when comparative study of the management of Japanese and American corporations was quite popular, including those studies implicitly attempting such a comparison, without explicitly taking such a viewpoint.

Numerous comparative studies of such a nature were conducted in Japan as well as in North America in this period, among which the aforementioned research by Kagono *et al.* (1983) can be named as a representative work. In this study, research was carried out in areas such as corporate environment, management targets, management strategies, organizational structure, and organizational climate in both Japanese and American corporations, and a comparative analysis based on the results of this research was explored.

Having done some comparison, Kagono *et al.* (1983) dared not decide which of the two was absolutely superior, which distinguishes this study from the then prevalent tone of argument. Indeed, Japanese corporations had superior competitiveness over the Americans in industries such as consumer appliances, electronics, and automobiles, while in other industries such as natural resources extraction (including petrochemical and mining), chemicals, food, pharmaceuticals, apparel, distribution, financial services, etc.), the American corporations still maintained overwhelming competitive advantages. Of all the differences between the Japanese and American corporations identified as a result of such a management comparison, the four points as follows can be mentioned as those of particular relevance to the discussion hereafter in this paper.

3.2 Flexible deployment of resources vs. cumulative reserve of resources

A comparative analysis of the strategic behavior of Japanese and American corporations revealed that the Americans tend to deploy resources flexibly based on a thorough analysis of the opportunities in their business environment and associated risks, where merger and acquisition serves as a realistic tool for such an exercise. This is an approach that enables a corporation to adapt promptly to the changing environment by restructuring its internal resources through market transactions, based on the analysis of opportunities in the corporation's business environment.

Compared with this, Japanese corporations are said to be inclined to take an approach in which they seek to accumulate internal operational resources to an abundant enough level to cope with any contingency in their business environment, rather than meticulously analyzing their business environment to find a way to adapt to it. It was observed that as a result of such an approach, Japanese corporations appeared to remain emotionally committed to their existing business operations, without adequate agility and decisiveness in the face of the need to restructure their business operations. In the event of launching new businesses, they also tend to internally build up their own new business units from scratch, rather than acquiring existing business operations from the outside. A comparison of the business profile of Japanese and American corporations on the PPM (Product Portfolio Management) matrix indicates that Japanese corporations generally embrace more "problem children" and "underdogs," while American corporations keep more "stars" and "cash cows." This reveals that the American corporations are more focused on flexible allocation of resources and short-term investment efficiency.

3.3 Deductive/logical approach vs. functional/fine-tuning approach

The findings described in the above section concern the trend of corporate decision-making with respect to a company-wide business portfolio (or characteristics of company-wide strategies). Some Japanese–American differences were observed also on the competitive strategy level (business strategies), pursuing the establishment of competitive advantage at each business unit. American corporations typically take a logical/deductive strategy-making process based on a preconditioned rationality, where specific action plans are developed and implemented based on the concepts formulated by the strategic staff.

On the other hand, within a typical Japanese corporation, the development process of competitive strategies is not clearly separated from the implementation process. The typical procedure is to take action first, and then apply incremental fine-tuning, paying attention to the current business environment and competitive circumstances, to finally achieve competitive advantages. For instance, new products are introduced first, and various experiments are conducted through regular sales activities. Customer response and market information are promptly fed back, to change production quantity and product specification, or sometimes even the product concept and sales strategies themselves.

3.4 Difference in the nature of budget as caused by the difference in the formulation process of business strategies

In association with the findings by Kagono *et al.* (1983), I would like to make some comments on the difference in the nature of budgets between Japanese and American corporations. A difference in the strategy formulation approach makes a remarkable difference in the meaning of business plans (overall budget). In the deductive approach adopted by American corporations, innovativeness of the product concept, compatibility between the product concept and sales strategies, systematic integration between sales strategies and the strategy-implementing functions, etc. are important preconditions for achieving competitive advantages. Operational performance in conformity with strategic plans is emphasized at the strategy-implementing functions from which market information is fed back through the regular monitoring of deviations from the projection. After all, a deviation from the projection (budget) is "something that should not exist" and "something that ought to be eliminated or repressed" as much as possible in such a strategy-formulation approach.

On the contrary, in the improvisation-oriented strategy-formulation process named as the characteristics of Japanese corporations by Kagono *et al.* (1983), refinement of the product concept and sales strategies through daily activities are the preconditions to achieving competitive advantages. Under this approach, as the plan itself is not so much an enforceable norm, analyzing deviations from the plan is not of great relevance. What really matters is the straightforward feedback of the market information, whereby constant improvement of the product concept and sales strategies can be realized.

Kagono *et al.* (1983) argue that the option whether adhering to a plan rationally formulated in advance or leaving room for flexible fine-tuning is found also in the quantity adjustment method in the production process. For an example, in the Toyota Production System (TPS), various car models are assembled in a single production line, where production quantity is fine-tuned between each model according to the orders from the market. On the other hand, in the North American automotive manufacturers' system, production is carried out by adhering to the production plan scheduled beforehand for each car model. Given the uncertainty in the business environment, the fine-tuning approach is believed to be appropriate by the Japanese corporations, as a way to respond to the changes in the market, where the effort to prepare rational plans in advance is given up to a degree, allowing flexibility in the production/sales system instead.

3.5 *Strategic hierarchy vs. improvising network*

The contrast between Japanese and American corporations is clearly visible in their organization structure and internal administration system. The results of a questionnaire indicate that American corporations tend to employ divisional organization (94.4% of the respondent US corporations, while 59.8% of their Japanese counterparts), with higher self-sufficiency (i.e., ratio of retaining various functions within each division). Furthermore, the headquarters' accounting department is given relatively great authority to assure the aforementioned flexible corporate strategies. Typically, these departments manage a number of divisions, with each operating within a clearly defined business domain based on the relevant product concept, where each division is controlled by such financial measures as ROI.

On the other hand, Japanese corporations tend to employ functional organization, where divisions, if they exist, tend to be functional divisions with lower self-sufficiency and clear separation of production and sales. As a result, a performance comparison between divisions is not relevant, and no great emphasis is placed on ROI, while management control is based on criteria such as market share and ROS (return on sales).

The evaluation of divisional performance is mainly based on return on investment (ROI or residual income), which in turn serves as the basis for the allocation of resources among divisions.

3.6 Concepts behind methodologies of adaptation to environment

As described in the work by Kagono *et al.* (1983), organizational management in Japanese corporations originally does not involve such management concepts as divisional allocation of resources and financial control, as often observed in American corporations. It should be pointed out that while the organizational structure and management in an American corporation are designed and operated in an orderly fashion, as if in the military with emphasis on logical methodology, Japanese corporate organization, despite its clearly defined official structure on its organizational chart, is actually designed to operate with some flexibility to allow adequate room for autonomous fine-tuning on the frontlines. Japanese corporations generally operate on the frontline-oriented principle, enabling incremental adaptation to the environment across all organization units.

There is no telling which of the two is absolutely superior, but either has relative advantage depending on the environmental conditions. The philosophy behind the adaptation method of American corporations fits the business environment in which environmental changes are predictable on a longer-term basis, while customer needs are relatively constant. This philosophy, however, is flawed in that it is incapable of partial fine-tuning to the organizational structure and management strategies. The philosophy of the Japanese corporations in their adaptation to environment is effective in an environment where customer needs are continuously changing. But this method can possibly stop working in a circumstance where partial fine-tuning cannot provide solutions.

Summarizing the above argument, the approach taken typically by American corporations seeks to adapt to the environment by exercising management, adhering to the optimum business plan (i.e., budget) developed in reliance on the preconditioned rationality (planning-oriented adaptation by bureaucratic dynamics). Bureaucratic dynamics is defined as "a method of organizational structuring, meant to achieve organizational integration and address environmental variety through rules and planning, based on the development of formulated organization and hierarchy" (Kagono *et al.*, 1983, p. 174). On the other hand, the approach taken typically by Japanese corporations seeks to adapt to the environment, by continual experiments and .fine-tuning from time to time, taking a skeptical standpoint with respect to the preconditioned rationality (fine-tuning-oriented adaptation by group dynamics). Group dynamics is defined as "a method of achieving organizational integration while addressing environmental variety, through frequent interactions between member staff as well as groups, based on the shared value and information" (p. 174). Generally, the latter is more effective in a rather uncertain environment, while the former is advantageous when environmental variation is predicable to a degree.

4   Compatibility between a Budgetary Control System and an Organization Model

When management accounting was established as an academic discipline in the 1920s, the budgetary control system was positioned as the discipline's central tool along with standard cost accounting. Behind the establishment of management accounting was the calling of time seeking a methodology, competent enough to manage the unprecedented scale and complexity of the so-called modern big businesses emerging in the United States from the late 19th century to the early 20th century (Hiromoto, 1993). The bureaucratic organization model was adopted to manage those large and complex organizations at that time. The traditional budgetary control system has been designed and operated based on the bureaucratic organizational structure, in which problem solution and internal adjustment is carried out through a hierarchical chain of authority, where responsibility and authority were clearly defined. Hiromoto (2005, 21) says, "It can be said that J. O. McKinsey who invented the traditional management accounting, originated the argument for his case by explaining about a centralized functional organization, and then developed the management accounting theory as a standard corporate ideology, where function of management accounting that supports the operation of bureaucratic organizations was envisaged, attaching particular importance to procedural standards as well as budgetary control (operational standards)," reminding that management accounting in its early days assumed bureaucratic organizations as its organization model.

Bureaucratic organizations work effectively as long as the external environment is relatively stable, whereas it is difficult for them to adapt quickly to the environment with greater uncertainty. Desirable organizations under the corporate environment nowadays are the ones with autonomy, capable of spontaneous adaptive behavior at the frontline. A management control system in an autonomous organization is desired to be furnished with functions such as (i) an information provision function that helps each staff member to clearly see what is going on in the organization and what impact his/her own action has on the whole organization and (ii) a learning facilitation function that supports flexible adaptation to an ever-changing corporate environment (Hiromoto, 2005, p. 25). The traditional budgetary control system assumed from the Beyond Budgeting point of view, as represented by Hope and Fraser (2003), is far from meeting these requirements, and thus is incompatible with autonomous organizations, allowing us to conclude that an autonomous organization better matches the Beyond Budgeting model, while the traditional budgetary control model works better in a bureaucratic organization.

5 Budgetary Control Practice in Japanese Corporations and Beyond Budgeting

In the budgetary control practice by Japanese corporations, we find particular relevance in two points, i.e., its relationship with compensation calculation system and its enhanced prediction accuracy by the adoption of a rolling budget, as they are compatible with the assertion in support of the Beyond Budgeting model. Let us review these points in turn.

5.1   *Separation between compensation calculation system and budgetary control system*

Management accounting systems have often been operated separately from the short-term compensation calculation processes in Japanese corporations.[3] Yokota (1998) defines such separation between management accounting system and compensation calculation, as "divided structure of the management control process in Japanese corporations." The management control process generally assumes compensation to be calculated in accordance with the results of a performance evaluation, whereas in Japanese corporations, compensation calculation has been practiced without much regard to short-term financial performance, but as part of the staff administration system independent of the management accounting system (Yokota, 1998, pp. 67–69).

In the generally practiced management control process, a plan that has been set beforehand is implemented. Its performance status is monitored and then evaluated against some kind of performance evaluation criteria, in order to provide a basis of compensation calculation, whereas in the management control process typically practiced in Japanese corporations, the management accounting system operates separately from the staff administration system.

In the management control process often observed in Japanese corporations, management accounting information has not been regarded as very relevant in the calculation of compensation. In that sense, the need to get rid of the "annual performance trap" claimed by Beyond Budgeting did not exist in Japan in the first place.

5.2   *Adoption of rolling budget*

Many Japanese corporations are adopting a rolling budget (also known as revolving budget, continuous budget, or continual budgeting), which is another practice recommended for better planning accuracy in the Beyond Budgeting model. An increasing number of corporations are practicing rolling budget these days. Rolling budget refers to a budgeting method in which an annual budget is prepared first, say, for period

---

[3]Due to the increasing popularity of meritocracy since the 1990s, an increasing number of corporations have come to include budget performance in the measurement parameters for compensation calculation.

April/2006–March/2007, then after the lapse of one month, figure for the single month of April/2006 is dropped while the single month of April/2007 is added, to make an annual budget for period May/2006–April/2007.

For example, Nikon was known to be employing a quarterly rolling budget system reviewing every three-month period, which was introduced in the following circumstances: "Sales turnover of the company drastically decreased, through the strong yen-caused recession from 1986 to 1987, and in a deteriorated business environment due to the 'semiconductor recession.' In such a circumstance, if production outsourcing and procurement of materials within manufacturing divisions, or promotion and advertising within sales divisions went ahead by contracting outside providers as originally planned, on the basis of the initial sales budget, cost for those activities could have drastically deteriorated the company's profitability, resulting into increases in stock and financial crunch. This question gave rise to an argument about how budgetary control should operate in such a volatile, difficult-to-predict period, leading up to the eventual introduction of quarterly budgeting as a solution to cope with environmental changes" (Tanaka, 1993, pp. 104–105). As discussed above, in a situation in which an unpredictable corporate environment makes it difficult to prepare plans in advance, rolling budgeting proves effective as it increases the frequency of feedback as well as budget revisions by shortening the budget period. According to Tanaka (1993), quarterly budgeting has the following advantages:

(a) Shortening the budget period enables a prompt review of operational plans and timely revisions of the budget, in response to the changes in the business environment.

(b) Corporate top management has access to the latest information through the budgeting process, and thus remains alerted enough to take measures to rectify problems as needed.

(c) Leveling off of sales turnover and expenditure is facilitated through quarterly budget preparation. Bi-annual sales budgets can be performed in six months' time, while under quarterly budgets, quarter-to-quarter fluctuation of the sales projections tends to cause greater volatility in profitability. Thus, the utmost effort to eliminate volatility at the stage of sales projection is required in order to secure a constant profit. The same is true in expenditures. For instance, as expenditures recorded on a payment basis could create volatility in quarterly profits, expenditures should be switched to an accrual basis.

(d) There is greater likelihood of reduced lead time. Introducing quarterly budgeting will not immediately reduce lead time. As the input budgeting and inventory planning in production projection is run on a quarterly basis, the utmost effort must be made to squeeze the lead time into the three-month time frame. It can be said that quarterly budgeting obliges each division to take an active stance in adapting itself flexibly to the environmental changes.

6 Summary and Conclusion

The budgetary control theory in recent years is said to be classified into two streams, namely (1) an approach pursuing to refine corporate budgeting (ABB, Activity-Based Budgeting) and (2) an approach to scrap budgeting itself (Beyond Budgeting). As (1) takes a stance that focuses on the causation of budgeting in an attempt to refine the budgetary control system, it can be presumed to be as an extension of the hitherto evolving process of budgeting systems, which is an attempt that is readily justifiable. A major issue in the performance-based management accounting theory (budgetary control theory) is how to evaluate the argument in (2).

In this chapter, budgetary controls practiced in Japanese corporations, in association with the Beyond Budgeting theory, have been discussed. Specifically, an analysis of the budgetary control systems in Japanese corporations, in terms of the linkage between performance evaluation and compensation system, as well as the adoption of rolling budget as advocated by Beyond Budgeting, was presented. Through the above process, the "information-oriented budgetary control system" observed in a number of Japanese corporations can be positioned as an antithesis of the "control-driven budgetary control system" closely linked to performance evaluation as observed more often in Western corporations. Meanwhile, as the operational characteristics of the budgetary control system were typically observed in Japanese corporations, we can point out a finding that has been, at least hitherto, clearly separated from the short-term compensation calculation process (introduction of meritocracy is changing the climate, though), and that enhancement of planning accuracy by adopting a rolling budget was consciously envisaged. These facts provided confirmation that the principal elements promoted by the Beyond Budgeting model were already in existence in the Japanese budgetary control system.

References

Anthony, R. N. (1965). *Planning and Control Systems: A Framework for Analysis*, Harvard University Press.

Anthony, R. N. (1988). *Management Control Function*, Harvard Business School Press.

Anthony, R. N. and Govindarajan, V. (2003). *Management Control Systems*, 11th ed., McGraw-Hill.

Flamholtz, E. G. (1983). Accounting, budgeting and control systems in their organisational context: theoretical and empirical perspectives, *Accounting, Organisations and Society* 8-2/3, pp. 153–169.

Hansen, S. C. and Torok, R. (2003). *The Closed Loop: Implementing Activity-Based Planning and Budgeting*, Bedford, TX: CAM-I.

Hiromoto, T. (1993). *Historical Development of the Management Accounting Theory in the United States*, Moriyama Shoten (in Japanese).

Hiromoto, T. (2005). Autonomous organization and management accounting: from the market-oriented management point of view, *Kigyou-Kaikei* 57-12, pp. 18–26 (in Japanese).

Hope, J. and Fraser, R. (2003). *Beyond Budgeting: How Managers Can Break Free from the Annual Performance Trap*, Harvard Business School Press.

Horngren, C. T. (2004). Management accounting: some comments, *Journal of Management Accounting Research* 16, 207–211.

Jensen, M. C. (2001). Corporate budgeting is broken: let's fix it, *Harvard Business Review*, November, pp. 94–101.

Johnson, H. T. and Kapalan, R. S. (1987). *Relevance Lost: The Rise and Fall of Management Accounting*, Harvard Business School Press.

Kagono, T., Nonaka, I., Sakakibara, K., and Okumura, A. (1983). *A Management Comparison Between US and Japanese Firms: Theory of Strategic Adaptation to Environment*, The Nihon Keizai Shinbun-sha (in Japanese).

Mintzberg, H. (1994). *The Rise and Fall of Strategic Planning*, Prentice-Hall.

Mintzberg, H., Ahlstrand, B., and Lampel, J. (1998). *Strategy Safari: A Guided Tour Through the Wilds of Strategic Management*, 1st ed., Simon & Schuster.

Otley, D. (2006). Trends in budgetary control and responsibility accounting, in *Contemporary Issues in Management Accounting*, edited by Alnoor Bhimani, Oxford University Press, pp. 291–307.

Simons, R. (1994). *Levers of Control: How Managers Use Innovative Control Systems to Drive Strategic Renewal*, Harvard Business School Press.

Tanaka, N. (1993). Nikon's internal control system, in *A Case Study of Management Accounting System of the Japanese Corporations*, Yasuo Sato, edited by the Society for the Study of Industrial-Academic Cooperative Management Accounting, Hakuto Shobo (in Japanese).

Yokota, E. (1998). *Management of a Flat Organization and Its Psychological Aspect: Management Control in a Changing Times*, Keio University Press, Inc. (in Japanese).

Questionnaire Survey on the International Financial Control Affecting the Responsibility Accounting of Overseas Subsidiaries

Makoto Tomo

Associate Professor, Faculty of Economics
Seijo University

1 Introduction

For globally developed businesses operated by multinational enterprises (MNEs), it has been indicated that "managerial localization" for authorizing the preferment of local staff and the transfer of authority in overseas subsidiaries is quite important. However, many Japanese MNEs have introduced a financial system known as "the global cash management system" (hereinafter referred to as GCMS) for the efficient control of capital and exchanges by aiming to secure maximum company-wide profits after taxation. Hence, practically, there are two different methods for controlling MNEs, i.e., by means of decentralization and centralization.

As a result of analyzing the questionnaire survey of Japanese MNEs executed in 1998, it has been indicated that there is a trend for MNEs to introduce centralized financial methods. Based on this indication, a hypothesis on the possible influence affecting the evaluation of business results on the part of individual overseas subsidiaries is set up. Hence, based on the mail survey results regarding the budget control system and the financial control system executed in 2001, the influence on the performance indicator carried out via the GCMS and the relationship between the GCMS and tax reducing management are discussed.

2 Influence of the Financial Centralization Method

The MNEs use various financial methods, such as forward exchange contract, currency swap, currency option, leads and lags, matching, netting, re-invoicing, etc. These financial techniques are divided into two types of methods from a perspective of whether a subsidiary uses these independently or not. One type of the method we name is the financial centralization method. Leads and lags, matching, netting, and re-invoicing are included in this type. The other type is non-centralized financial method. Forward exchange contract, currency swap, and currency option fall under this type.

(1) Leads and lags: A technique of paying early (leads) or paying late (lags) to shift the financial liquidity between subsidiaries.
(2) Matching: A technique of marrying receivables with the same amount of currency payables within MNEs group firms.
(3) Netting: A technique of concentrating settlements with invoicing and payment information among subsidiaries to reconcile.
(4) Re-invoicing: A kind of offshore trade — A manufacturing subsidiary sends goods direct to a distribution subsidiary. A re-invoicing center mediates their payments. The distribution subsidiary pays to a re-invoicing center, and then the manufacturing subsidiary receives the payment from the center.

The financial centralization method contributes to efficiency in MNEs' operations for the following reasons. First, financial officers come to deal with their financial operations with global perspective. Second, fund accommodation among subsidiaries saves group-wide cash and extra liquidity. It reduces costs arising from remittance charges, interest, and tax.

At the same time, the financial centralization method affects a subsidiary's financial statements, since its main purpose is to maximize MNEs' in-group cash flow, but it seldom incorporates the subsidiary's decision in finance (Figure 1). Shapiro (1992) pointed out that the actual result of manipulating transfer prices on goods and services, adjusting dividend payments, and leading and lagging remittances cause destruction on incentive systems of profit center based management and eventually cause confusion and computational chaos.

Due to the above problems, it has been pointed out that evaluating the operating performance of foreign subsidiary managers should be separate from judging the subsidiary as an investment (Gernon, 2001, p. 158). However, according to the survey by Borkowski (1999) only 10% of surveyed Japanese enterprises keep two sets of books to circumvent the effect of transfer pricing on performance evaluation.

Balance sheet	Income sheet	Cash flow
Leads and lags		
Amount of credit and debt increases or decreases.	Interest on credit and debt increases or decreases.	Cash flow increases or decreases by the change of settlement timing of credit and debt.
Matching		
Amount of local currency based credit and debt increases or decreases	Exchange gains and losses accrue from credit and debt	Exchange gains and losses accrue from local currency based credit and debt.
Netting		
There is same influence as the leads and lags by settlement timing change of credit and debt.		
Re-invoicing		
There is same influence as "leads and lags" and "matching." In addition, the following influences exist.		
	Amount of profits and tax increases and decreases by transfer pricing.	Cash flow increases or decreases corresponding to profits and tax change.

Fig. 1   Influence of the financial centralization method on subsidiary's financial statements

Thus, the following working hypotheses are drawn:

H1: With the globalization maturing of MNEs, there is a trend for Japanese MNEs to employ the GCMS for the company-wide financial efficiency.

H2: The degree of importance of financial performance indicator has lessened for the MNEs which employ the GCMS.

H3: The awareness of cash and foreign exchange management is adversely affected for the MNEs which employ the GCMS.

3   Overview of the Survey

3.1   *Overview of the questionnaire survey*

The survey was conducted from October 2001 to November 2001. Questionnaires were sent to 512 Japanese manufacturing enterprises listed in the Tokyo Stock Exchange whose consolidated sales were more than ¥40 billion. The questionnaires were addressed to staff in charge of the accounting and financial departments. Valid response was 110. The valid response rate was 21.5%.

For the questionnaire survey, since a survey was also conducted on the budget control systems adapted by Japanese and Korean industrial enterprises at the same time, only those global enterprises were not specifically selected. But, only those enterprises that responded to items being surveyed related to overseas financial management such as employing the GCMS as a subject for analysis were solely dealt with.

3.2 *Overview of the MNEs who responded to the questionnaire*

Figure 2 shows the average company size (including sales-volume and number of employees) of MNEs who responded to the questionnaire. The arithmetic average of consolidated sales is ¥660 million. The median is ¥201 million. The reason for the discrepancy between the arithmetic average and median is caused by the inclusion of MNEs exceeding ¥1 trillion. The average number of consolidated employees is 17,700, and the median is 5,800.

The proportion of an overseas subsidiary in consolidated sales is 2.3% on the average. In the case where there are mutual transactions between the head offices in Japan and overseas subsidiaries, the percentage of an overseas subsidiary in consolidated sales is 9.2% on the average; its median is 4% and the number of MNEs is 61 (55%). The number of MNEs having mutual transactions in more than 5% of consolidated sales is 35. In the case where there are mutual transactions between the overseas subsidiaries, the percentage of mutual transactions in consolidated sales is 5.4% on the

	N	Avg.	25%	50%	75%	Std.
Consolidated sales (billion ¥)	110	660.5	85.8	201.5	704.0	1,236.0
Employee (thousand)	110	17.7	2.6	5.8	19.2	37.9
Mutual transactions:						
between subsidiaries (%)	70	5.4	0.0	0.1	4.0	13.7
Head office and subsidiaries (%)	74	9.2	0.5	4.0	12.0	13.8
Overseas subsidiaries sales (%)	104	2.3	1.0	2.0	3.0	1.7

Fig. 2   The size of MNEs that responded to the questionnaire

average; the median is 0.1% and the number of MNEs is 37 (37%). Further, there are 16 MNEs who have mutual transactions between the overseas subsidiaries in more than 5% of consolidated sales. Compared with the number of MNEs and sales, the percentage of mutual transactions between the overseas subsidiaries is twice the percentage of mutual transactions between the overseas subsidiaries.

3.3 *The responsibility center type of overseas subsidiaries*

As shown in Figure 3, 43% of MNEs recognize overseas subsidiaries as cost centers. Profit centers are 30% and investment centers are 26%. When it concerns the foreign sales subsidiary, 42% of MNEs recognize overseas subsidiaries as profit centers or revenue centers. Conversely, 48% of MNEs recognize overseas subsidiaries as investment centers. It is thought that foreign subsidiaries assume a self-concluding authority and responsibility, because they have functions from manufacturing to sales.

4 Utilization of GCMS and Influence on Overseas Performance Accounting

4.1 *Utilization of GCMS*

Figure 4 shows whether to use GCMS. In this section, the data was limited to the enterprises where the subsidiary existed in foreign countries. Of those five methods, the utilization ratio of netting is highest (52%), followed by

	Overseas manufacturing subsidiaries	Overseas marketing subsidiaries	Overseas mfg/marketing subsidiaries
Revenue center	1 (1%)	32 (42%)	5 (6%)
Cost center	32 (43%)	0 (0%)	2 (3%)
Profit center	22 (30%)	32 (42%)	38 (48%)
Investment center	19 (26%)	12 (16%)	34 (43%)
Average	2.8	2.3	3.3
Standard deviation	0.8	1.2	0.8
Number of responses	74	76	79

Fig. 3   The responsibility center type of overseas subsidiaries

matching, re-invoicing, and cash-pooling method. Leads and Lags method is used only 11%. There are 51 MNEs which use one of the above five methods.

Compared to the previous survey conducted in 1998, the above survey proved that the utilization ratio of the above five means, especially netting and re-invoicing methods, increased.

The cash-pooling method was mainly used by MNEs aiming to reduce capital cost. The Leads and Lag and matching methods were mainly used aiming to minimize exchange risk exposure. The netting and re-invoicing methods were aimed to reduce capital cost and minimize exchange risk exposure. In contrast, tax-reduction purpose was only for 5 cases. 4 of them were the purpose of re-invoicing method. The re-invoicing is the payment and settlement system of a triangular trade. And the re-invoicing center is used for every transaction. There might be room created for tax-reduction strategy using the re-invoicing method.

	Leads and Lags	Matching	Netting	Re-invoice	Cash-pooling
Not being used	52	37	33	45	44
No knowledge	19	16	5	11	11
Actually being used	9	27	41	24	23
Reducing cost of fund	1	1	20	6	20
Minimizing exchange Risk exposure	8	22	15	12	2
Tax-reduction	0	1	0	4	0
Exchange risk Exposure/tax-reduction	0	3	6	2	1
Total	80	80	79	80	78
Rate of use	11%	34%	52%	30%	29%
Rate of use (past 1998)	6%	23%	25%	11%	-
Ratio of purpose					
Reducing cost of fund	11%	4%	49%	25%	87%
Minimizing exchange Risk exposure	89%	81%	37%	50%	9%
Tax-reduction	0%	4%	0%	17%	0%
Exchange risk Exposure/tax-reduction	0%	11%	15%	8%	4%

Fig. 4   Purpose of the GCMS

4.2 Relationship between globalization maturity of MNEs and use of the GCMS

Figure 5 is a cross-tabulation table. The abscissa axis was categorized by whether an initial establishment year of overseas subsidiary was before 1974 or after. This is a proxy variable of globalization maturity. The number of MNEs using GCMS methods was plotted in the vertical axis. In the first row, the number of MNEs using methods in GCMS is 0; frequency after 1975 category is 79% (22 MNEs). In contrast, in rows 4 and 5, frequency after 1975 category is both 0%. According to the test of mean difference between the two categories, the p-value was 0.00. Statistically, there is significant difference. Thus, the number of MNEs using methods of GCMS increases as the globalization maturity rises.

4.3 Relationship between the performance indicator for managers in overseas subsidiaries and the use of GCMS

The relationship between the number of MNEs using GCMS and overseas managers was analyzed by the test of mean difference. The MNEs were categorized into two types, the MNEs which used over one GCMS methods were group A, and others were group B. Before the test, the importance was converted into the numerical value, primary into 3, secondary into 2, tertiary into 1, and others into 0.

Figure 6 shows that only the cash flow indicator is statistically significant. By comparing the average values, group A shows high use of the cash

GCMS adapted number	Initial establishment year of overseas subsidiary		
	Before 1974	After 1975	Total
0	7	22	29
1	5	11	16
2	11	4	15
3	7	2	9
4	7	0	7
5	4	0	4
Total	41	39	80

Chi-square of Pearson = 27.0; Degree of Freedom = 5, p-value = 0.00.

Fig. 5 Initial establishment year of overseas subsidiary and GCMS adapted number

	Group B N < = 1	Group A N > = 2	t-value	df	p-value
Return on sales (ROS)	0.78	1.06	−1.02	78	0.31
Controllable profit	0.60	0.74	−0.54	78	0.59
Divisional profit after home office cost	0.82	0.83	−0.02	78	0.98
Return on investment (ROI)	0.80	0.40	1.71	78	0.09
EVA	0.31	0.09	1.39	78	0.17
Sales	0.64	0.83	−0.73	78	0.47
Sales growth rate	0.22	0.49	−1.48	78	0.14
Market share	0.40	0.31	0.50	78	0.62
Cash flow	0.47	0.86	−2.05	78	0.04
Total assets turnover	0.07	0.06	0.14	78	0.89
Labor productivity	0.09	0.00	1.47	78	0.15
Equipment productivity	0.04	0.00	1.26	78	0.21
Quality	0.36	0.09	1.74	78	0.09
Delivery	0.04	0.00	1.26	78	0.21
Cost	0.16	0.17	−0.15	78	0.88
Customer satisfaction	0.20	0.09	0.96	78	0.34
Number of cases	45	35			

Fig. 6   Applicable extent of the GCMS and targets for overseas managers

flow indicator than group B. Other indicators, including non-financial performance indicators, do not have a statistically significant difference. The working hypothesis 2 is not supported in this result.

4.4   *Relationship between the GCMS and the awareness of cash management and foreign exchange management*

Figure 7 shows the practical influence of the GCMS on performance evaluation and the awareness of cash management and foreign exchange management. For a start, 82% of the MNEs responded that the GCMS do not affect performance evaluation significantly or at all. This result is consistent with Figure 4; there were few MNEs using the GCMS for reducing tax.

Secondly, 59% of the MNEs responded that GCMS considerably or slightly affect the awareness of cash management and foreign exchange management. Since GCMS is a system for the cash transfer, it is natural. Conversely, 82% of the MNEs responded that the GCMS do not affect overseas subsidiary performance. Conceivably, this is because the MNEs do not evaluate their cost of fund.

	Influence on performance	Influence on awareness of cash/ foreign exchange management
Not affected at all	26 (32%)	14 (17%)
Not that much affected	41 (50%)	20 (24%)
Slightly affected	14 (17%)	41 (50%)
Considerably affected	1 (1%)	7 (9%)
Total	82 (100%)	82 (100%)
Average	1.9	2.5
Standard deviation	0.7	0.9

Fig. 7 Relationship between the GCMS and the performance or the awareness of cash management and foreign exchange management

The relationship between globalization maturity of MNEs and the awareness of cash management and foreign exchange management was analyzed by the test of mean difference. First, the MNEs were categorized into two, whether initial establishment year of overseas subsidiary was before 1974 or after. Figure 8 shows the influence on performance of overseas subsidiaries have a statistically significant difference. Secondly, the MNEs were categorized into two, whether the MNEs used over one GCMS methods or less.

Figure 9 shows the influence on performance of overseas subsidiaries also have a statistically significant difference. There was no statistically significant difference in the influence on awareness of cash management

	Average		Statistical values			
	Before 1973	After 1974	t-value	df	p-value	Leben's p-value
Influence on performance of overseas subsidiaries	1.67	2.14	−2.95	76	0.004	0.329
Influence on awareness of cash/ foreign exchange management	2.52	2.53	−0.02	76	0.984	0.178
Number of cases	42	36				

Fig. 8 Relationship between the GCMS and the performance or the awareness of cash management and foreign exchange management relative to the initial establishment year of overseas subsidiary

	Average		Statistical values			
	Below one kind of GCMS	Above two kinds of GCMS	*t*-value	*df*	*p*-value	Leben's *p*-value
Influence on performance of overseas subsidiaries	2.05	1.67	2.34	77	0.022	0.509
Influence on awareness of cash/ foreign exchange management	2.51	2.53	–0.08	77	0.937	0.553
Number of cases	43	36				

Fig. 9 Relationship between the number of MNEs using methods of GCMS and the performance or the awareness of cash management and foreign exchange management

and foreign exchange management. But the majority of the MNEs conceived that the GCMS could affect their awareness of cash management and foreign exchange management to some extent.

The comparison of the average values of the influence on performance of overseas subsidiaries: the average value of group A (before 1973) was lower than group B (after 1974), and the average value of group D (above two kinds of GCMS) was lower than group C (below one kind of GCMS), although in the working hypothesis 3, the analyzed result turned out to be contrary. This is because the matured MNEs might have already established a system for controlling their overseas subsidiaries as highly independent organizations.

5 Conclusion

The relationship between the GCMS and the responsibility accounting in Japanese MNEs was investigated through the questionnaire survey. The GCMS are used to maximize profit of MNEs. They may also harm incentive systems in profit center based management, though it improves company-wide profits. From these aspects three working hypotheses have been tested. In conclusion, the H1 was supported. However H2 and H3 were not supported.

With gradual maturity as MNEs, many of them have introduced the GCMS to centralize the financial management control. At present, the

GCMS are mainly used for efficient control of the uneven distribution of cash and/or the foreign exchange exposure. However, there were only 17% of MNEs applying the GCMS (re-invoicing) for the global group tax-reduction strategy.

Due to the transfer price taxation and the anti-dumping tariff, it is difficult to operate the global group tax-reduction strategy. Although the majority of MNEs aim for the maximization profit after tax, only a few of them practically execute global group tax-reduction strategy, so that it may not affect the profit of overseas subsidiaries. Those MNEs might consider that decentralization management of overseas subsidiaries is more important than the global group tax-reduction strategy. In other words, the MNEs do not use the GCMS to eliminate the adjustment of performance influenced by them. Although 59% of the MNEs responded that the GCMS affect the awareness of cash management and foreign exchange management, they considered that there is no need to adjust the performance of overseas subsidiaries for these MNEs.

References

American Accounting Association (1973). Report of the committee on international accounting, *The Accounting Review, Supplement*, pp. 120–167.

Asada, T. (1996). Management control systems of global enterprise, *Kaikei* 149(2), pp. 276–278; 149(3), pp. 395–404 (in Japanese).

Asada, T. (1997). Progress and globalization of budget control system for Japanese enterprise and management control systems of global enterprise, *Kaikei* 149(2), pp. 276–278; 149(3), pp. 395–404 (in Japanese).

Borkowski, S. C. (1999). International managerial performance evaluation: a five country comparison, *Journal of International Business Studies* 30(3), pp. 533–555.

Carlos, J. V. and Goetschalckx, M. (2001). A global supply chain model with transfer pricing and transportation cost allocation, *European Journal of Operational Research* 129(1), pp. 134–158.

Collins, J. H. and Shackelford, D. A. (1998). Global organizations and taxes: an analysis of the dividend, interest, royalty, and management fee payments between U.S. multinationals' foreign affiliates, *Journal Accounting and Economics* 24, pp. 151–173.

Eiteman, D. K., Stonehill, A. I., and Moffett, M. H. (1998). *Multinational Business Finance*, 8th ed., Addison Wesley.

Galbraith, J. R. (2000). *Designing the Global Corporation*, Jossey-Bass Pub.

Gernon, H. and Meek, G. K. (2001). *Accounting: An International Perspective*, 5th ed., McGraw-Hill Higher Education.

Ito, H. (1995). *Globalization of Enterprise and Management*, Chuokeiza-sha (in Japanese).

Minagawa, Y. (1993). *Tax Management of MNCs*, Nagoya University Press (in Japanese).

Miyamoto, K. (2003). *Management Accounting of Global Corporation*, Chuokeiza-sha (in Japanese).

Nakajo, S. (1992). Exchange risk control system of European and American multinational, *Trade and Tariff*, July, pp. 60–67; August, pp. 58–65; September, pp. 42–48 (in Japanese).

Okawara, K. (2003). *International Tax Management Practice*, Chuokeiza-sha (in Japanese).

Radebaugh, L. H. and Gray, S. J. (1997). *International Accounting and Multinational Enterprises*, 4th ed., John Wiley & Sons, Inc.

Robbins, S. M. and Stobaugh, R. B. (1973). *Money in the Multinational Enterprise: A Study of Financial Policy*, Basic Books.

Schwarz, J. and Elina, C. (2006). Re-engineering multinational supply chains, *Bulletin for International Taxation* 60(5), pp. 187–193.

Shapiro, A. C. (1992). *Multinational Financial Management*, 4th ed., Allyn and Bacon.

Tomo, M. (1997). *Overseas Financial Management for Capital Efficiency*, LTCB Research Institute (in Japanese).

Tomo, M. (1999). The study of accounting and financial control for global enterprises, Master Thesis of Osaka University (in Japanese).

Tomo, M. (2002). Responsibility accounting and financial centralization method, *Kanrikaikeigaku* 10(1), pp. 53–62 (in Japanese).

Tomo, M. and Asada, T. (2002). The relationship between financial centralization and management accounting: a questionnaire survey of Japan-based multinational enterprises, *Asia Pacific Management Review* 7(1), pp. 41–59.

Zenoff, D. B. and Zwick, J. (1978). *International Financial Management*, Perican-sha (translated in Japanese).

Part 3

Cost Management

The Role of "Hidden Costs" in Cost Management

Seiichi Kon

Professor, Faculty of Management
Kyushu Sangyo University

1 Introduction

According to Sakurai, cost management, including cost planning, became important during the period of high-economic growth and remarkable technological innovation in Japan beginning in the 1960s (Sakurai, 2004, p. 267).

During the high-economic growth period, on the one hand, consumer tastes became diverse due to increases in income; on the other hand, we saw remarkable advances in production technology and information processing by which high-mix low-volume production made responding to this diversity possible. In such a managerial environment, it was more effective to focus on planned cost reduction through research and development than on cost control through attempting to restrict operating activities costs within standard costs or budget costs.

In 1969 when period of high-economic growth was about to come to an end, the Sangyo-Kozo Shingikai of the Ministry of International Trade and Industry published a report called "Cost Management." In the report, cost management was defined as the clarification of the goal to reduce costs as a necessary part of profit management for an enterprise's stable growth, the establishment of a plan to achieve this goal, and all the control activities to realize this plan (Sangyo-Kozo Shingikai, 1969, p. 128).

In short, cost management is "business management with an emphasis on planning that primarily utilizes cost information as part of profit management."

However, since the major managerial goal for modern enterprises has changed from simply increasing profits to creating enterprise value, it is necessary for us to discuss cost management in the framework of value-based management.

This paper aims to clarify the role of "hidden costs" (implicit costs) in cost management. A variety of problems that cost management deals with can be summed up as problems of managerial decision-making for the purpose of achieving managerial goals. The concept of cost to support rational decision-making is the concept of opportunity cost in economics, which is comprised of explicit cost and implicit cost. Consequently, the argument here will be developed from an opportunity cost perspective.

Section 2 discusses opportunity cost in economics and clarifies the significance of "hidden cost." We also examine the difference in how opportunity cost is understood in economics and accounting.

Section 3 proposes a heuristic way of analysis of financial costs (costs measured in monetary units) that has been discussed in accounting; it also considers the way of dealing with the financial costs that are included in traditional cost management techniques.

Section 4 considers the significance of "hidden non-financial costs" and "cause variables of value" through a sequential managerial decision-making process example. In addition, the present state and future prospects of cost management centered on "hidden costs" are considered.

There are a few studies on "opportunity cost in accounting," but many of these emphasize the uniqueness of opportunity cost or deal with an extremely limited aspect of managerial decision-making. Consequently, this study is different from these previous works.

2   The Opportunity Cost

2.1   *The meaning of opportunity cost and decision-making*

In economics, cost is defined as the maximum goods' value (utility) acquired from alternative uses of a resource. In this context, cost refers to "opportunity cost." In other words, this concept of cost describes correctly the essence of cost in decision-making. Opportunity cost is a concept recognized when we input a scarce resource (means) and decide to produce one of a possible number of goods (purposes) that share the same resource input. Since such a situation is seen in all economic activities, opportunity cost is allegedly a universal concept (Kumagai *et al.*, 1992, pp. 193–194).

In a market economy, enterprises usually have a variety of alternatives in which they input multiple resources with different ratios at various times. Each alternative produces goods, and the value of goods is accumulated to form a corporate value. Sequential managerial decision-making processes in a real enterprise are not as simple as that of Robinson Crusoe's case.

In order to consider the opportunity cost in various situations enterprises face, we divide the decision-making types into three for the sake of convenience.

The first type is that if we select one choice out of multiple apparent alternatives. This is simply a decision of "what to choose." This is the basic type of decision-making. We regard an alternative that can serve as a standard alternative, and other alternatives that are compared with this as comparative alternatives.

Second, if a comparative alternative is not apparent, the decision simply becomes a "to do or not to do decision." For example, in the case of continuous improvement activity on the shopfloor, comparative alternatives may not necessarily be apparent.

Third, if we are not clearly aware of a standard alternative, it is essentially a decision "not to do anything new." It may be an indication that managers are negligent.

Managers are responsible for continuously seeking hidden uses of the resources, improving the third type situation, and increasing the corporate value. Consequently, as for alternative uses of the resources, we have to examine all the alternatives (standard, comparative, and non-apparent alternatives). When there are not any alternative uses of the resources, by definition, opportunity cost is not incurred.

2.2   *Classification of opportunity costs*

Opportunity cost is not a concept inherent to resources, but it is a relative concept depending on goals and the situation, and it is difficult to comprehend its contents. Let us classify opportunity cost here (see Figure 1).

Opportunity cost that involves money outlay is called explicit cost while opportunity cost that does not involve money outlay is called implicit cost (Iwata, 1993, p. 138). We use "hidden cost" as a different name for implicit cost.

Furthermore, we classify "hidden cost" into two groups: "hidden financial costs" that are not paid for in money but measured in monetary units and "hidden non-financial costs" that are not measured in monetary units. In the following argument, we may omit "hidden" concerning hidden non-financial cost. The value of resources that has no market price such as the

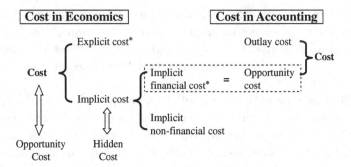

* "Explicit cost" and "implicit (hidden) financial cost" constitute "financial cost."

Fig. 1   Cost in economics and cost in accounting

natural environment is a typical non-financial cost of an alternative that uses the resources.

Last of all, explicit cost and hidden financial cost may be integrated into the concept of "financial cost" in the sense that they are measured in monetary units. According to this classification, opportunity cost in accounting is equivalent to implicit financial cost.

2.3   *Opportunity cost in accounting*

Although opportunity cost in economics is an indispensable measure for the optimal allocation of resources, it has not been dealt with in accounting (Heymann and Bloom, 1990, pp. 103–104). The reason why opportunity cost has not been utilized as a core concept in accounting is that the definitions of cost in economics and accounting are different.

The well-known definition of cost in the American Accounting Association's report of the fiscal year 1955 is the following:

"For business purposes, cost is a general term for a measured amount of value purposefully released or to be released in the acquisition or creation of economic resources, either tangible or intangible. Normally it is measured in terms of a monetary sacrifice involved." (Committee on Cost Accounting Concepts and Standards, 1956, p. 183)

This cost concept is examined in detail and defined. However, explaining outlay cost and opportunity cost in a unified way means that opportunity cost is a subordinate concept of cost in general.

Today, opportunity cost in accounting is considered to be a special concept that is used for project evaluation such as the decision to accept or reject orders. Consequently, it does not apply to general arguments of managerial decision-making issues. It is necessary to return to the concept of opportunity cost in economics and review cost management again.

3   Heuristic Analysis of Financial Costs

3.1   *Explicit costs and outlay costs*

In enterprises, the first type of opportunity cost is explicit cost. Assuming perfect competition and discounting problems of economic externality, explicit cost is believed to correctly represent the maximum value of goods exchanged for money (Kumagai *et al.*, 1992, p. 193). Outlay costs in accounting are identical with the explicit costs that satisfy the above conditions at the time of outlay.

However, the outlay costs described in financial statements are different from the explicit costs as follows:

- The market that an enterprise faces is in general imperfect, and economic externalities do in fact exist.
- Outlay costs are determined by internal calculations such as the allocation of fixed costs and joint costs.
- As time passes, the value of resources changes due to changes in the business and managerial environment.

In other words, outlay costs approximately indicate explicit costs when the influence of the above factors is small. For example, the purchasing cost of multipurpose parts that are traded in a large volume in the market may not differ greatly from the explicit cost if the enterprise's business does not change. However, the unamortized balance of specialized equipment no longer indicates the explicit costs even if the market exists.

The outlay costs reported in financial statements as assets, period cost, or loss, in general, are costs that are not directly related to the managerial decision-making. In short, they are sunk costs.

3.2   *Heuristic analytical method of financial costs*

The second type of opportunity cost for enterprises is the hidden financial cost. Since this is opportunity cost in accounting, we will leave detailed discussion to textbooks and papers of managerial accounting and costing (Miyasaka, 1980; Monden, 2001), proposing a heuristic analytical method of financial costs here.

In principle, we can devise a plan of the optimal allocation of resources using mathematical techniques. Since a linear programming model has high operability based on the linear assumption, it is one of the most often utilized mathematical techniques.

A profit planning model formulated by linear programming can provide the optimal solutions (the best product mix) and the imputed value of the resources. This imputed value of a given resource is a measured figure of hidden financial cost, and the imputed value per unit of the resource is called the "shadow price." Since mathematical techniques can provide a variety of insights into the process of managerial decision-making for individual planning and profit planning, they become a powerful tool for business management.

However, in general, it is difficult to implement the optimal solutions of a mathematical model. The most important reason is that though it is theoretically possible to build an appropriate model of all the factors that may influence managerial goals, these factors are considered to be too complex to make a model in reality.

For example, in case the linear assumption is not applicable, we can alternatively use non-linear programming, target profit can be modeled by goal programming, inseparability of resources can be modeled by integer programming, and different timing of resource input can be modeled by dynamic programming; however, it is extremely difficult to model all of them at once. Consequently, in place of a mathematical model, a heuristic analytical method that can be utilized in managerial decision-making is necessary.

The author proposes that we use a "differential financial cost analysis sheet" supported by the traditional differential cost and revenue analysis sheet (see Figure 2). The major characteristic of this method is that concerning all resources such as raw materials, labor force, and capital asset input in an alternative, we use financial costs calculated assuming alternative uses. This method is only a generalization of the traditional method of differential cost and revenue analysis, that is, a method of booking opportunity cost such as income from leasing a capital asset.

As for the financial cost of resources held, we must first list up feasible alternative uses of these resources such as production, resale, lease, and disposal; second, we must estimate the net value; and third, we must select the largest among them. Subsequently, the largest net value serves as a provisional value of the opportunity costs and becomes the starting point for a sequential managerial decision-making process.

		Standard alternative	Comparative alternative	Difference
Goods' financial value	Monetary revenue	$ 1,000	$ 1,200	$ ☆200
Resources' financial costs	Monetary expenditure	500	800	☆300
	Cost of inventory*	30	70	☆40
	Cost of fixed assets*	200	40	160
	Cost of labor force*	70	70	0
	Cost of capital	50	80	☆30
	Sum of financial costs	$ 850	$ 1,060	$ ☆210
Net value	(at the end of the project)	$ 150	$ 140	$ 10
Opportunity cost	Net value of the comparative alternative	140		
Excess value	(at the end of the project)	$ 10		

* Hidden financial costs calculated assuming alternative uses.

Fig. 2   An example of differential financial cost analysis sheet

On the one hand, an unavoidable reason why we estimate the net value of alternative uses is that we fall in a circular argument if we have to calculate the value of alternatives through the same process of considering other alternative uses.

On the other hand, essentially, managerial decision-making requires relevance and rapidity rather than precision of information. Since managers are familiar with how resources in their enterprise are employed, this is a realistic method to provide information in a relevant and rapid manner. Nevertheless, in order to provide information concerning financial costs that may be overlooked by managers, it is recommended that we use mathematical models in a supplementary manner.

Then, we take into consideration the "cost of capital" that is generated when we use capital (funds). Prospective expenditures on resources and the maximum amount of net value among alternative uses of resources held are equivalent to the principal of the financial cost of resources that are input into the alternatives. The cost of capital of the alternatives is calculated based on the amount of monetary revenue and financial cost (principal) of the alternatives.

In the first basic decision-making type, we calculate excess value of the standard alternative by deducting the net value of the comparative alternative from that of the standard alternative. This procedure is meaningless in a mathematical method to find the optimal solutions, but it is indispensable for our proposed heuristic approach.

This differential financial cost analysis sheet may be applied to the analysis of the alternatives with different kinds of resources, input ratios, and input timings, and to the analysis of the second type of decision-making in which comparative alternatives are not apparent. The net value of the analysis sheet may also be utilized as a transfer price that leads to improvement of enterprise value, considering the total activities of a given department as an alternative.

3.3 *Financial cost in cost management techniques*

Cost management techniques have skillfully incorporated, if not systematically, financial cost.

The profit measured by internal calculation based on absorption costing does not represent the net value of the alternative. Since "marginal profit" represents the financial value of goods after deduction of the marginal explicit cost, it is appropriate for measuring the financial net value of the alternative. Variable profit and throughput are in principle based on the same way of thinking as that of marginal profit.

The Theory of Constraints (TOC) makes it possible to use capital assets effectively by adopting the management method of focusing on the specific facility that becomes a bottleneck and producing products in descending order of their throughput per time, without attributing throughput to the facility. In this sense, the TOC is a practical cost management technique that incorporates financial cost.

Operating cash flow and free cash flow are widely employed in value-based management since they are free from internal calculation and problems arising from the passage of time that may cause separation of outlay cost from explicit cost, and go hand-in-hand with the calculation of enterprise value.

4 Cost Management Centered on "Hidden Costs"

4.1 *Hidden non-financial cost and cause variables of value*

The value of goods an enterprise produces and the opportunity cost of resources that depends on the value are, in the end, determined by monetary evaluation in the market. However since managerial decision-making takes place before the evaluation, the financial net value of an alternative is only the value predicted by managers.

In order to understand the process of managerial decision-making in enterprises, let us consider an IT project. Suppose we implement this project spending three million dollars of explicit cost, then we expect to generate six million dollars in revenue through the improvement of customer service, but one million dollars of cost of capital will be incurred during the project. Since the financial predictive net value at the end of the project is two million dollars, we should adopt this project.

However, our experience tells us that a manager may reject this project. When there is no comparative alternative, he/she must judge that the IT project's "total value" (total utility) combining the project's financial net value and non-financial net value is negative. When there is a comparative alternative, he/she must judge that its total value is lower than that of the comparative alternative.

In order to clarify the factors involved in the managers' evaluation, let us examine some examples of the IT project's attributes (Figure 3).

We recognize that the below examples include direct, indirect, and secondary attributes of the project, and the degree of convertibility into financial value is different. In real managerial decision-making, it is necessary to understand the attributes of the alternative in a broader sense from the perspective of the "effect on enterprise value."

In order to reduce trouble arising from inexperience, it may be necessary to have at least half a year period of preparation. For the improvement of employees' IT abilities, educating them through a method of supporting their voluntary learning may be effective. We may consider these actions that lead to changes of attributes of the alternative as the "cause variables

	Attributes easy to convert into financial value	Attributes difficult to convert into financial value
Positive attributes	• Improvement of customer service	• Desirable effects on outsiders' confidence • Improvement of employees' IT abilities
Negative attributes	• Additional resources consumed for IT education (secondary attributes)	• Trouble arising from inexperience and its undesirable effects on motivation

Fig. 3   Examples of the IT project's attributes

of value." They may be redefined by other variables and form a variety of causal chains.

In light of the concepts discussed here, the steps involved in a real sequential managerial decision-making process will probably be:

- Estimate the financial values of attributes and financial costs of resources that are easily convertible into financial value, and calculate the financial net value.
- Search for attributes that are difficult to convert into financial value, and collect information about the cause variables of value and decide what action to take. Repeat the former step until ideas are exhausted.
- Combine the "financial net value" with the "non-financial net value" and find the "total value" based on the utility function of the managers themselves who are the main actors in the decision-making process. When the total value is negative, reject the standard alternative. (Finish the process when confronted with a decision of the second type.)
- When the total value of the standard alternative is positive, find the total value of the comparative alternative using the same procedure above.
- Find the "excess total value" (excess total utility) of the standard alternative by deducting the total value of the comparative alternative from that of the standard alternative.
- When the "excess total value" of the standard alternative is positive, adopt it. When it is zero, the manager must choose between the two. When it is negative, reject it.

The last type of opportunity cost for the enterprise is the "hidden non-financial cost" of the resources that are input into the alternative. It indicates the non-financial net value of resources for an alternative use that was not measured in monetary units. However, similar to the argument concerning hidden financial costs in the previous section, the argument about non-financial costs falls into a circular argument.

In real managerial decision-making, an approximate approach is necessary, taking into consideration only the prominent non-financial net value, in addition to the financial net value as the value of the alternative use. For example, suppose the non-financial net value of the utilization of resources with little environmental burden (friendly to environment) receives a higher evaluation in comparison with that of another usage. If we input these resources into an alternative, we must assume that the resources' non-financial cost is larger.

4.2 *The present state and future prospects of cost management centered on "hidden costs"*

We believe that sharing of information about the "hidden cost" within and among organizations is effective. Sharing of information means not only avoiding hoarding information but also creating and exchanging information and using it for action by members of the organization in order to achieve the managerial goals.

Suppose all managers and employees carry out cost management participating in the managerial decision-making process mentioned above. With a proper managerial control system and enterprise culture, they will recognize factual information such as attributes of alternatives that are strategically important and causal variables of value on the shopfloor, and exchange them. They eventually recognize the importance of "hidden costs," and this recognition begins to shape their behaviors.

Cost management that includes sharing information on the "hidden costs" leads to a high probability that the managers and employees voluntarily find obsolete combinations of resources and create new alternatives for a better resource combination. The creation of the new alternatives means the enrichment of choices available for managerial planning on which the cost management puts emphasis.

We believe that cost management systems that incorporate the sharing of information about "hidden costs" already exist. In Japanese cost management with an emphasis on process, the symbolic concepts of *muri* (unnatural), *muda* (waste), and *mura* (unevenness) may sometimes explain causal variables of value. The system successfully promotes the sharing of information through personal interaction on the shopfloor and leads to the incorporation of causal variables of value into individual goals rather than simply making such variables explicit.

For example, the Toyota System points out that the "waste of overproduction" will cause a four-stage excessive input of resources. Above all, "working too fast" is the worst waste, which in the end will lead to increasing the product cost (Monden, 1991, pp. 42–45). In order to remove such waste, daily efforts of continuous improvement of individual causal variables such as operation, machines, people's movement, and equipment, are emphasized.

The Balanced Scorecard (BSC), which is said to have developed from the introduction of Japanese-style managerial techniques into the United States, incorporates non-financial measures that function as performance drivers (causal variables of value) such as "responsible delivery of products." We believe that performance drivers (leading indicators), going through a variety of causal chains, will be integrated into the managerial goal of creating an enterprise value (lagging indicator). Above all, the BSC emphasizes recombination of resources in order to create its own "value proposal" for target customers (Kaplan and Norton, 2001, pp. 1–27).

In considering the future of cost management centered on "hidden costs," we cannot ignore external causal variables of value. Modern enterprises have many stakeholders. They evaluate not only the quality of goods that an enterprise produces but also the combination of resources as well as the quality of management in accordance with their own interest criteria. Since the stakeholders' evaluation is a causal variable that may influence the value of the enterprise as a whole, it is necessary for managers to foresee and incorporate stakeholder evaluation into the managerial strategy and managerial control processes.

Shareholders and employees, the enterprise's core stakeholders, consider possibilities of value creation employing resources from their own perspectives. For example, one of the conditions common among takeover targets is the holding excess resources (excess funds and underutilized real estate). In other words, in such an enterprise, "doing nothing new" is unacceptable from a perspective of value-based management.

Environment cost management and corporate social responsibility accounting can be considered products of a managerial philosophy that tries to positively respond to a value criterion for the general public. Recent concepts of corporate social responsibility involve a wide variety of issues: environment conservation, the employment rate of the handicapped, prevention of misconducts, and so forth.

The "hidden costs" arising from neglecting to consider these interests are literally "immeasurable." It is clear that enterprise managers have already begun to recognize the importance of value created from considering and adopting the interests of a variety of stakeholders into their management practices.

5　Conclusion

This paper clarified that opportunity cost in economics is applicable to managerial decision-making and proposed a heuristic analytical method based on differential financial cost analysis in place of mathematical models as devices for cost management. Analyzing an example of sequential managerial decision-making processes in enterprises, it also demonstrated the significance of "hidden non-financial costs" and "causal variables of value."

Finally, the problem of the "hidden costs" in cost management should be discussed in detail in conjunction with knowledge from business administration. However, this effort is beyond the bounds of this paper.

Nevertheless, the attempt to systematize cost management developed from a perspective of opportunity cost offers a new and hopefully useful perspective.

Subjoinder

After receiving permission for republication in this Book Series, I wrote this paper altering much the original manuscript, "A Sketch of Cost Management from a 'Hidden Cost' Perspective," (in Japanese) published in *Accounting Research* (The Institute of Accounting Research of Chuo University) Vol. 48.

Acknowledgment

I would like to express sincere appreciation to Professor Yasuhiro Monden of Mejiro University who gave me precious advice in order to complete this paper.

References

Committee on Cost Accounting Concepts and Standards (1956). Tentative statement of cost concepts underlying reports for management purposes, American Accounting Association, *The Accounting Review* Vol. 31.

Heymann, H. G. and Bloom, R. (1990). *Opportunity Cost in Finance and Accounting*, Greenwood Publishing Group, Inc.

Iwata, K. (1993). *Seminar: Introduction to Microeconomics*, Nihon Keizai Shinbunsha (in Japanese).

Kaplan, R. S. and Norton, D. P. (2001). *The Strategy-Focused Organization: How Balanced Scorecard Companies Thrive in the New Business Environment*, Harvard Business School Publishing Corporation.

Kumagai, H., Shinohara, M., *et al.* (eds.) (1992). *Dictionary of Economics*, 2nd ed., Toyo Keizai Shinposha (in Japanese).

Miyasaka, M. (1980). Opportunity Cost — Accounting Study (I), *Bulletin of Nagano University*, 1(3/4) double number (in Japanese).

Monden, Y. (1991). *New Toyota System*, Kodansha (in Japanese).

Monden, Y. (2001). *Managerial Accounting — Strategic Finance and Control of Decentralized Organization*, Zeimu-Keiri Kyokai (in Japanese).

Sakurai, M. (2004). *Managerial Accounting*, 3rd ed., Dobunkan (in Japanese).

Sangyo-Kozo Shingikai (1969). Cost management — new principles and methods of cost reduction, in *Profit Planning and Organization for Control*, edited by Sangyo Kozo Shingikai, Ministry of International Trade and Industry, Nikkan Kogyo Shinbunsha (in Japanese).

Target Costing Brings Another Competitive Edge: Creation of Capacity Surplus through Information Capital Readiness by IT

Yoko Ogushi

Associate Professor, Faculty of Economics
Niigata University

1 Introduction

Target costing is used as a tool for cost reduction to achieve lower price and to yield investment surplus for model change or development of the next generation products. However, the effect of target costing goes beyond these merits. When target costing is continuously implemented, the long-term learning effect or experience effect (i.e., reservoir of target costing knowledge) is accumulated, leading to speedy and sophisticated target costing. As a result, the whole lead-time required, from the initial concept planning, design, final prototyping, etc., is shortened, and a surplus in planning ability and design is achieved.

Using this surplus capacity to create the next model or new products shortens development lead-time. Furthermore, when there is cost reduction in the development phase, including processing costs at each manufacturing stage, the surplus capacity can affect the total manufacturing phase efficiency. Information Technology (IT) accelerates to accumulate the surplus. This surplus has become information capital over time. Thus, it is very important to create the accumulation system; it is called as information capital readiness, on purpose. It might have a strong influence on competitive superiority.

This paper begins with a definition of target costing and its aspects. It then describes the importance of sharing and utilizing latest information on product cost throughout a company, including suppliers. Finally, a case study shows that target costing with IT plays a key role in creating competitiveness for companies.

2 Target Costing as a Strategic Weapon

A company must produce a proposed product with specified functionality and quality under the condition that the product is profitable at its selling price. In other words, it is essential to reduce the unit cost required for manufacturing, sales, and management without affecting the quality of products.

Many of the accounting literature have made a splendid contribution to further the understanding of target costing (Monden and Hamada, 1991; Monden, 1995; Kato, 1993; Tanaka, 1995). Then, target costing has been regarded as an essential tool for realizing desirable profit. While most of the articles tend to focus on target costing through case studies in the electronics or automotive industry, particularly among Japanese firms, its importance is recognized enough in other industries as well.

With the emergence of global competition, companies face ever-increasing competition. To survive in the market, target costing is primarily a technique to strategically manage a company's future profits.

2.1 *Formula and six key principles*

Target costing used to be a simple calculation system which brings together material prices and labor charge. Now, it is considered as an established method to close the gaps between current and desired cost, to enhance the functionality and quality without extra expense. Significant improvement of new and renewed product development processes result from changes in accounting, engineering, operations management, and purchasing division.

The overall target costing for a product or services is showed by the following formula:

Target Costing = Estimated Selling Price − Desired Profit

The formula is quite simple and straightforward. However, the target costing processes are quite complex and always require a lot of challenges. The main reason is that an estimated selling price is only derived from market, which includes customer requirement and competitive offerings. In many cases, the estimated sale price is lesser than the expected sale price.

In addition, the desired profit comes mainly from the shareholders' expectation. Moreover, to achieve the target cost, it is necessary to focus not only on the price, but also on the product quality, process design, meeting delivery schedule, and continuous improvement throughout the product lifecycle.

According to Ansari *et al.* (1997), target costing has six key principles:

- Price-led costing: Market oriented price leads to target cost (see the above formula).
- Focus on customers: Only when the customer satisfies the value of product, the cost is justified.
- Focus on design: Cost management in target costing requires excellence in product and process design. Reducing cost without this will be very difficult.
- Cross-functional teams: Cross-functional target costing teams are responsible for managing new and renewed products from initial development stage. The team should involve in all divisions of production processes.
- Value chain involvement: Target costing activities require participation from outside members who are connected via value chain, such as suppliers, dealers, distributors, and so on. Otherwise, the effect of target costing becomes restrictive.
- Life cycle costing: Target costing needs to be considered to reduce the life cycle cost of a product from the product concept for the organization is no longer responsible for the product.

2.2 *Target costing process*

Figure 1 illustrates the stream of the process by six steps in target costing approach. Organizations use this to support both the existing and new products.

As target costing processes are quite systematic and involve cross-division activities, it is very important to speed up and to perform them effectively. Furthermore, the wider the cover area of the target costing is, the more the possibility extends.

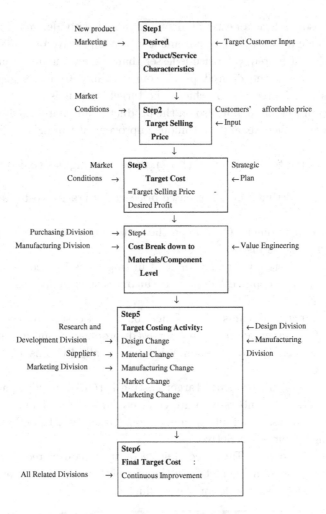

Fig. 1   Target costing process

2.3   *A serious cost reduction effect at the design stage*

Control costs during a product design stage mainly rely on a combination of target costing and value engineering. It is said that the easy way to reduce manufacturing cost is by changing the design or by making the design process efficient. In fact, the possibility of cost reduction is highest during the design stage (Figure 2).

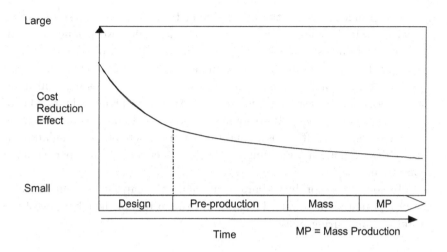

Fig. 2   Possibility of cost reduction

2.4   *Information sharing across divisions and suppliers*

In addition to the cost reduction at the design stage, collecting and sharing of information across divisions are necessary to improve target costing itself continuously. The role of the purchasing activity should also be focused.

However, ECN (Engineering Change Note) issues often arise even after a formal design released. When the design division changes any design, parts, material, or ways of manufacturing, interested people who belong to the business process need to know the change as soon as possible. They have to modify parts and change the schedule depending on the contents of an ECN. Promptness is requested though the number of parts and functions to treat in the design division keeps increasing in the recent years. Thus, it is actually very difficult to obtain latest data instantly in all the related divisions without IT.

3   IT for Efficient Target Costing

Although the importance of target costing is already recognized in the world, it is difficult to realize the concept of target costing throughout all business processes. In fact, a lot of business processes are divided into small sections. It easily causes inefficient information use. Clearly IT helps *kaizen* costing and continuous target costing activities by efficient data management.

The problem is that the articles tend to focus on the cost reduction scheme itself. Besides, engineers in a design section work long hours in cost estimation tasks of collecting parts information on price, quality, and delivery. In other words, precious managerial resources such as time and workforce might not be used to plan on strategic target costing, which are really essential to create additional value. Moreover, precious knowledge of target costing belongs only to some specific staffs. Enough communication among divisions is often costly and takes time. Therefore, sharing and utilizing data among a wide range of business network do not persist for a long time.

To solve these problems and accumulate the capacity surplus for corporate potential capability, IT can play a main role in the efficiency of the total manufacturing phase.

3.1   *Functions required for target costing*

In order to carry out effective target costing activities, continuous and broad efforts are required for all business processes. Especially, the following three points are important.

3.1.1   *Strengthening of a search function*

At the earlier stage of a product design, data required for estimating cost must be able to be used simply. As we see in Figure 2, the cost reduction effect in this stage is the largest. In reality, engineers' expense time and their capability for gathering data and/or adjusting repeated design changes. Even though some parts were used in the past and the data about their quality or accuracy were already accumulated, it was difficult to search them in many cases. One of the reasons for it is that BOM (Bill of Materials) differs according to the purpose. The decomposition viewpoints of BOM are based on the functions of the unit of manufacture. In fact, necessary BOM is different in each section of the design, procurement, production, and sales. Thus, enabling easy search of the earlier design data and related technical-writing documents contributes to increase the efficiency in the earlier stage of the product design.

3.1.2   *Auto cost estimation from component formation*

Engineers need to carry out the design being cost conscious from the development stage in order to secure desired profit, then desired cost.

Therefore, present cost must be able to be grasped during every change, rearranging component formation so that a demand function and quality are fulfilled. To grasp cost is not difficult if there are a few number of parts and combination patterns. However, it is usual that a number of parts and combination patterns are complicated in practice. Therefore, recalculation task of estimating cost by engineers accompanies a serious load. Therefore, system architecture, which enables to check total cost information per product at every change, is desirable. On this occasion, cost estimation synchronizes with CAD (Computer Aided Design)/ CAM (Computer Aided manufacturing) and will be done by the automatic operation.

3.1.3 *Concurrent information sharing*

It is important to prepare the system where the newest data about the planned product is shared efficiently through all business processes. Not a division unit but a process unit attracts attention to manage target costing. Besides the process units inside corporations, inter-organizational cost management is essential. Inter-organizational cost management occurs primarily between the buyer and the supplier. Target costing becomes effective when they are linked to form a chain through business processes. In the chain, the output of a buyer's target cost becomes an input to the suppliers' target costing. To make effective chained target costing, the buyer needs to share the latest information with the suppliers through all processes within the network.

3.2 *System architecture for realizing the functions*

As the premise of the above functions, newest and exact data in the integrated database is indispensable. For example, PDM (Product Data Management) is a system which realizes the concept to manage various engineering data from the design phase to the sales phase. In order to carry out PDM smoothly, it is necessary to use BOM effectively.

However, BOM does not play a main role at this time. The reason is that the primary purpose of BOM is part arrangements and not a tool for price examination. There is no direct relation between BOM and PDM. Then, the construction of the system that makes BOM and PDM link well is important to manage the target costing scheme.

Moreover, integrated system management with a common cost database is really important.

3.3 *System architecture for global optimal manufacturing*

An arrangement and consolidating parts cost information including not only domestic but also the overseas branches are indispensable for parts selection. Even the same parts have a variously different cost depending on its aim, time, and place. In economic activities that transcend national borders, there are a lot of factors that influence the product cost. Thus, construction of a global, integrated database is also indispensable because various factors that influence the cost are accumulated in the database. In that case, standard parts and optional parts are clarified.

Standard parts are designed and made a fundamental function for the quality and the cost thoroughly by the design section in the headquarters. The design section in each production center designs regional specified parts. As a result, the headquarters takes the responsibility for the main parts and each region can change other parts flexibly according to various regionally specific demands (Figure 3).

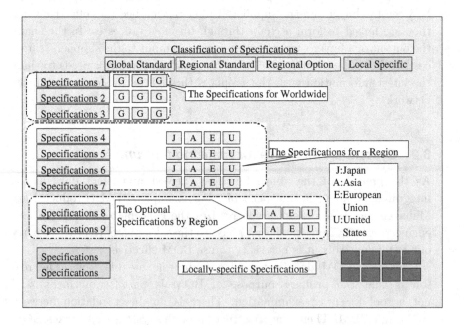

Fig. 3   Flexible component formation in global markets

4 Creation of Capacity Surplus Through Information Capital Readiness

Effective use of IT accelerates the speed of development processes without any extra cost. In fact, it is necessary to manage a lot of information in the target costing processes.

The integration of data used in every section and the utilization of them with IT are very important in the processes. Repeating these activities have been accumulating in a long term, and then, creating capacity surplus through information capital. Moreover, information capital, which derives from its readiness, becomes intangibles as follows.

4.1 *Intangibles and information capital*

Intangibles such as a valuable accumulation of know-how and improvements of capability are regarded as a key to success.

Itami (2004) insists that only intangibles can be the true source in the competition era, and be the source of the correspondence power to the change in the business environment. He has enumerated the following three features as the intangibles:

- It is not possible to buy easily.
- It takes time to make it.
- Concurrent multiple use of it becomes possible, once it is made.

In fact, it is difficult to accumulate intangibles because it is a strenuous effort and takes long hours. However, it works wonders when it is correctly used, eventually deriving most of intangibles from information capital. As the result, when target costing is continuously implemented, the long-term learning effect or experience effect is accumulated as information capital.

4.2 *Information capital readiness and capacity surplus with IT*

Information capital depends on information capital readiness with IT. The concept of "Information capital readiness" in the strategy map is paid much attention when investment in information equipment for the strategy execution is evaluated (Kaplan and Norton, 2001, 2004). As information capital derives from information capital readiness, it is quite important. Of course it will be ready and accomplished with IT. Architecture of IT must be supportive for making good readiness because it is a foundation for strengthening company's competitiveness.

5 Case Study: Mazda

To examine the creation of capacity surplus through information capital readiness by IT, we will see the case with Mazda Motor Corp. The name of the project is the Mazda Digital Innovation (MDI) program.[1] They needed to enhance the quality of process design with cost reduction and shorten development period.

- Project aim: To virtually simulate the production processes by introducing the newest integrated digital development system.
- Challenge: To integrate different kinds of CAD, BOM, and CAE applications and make one database which can be accessed from around the world.
- Main achievements:
  — Shortening the development period from design-fix to mass production from 27 months to 18 months.
  — Reducing Research and Development staff hours by 30%
  — Cutting development cost by 20%
  — Decreasing facility investment by 40%

6 Conclusion

In addition to achieving lower price and producing investment surplus for model change or development of the next generation products, the effect of target costing goes beyond these merits. When target costing is continuously implemented, the long-term learning effects and experience have been accumulated as knowledge of the developing processes. It can be a part of information capital, and then, becomes intangibles in the end. Thus, the concept of how to make ready information capital by IT, which is equal to information capital readiness, is regarded as a key to success in this era.

---

[1]Please refer to the following URL for details of The Mazda Digital Innovation Program: http://www.ugs.jp/about/client/mazda.html

Of course, information capital is able to be ready without IT, but IT accelerates its accumulation and is able to use the capital efficiently. As a result, the whole lead-time required, from the initial concept planning, design, final prototyping, etc., is shortened, and a capacity surplus in planning ability and design is achieved by IT.

In the case of MDI program, it was clear that their new IT and its architecture improved and enhanced the quality of process design. In other words, they were just on the start line with the program. Only continuous improvement of target costing with IT gives a chance to survive in the competitive environment.

References

Ansari, S. L., Bell, J. E., and the CAM-I Target Cost Core Group (1997). *Target Costing: The Next Frontier in Strategic Cost Management*, Chicago, IL: Irwin Professional Publishing.

Ellram, L. M. (2000). Purchasing and supply management's participation in the target costing process. *Journal of Supply Chain Management*, 36(22), pp. 39–51.

Itami, H. (2004). Dynamic stream of information, in *Strategy and Logic of Intangible Assets*, edited by Itami, H. and Karube, M., Nippon-Keizai-Shinbunsya, pp. 40–72 (in Japanese).

Kaplan, R. S. and Norton, D. P. (2001). *The Strategic-Focused Organization*, Boston, MA: Harvard Business School Press.

Kaplan, R. S. and Norton, D. P. (2004). *Strategy Map*, Boston, MA: Harvard Business School Press.

Kato, Y. (1993). *Target Costing: Strategic Cost Management*, Nippon-Keizai-Shinbunsya (in Japanese).

Monden, Y. and Hamada, K. (1991). Target costing and kaizen costing in Japanese automobile companies, *Journal of Management Accounting Research*, 3, Fall, pp. 16–34.

Monden, Y. (1995). *Target Costing and Kaizen Costing*, Portland, OR: Productivity Press.

Noboru, Y. and Monden, Y. (1983). Total cost management system in Japanese automobile corporations, *Kigyoukaikei* 35(2) pp. 104–112 (in Japanese).

Tanaka, M. (1995). *Target Cost Management and Profit Engineering*, Chuo-Keizaisya (in Japanese).

Worthy, F. S. (1991). Japan's smart secret weapon, *Fortune* 124(4), pp. 72–75.

A Framework for Performance Evaluation Methods in Continual Improvement Activities

Hiroshi Ozawa

Associate Professor, Graduate School of Economics
Nagoya University

1 Introduction

Many Japanese companies are working on continual improvement activities. Of these, there are also many companies that have adopted methods for evaluating performance improvements that have been devised in a variety of ways in order to effectively conduct improvement activities. In particular, instead of using non-financial indices for improvement results such as lead time and the defective ratio, evaluating using a financial scale by converting these into monetary values is said to be a more effective way of improving the motivation of workers.

In many cases, evaluation of improvement performance is implemented like a game for increasing motivation for workers to make improvements, and is not strictly intended for evaluation. Except in cases where small one-off bonuses are paid, there are virtually no cases in which evaluation is linked to financial compensation such as wages. Because of this, little thought was given to the details of performance evaluation methods.

However, the rules of the game, or the method for evaluating performance, could have an impact on workers' behavior if they actively participate in the game. Put simply, the design of the evaluation method can point improvement activities in a certain direction or incite opportunistic behavior.

Although there have been many reports on efforts regarding improvement activities in the past, most simply outline the practical procedures, and very few have made detailed examinations of the evaluation methods

129

used, what is being evaluated and what is not, and how improvement activities are directed.[1]

This paper attempts to show a basic framework for considering the methods used to evaluate improvement performance that many companies have built over time through trial and error, and attempts to simply examine evaluation methods using the framework presented.

2   Framework for Evaluation of Improvement Value

When making a monetary evaluation of improvement performance, it is necessary to differentiate the contributions of the improvements to financial performance from the value of the improvement proposals themselves. The same improvement proposal has a different impact on financial performance depending on the conditions it is implemented under. Furthermore, improvements that are favorable for a company do not necessarily contribute to financial performance. If this differentiation is not recognized, favorable improvements could be disregarded because of the small contribution to financial performance, or opportunistic behavior such as implementing the same improvement proposal under favorable conditions could be overlooked.

It is believed that there are three factors that cause the difference between the improvement proposal's contribution to financial performance and the value of the improvement proposal. The first is the difference caused by whether a planned production volume or actual production volume is used in evaluation. An actual production volume is used to evaluate the contribution to financial performance, while a planned production volume is used to evaluate the value of the improvement proposal.

The second is the difference caused by the timing of the implementation of improvements. When evaluating the contribution to financial performance, even the same improvement proposal can have a different impact on financial performance depending on when it is implemented within a financial year. Meanwhile, the value of an improvement proposal must be evaluated independently from the timing of the implementation of the improvement proposal.

---

[1]For example, see Factory Management (2000), Hamada (1989), Hamada and Monden (1989), Tani and Miya (1998), Miya *et al.* (1999), Yoshida and Matsuki (2001), Miya (2003), etc.

The third is the difference caused by whether the improvement is related to a direct cost item or related to a fixed cost item. Whereas improvements related to variable cost items are immediately reflected in financial performance, improvements related to fixed costs are often not reflected in financial performance straightaway. That is, evaluation methods that evaluate financial performance may not properly evaluate the value of improvements related to fixed cost items.

2.1 *Evaluation of improvements to variable cost items*

If direct consumption is lowered through improvements related to variable cost items, expenses are immediately lowered. Therefore, the value of the improvement proposal is directly reflected in financial performance.

The performance of improvements related to variable cost items is evaluated as the difference between the cost that is expected to be incurred without the improvement (ongoing cost, OC) and the cost that was actually incurred (actual cost, AC). The improvement value (IV) can be expressed using the following equation.

$$IV = OC - AC. \tag{1}$$

Here, the variable cost ratio from the end of the previous year is referred to as the ongoing variable cost ratio (VCR^O), and the variable cost ratio brought about as a result of the improvements is referred to as the actual variable cost ratio (VCR^A). The actual variable cost ratio is calculated by dividing the actual cost incurred for the current year (VC^A) by the actual production volume (PV^A). Based on this, Eq. (1) can be rewritten as follows:

$$VCR^A = VC^A / PV^A, \tag{2}$$

$$IV = (VCR^O - VCR^A) \times PV, \tag{3}$$

where PV = production volume.

The PV in Eq. (3) could be either the planned production volume (PV^P) or the actual production volume (PV^A). The evaluations for the improvement value based on PPV (IV^{PPV}) and the improvement value based on APV (IV^{APV}) are shown as follows (Figure 1):

$$IV^{PPV} = (VCR^O - VCR^A) \times PV^P, \tag{4}$$

$$IV^{APV} = (VCR^O - VCR^A) \times PV^A. \tag{5}$$

For improvements related to variable cost items, it is more appropriate to use the actual production volume than the planned production volume when evaluating the impact of improvements on financial performance. Conversely, as evaluations of the value of improvement proposals should not be affected by the production volume, it is more appropriate to make evaluations based on the planned production volume.

2.2   *Evaluation of improvements to fixed cost items*

In improvements to fixed cost items, production is made more efficient, but expenditure remains unchanged. That is, the results of the improvements are not reflected in financial performance. Only if the production volume increases due to increased production capacity, leading to increased sales, does this become reflected in financial performance in the form of contributing to profits. Because of this, it is more important to identify the difference between the value of the improvement proposal and the contribution to financial performance than in the case of improvements to variable costs.

If the production capacity before the improvements is referred to as the ongoing production capacity (PC^O), and the production capacity after the improvements is referred to as the actual production capacity (PC^A),

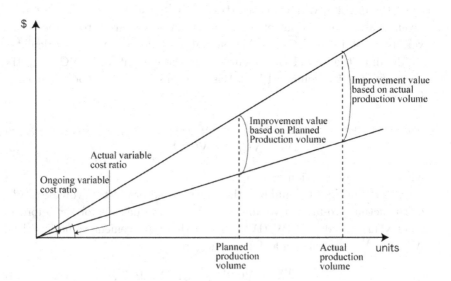

Fig. 1   Evaluation of improvements to variable cost items

the increase in production capacity (PC^I) can be expressed as follows:

$$PC^I = PC^A - PC^O. \qquad (6)$$

As mentioned above, improvements related to fixed expense items are not directly reflected in financial performance. However, the value of the improvement proposal can be evaluated as the value of the increased production capacity. The ongoing fixed cost ratio (FCR^O), the actual fixed cost ratio (FCR^A), and the value of new production generated $[IV(a)]$ can be found by the following equations (Figure 2):

$$FCR^O = FC/PC^O, \qquad (7)$$

$$FCR^A = FC/PC^A, \qquad (8)$$

$$[IV(a)] = (FCR^O - FCR^A) \times PC^O = FC - FCR^A \times PC^O, \qquad (9)$$

where FC = fixed cost.

Improvements to fixed cost items may also have an impact on financial performance. This occurs in cases when production capacity limits production volume despite there being sufficient demand. Such cases need to

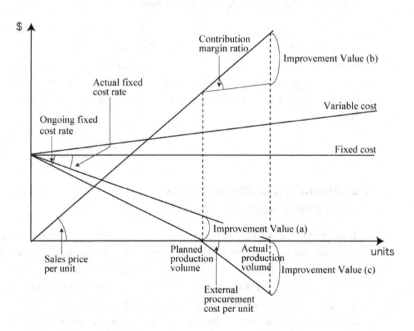

Fig. 2   Evaluation of improvements to fixed cost items

be considered separately as (1) cases in which no outsourcing is used and sales do not exceed production capacity, and (2) cases in which the lack of production capacity is handled through external procurement.

2.2.1   Cases in which no outsourcing is used and sales do not exceed production capacity

When production capacity limits production volume despite there being sufficient demand, use of production capacity generated through improvements increases sales and increases the contribution margin. Naturally, fixed costs do not change because of this. Therefore, the increase in the contribution margin is directly reflected in financial performance. In such cases, the improvement value (IV(b)) can be expressed as follows (Figure 2).

$$IV(b) = CMR \times (PC^A - PC^O), \tag{10}$$

where CMR = contribution margin ratio.

2.2.2   Cases in which the lack of production capacity is handled through external procurement

When production capacity is handled through outsourcing, internal production is made possible by increasing production capacity, and external procurement costs (PC^E) can be reduced. As fixed costs do not change, the reduction in external procurement costs is reflected in financial performance. In such cases, the improvement value (IV(c)) is expressed as follows (Figure 2):

$$IV(c) = PC^E \text{ per unit} \times (PC^A - PC^O). \tag{11}$$

2.3   Consideration of the timing of improvement implementation

The method of evaluating the improvement value mentioned above assumes that improvements are implemented at the start of the year. In reality, however, they occur during the year, and as the variable cost ratio and production capacity differ before and after the improvements, the use of the above calculations will result in calculation of the average variable cost ratio and production capacity from before and after the improvement. For this reason, caution needs to be given to two points.

The first is that improvements implemented at the end of the year are evaluated as having a smaller effect, which leads to an incentive to postpone the improvements to the start of the next year.

The second is that the results of improvements implemented at the end of the year are not sufficiently reflected in the financial performance of that year, and are instead reflected in the financial performance of the following year. This leads to the evaluation showing an improvement in the following year even though no improvements are carried out.

Incidentally, as it is only natural for the contribution of an improvement proposal to financial performance to differ depending on the timing at which it is implemented, the above method including the impact of the timing of implementation is suitable for evaluating the contribution to financial performance. However, in order to evaluate the individual value of an improvement proposal, it is necessary to exclude the impact of the implementation timing. The two methods below are conceivable for evaluating the value of an improvement proposal.

2.3.1 *Calculation of actual variable cost ratio giving consideration to the time of the improvement*

The time the improvement was implemented should be determined based on the production volume. For example, if the planned production volume is 600 units and 100 units were already produced at the time the improvement was implemented, the time of the improvement is "at production volume of 100 units." After the actual cost incurred (VC^A) is finalized at the end of the year, the actual variable cost ratio (VCR^A) is calculated using the following equation:

$$VCR^A = \{VC^A - (VCR^O \times PV^I)\}/(APV - PV^I), \qquad (12)$$

where VCR^O = ongoing variable cost ratio and PV^I = production volume at the time of improvement.

By multiplying the actual variable cost ratio (VCR^A) by the planned production volume (PV^P), it is possible to evaluate the value of an improvement proposal when the improvement is implemented at the start of the year and the planned production volume is produced (Figure 3).

$$IV = VCR^A \times PV^P. \qquad (13)$$

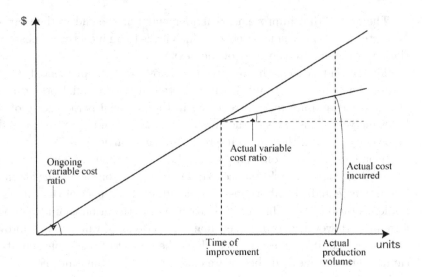

Fig. 3   Time of improvement and actual variable cost ratio

The actual fixed cost ratio (FCR^A) can similarly be calculated for improvements related to fixed cost items.

$$FCR^A = (FC - FCR^O \times PV^I)/(PC^A - PV^I), \tag{14}$$

where FC = fixed cost, FCR^O = ongoing fixed cost ratio, PC^A = actual production capacity, and PV^I = production volume at the time of improvement.

The difference between the amount obtained by multiplying this actual fixed cost ratio (FCR^A) by the ongoing production capacity (PC^O) and fixed costs is the increase in production capacity if the improvement is implemented at the start of the year (Figure 4).

$$IV = FC - (FCR^A \times PC^O). \tag{15}$$

2.3.2   *Calculations based on engineering methods*

Engineering methods based on approaches such as motion time analysis can also be used for the evaluation of improvements related to conversion costs. The PTS (predetermined time standard) system is applied in engineering calculations. Specifically, the PTS system is used to assign time values that are the standards for each component action to find the total work time

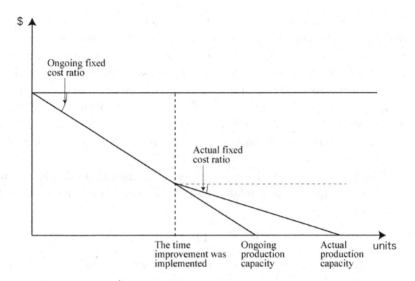

Fig. 4 Time of improvement and actual fixed cost ratio

eliminated by improvements. The total time is converted into a monetary value based upon the planned production volume (PV^P) and standard wage rate (SWR), and this is subtracted from the ongoing variable cost ratio (VCR^O) to calculate the actual variable cost ratio.

$$IV = \{ST^{EA}(\text{sec}) \times PV^P(\text{units})\} \times SWR(\$/h)/3600(\text{sec}), \qquad (16)$$

$$VCR^A = VCR^O - ST^{EA}(\text{sec}) \times SWR/3600(\text{sec}), \qquad (17)$$

where ST^{EA} = standard time value of eliminated actions.

This method is able to properly evaluate the value of improvement proposals regardless of the time of the improvement or the actual production volume because it uses the variable cost ratio after the improvement to evaluate the reduction in costs when producing the planned production volume.

3 Evaluation when Targets are Set

Improvement activities are not only evaluated by the results, but also set improvement targets in advance and evaluated by the level of achievement.[2]

---

[2]See Monden (1995, pp. 295–316) for details on target settings.

In such cases, the difference between the targeted improvement value (TIV) and the actual improvement value based on the planned production volume ($\mathrm{IV^{PVP}}$) is evaluated (improvement variance). The targeted improvement value is set during the budgeting process by giving consideration to profit targets. As targeted improvement values are obviously set during the budgeting process, they are set based on the planned production volume. The targets set are broken down and assigned to each manufacturing division. The method for calculating improvement variances is described below (Figures 5 and 6).

The improvement variance based on the planned production volume (V^{PVP}) for improvements related to variable cost items can be calculated as follows:

$$V^{\mathrm{PVP}} = \mathrm{TIV} - \mathrm{IV^{PVP}}. \tag{18}$$

However, when calculating the improvement variance based on the actual production volume (V^{PVA}), it is necessary to make corrections to the targeted improved value that was based on the planned production volume (TIV) in order to comply with the actual production volume ($\mathrm{PV^A}$).

$$\mathrm{TIV^{PVA}} = (\mathrm{TIV/PV^P}) \times \mathrm{PV^A}, \tag{19}$$

$$V^{\mathrm{PVA}} = \mathrm{TIV^{PVA}} - \mathrm{IV^{PVA}}, \tag{20}$$

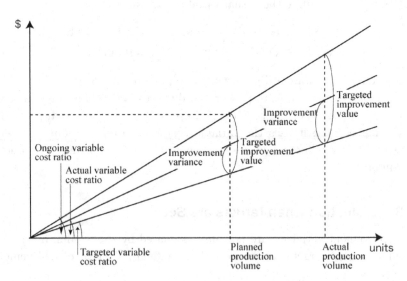

Fig. 5   Variable cost improvement variance

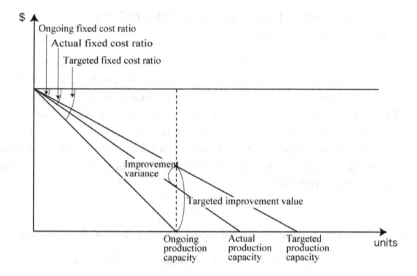

Fig. 6   Fixed cost improvement variance

where TIV^{APV} = the targeted improved value based on the actual production volume.

Meanwhile, the improvement variance related to fixed cost items (V) is the difference between the targeted production capacity (PC^{T}) and the actual production capacity (PC^{A}).

$$\text{FCR}^{\text{T}} = \text{FC}/\text{PC}^{\text{T}}, \tag{21}$$

$$\text{FCR}^{\text{A}} = \text{FC}/\text{PC}^{\text{A}}, \tag{22}$$

$$\begin{aligned}\text{TIV} &= \text{FC} - (\text{FCR}^{\text{T}} \times \text{PC}^{\text{O}}) \\ &= (\text{FCR}^{\text{O}} - \text{FCR}^{\text{T}}) \times \text{PC}^{\text{O}},\end{aligned} \tag{23}$$

$$V = (\text{FCR}^{\text{T}} - -\text{FCR}^{\text{A}}) \times \text{PC}^{\text{O}}, \tag{24}$$

where FCR^{T} = targeted fixed cost ratio, FCR^{A} = actual fixed cost ratio, FC = fixed cost, FCR^{O} = ongoing fixed cost ratio, and PC^{O} = ongoing production capacity.

4   An Example of Improved Cost Calculations in a Japanese Firm

There are some firms that organize small groups based on workplaces to encourage improvement activities, and track the improvement value for each small group. Of these, the examples of Sumitomo Electric Industries, NEC Saitama, and Kyocera are frequently mentioned. These have a variety of interesting characteristics other than the methods used to evaluate improvement performance, but these will be eliminated as consideration is only given to improvement value evaluation methods based on the basic framework described above.

4.1   *Sample calculation for Sumitomo Electric Industries*

Sumitomo Electric Industries Ltd. manufactures items such as wires and cables. The company has adopted a system called a line company system.[3] This is a mechanism in which the organizations of manufacturing divisions are restructured according to the product type, and each unit organization is deemed to be a *pseudo* profit center called a "Company" when calculating profits. The reason the "pseudo" label is used is that performance is evaluated based on profit despite each organization effectively being a cost center without any responsibility or authority over earnings.[4]

Profit calculations are made on a monthly basis in the line company system. There are a variety of patterns used in the calculation method depending on the plant. A typical example is shown below.

First, the profit that is the ultimate subject of evaluation is calculated as the difference between sales and costs.

$$\text{Profit} = \text{Sales} - \text{Costs}. \tag{25}$$

Sales are calculated by establishing the sale price by multiplying the unit cost before the improvement (the ongoing cost) by a certain coefficient, and then multiplying these by the actual production volume. The coefficient is

---

[3]See Factory Management (2000) and Yoshida and Matsuki (2001) for details on the line company system in Sumitomo Electric Industries.
[4]See Cooper (1995, pp. 279–282).

established to cover the company's administrative costs.

$$Sales = (Direct\ material\ costs\ per\ product\ unit$$
$$+ Processing\ costs\ per\ unit) \times Coefficient$$
$$\times Actual\ production\ volume. \qquad (26)$$

Meanwhile, costs are calculated based on the sum of the actual amounts for material costs, personnel costs, and indirect costs.

$$Costs = Actual\ material\ costs\ incurred + Processing\ costs$$
$$+ Indirect\ costs. \qquad (27)$$

This evaluation method evaluates the contribution of improvements to financial performance. Thus, improvements related to variable cost items are directly evaluated, but improvements related to fixed cost items are not directly evaluated. However, companies have the authority to accept work from other divisions to increase sales (production volume). Therefore, if production volume can be increased, the improvement performance is evaluated as being an increase in contributions to profits according to Eq. (13).

However, unless work to cover the increase in production capacity is assigned to a company, improvements related to fixed costs are not evaluated. The head of the company must play a sales-like role of accepting many jobs in order to ensure that improvement performance is evaluated appropriately. If there are several companies performing the same tasks under such an evaluation system, this creates competition between companies and is expected to encourage improvement activities.

Moreover, as this is a method for evaluating contributions to financial performance, there is little incentive to execute improvement proposals at the end of the month, while there is a greater incentive to postpone the proposal to the start of the next month when it will receive a higher evaluation. As a result, improvements are delayed and this could hamper improvements to annual financial performance.

4.2 Sample calculation for NEC Saitama

NEC Saitama Ltd develops, manufactures, and sells products such as mobile communication equipment. NEC Saitama also employs the line company system.[5] However, there are several differences in the methods used to evaluate improvements.

The first is that sales are estimated based on market prices instead of costs. Specifically, these are determined by giving consideration to the shipping price, recommended prices of other companies, budgeted processing costs, outsourced processing costs, the number of units required to break even and fairness between companies. Meanwhile, costs are estimated by tallying actual costs centered on items that should be focused upon for improvements.

$$\text{Costs} = \text{Personnel costs} + \text{Overtime costs} + \text{Equipment costs}$$
$$+ \text{Floor costs} + \text{Outsourced processing fees, etc.} \qquad (28)$$

Here, items subject to improvements such as equipment costs, floor costs, and personnel costs are treated as having a reduced expenditure due to improvements even if the expenditure is actually fixed. This enables the surplus capacity created by improvements to be immediately reflected in financial performance and evaluated. In this case, the improvement value is evaluated according to Eq. (12).

However, the condition of fixed costs being absent tends to bring about diminishing equilibrium behavior in which capacity is reduced if the production volume decreases. Because of this, there is no effect of encouraging internal competition like that in Sumitomo Electric Industries.

Moreover, only processing costs are included in costs, while material costs are excluded. This is because the large number of components for each model cannot be managed on-site, and sufficient improvements can be expected simply by reducing processing costs (particularly fixed costs).

Furthermore, costs do not include overhead such as development costs and administrative costs. This differs from Sumitomo Electric Industries' calculation method which accounts for administrative costs as a coefficient. By omitting administrative costs, etc. from costs, the cost of internally produced products is estimated to be lower than outsourced processing costs. As a result, this promotes a transfer from outsourcing to internal production. Even if there is a transfer from outsourcing to internal production, administrative costs, etc. remain unchanged. Meanwhile, increasing

---

[5]See Tani and Miya (1998) for details on the line company system in NEC Saitama.

internal production has the effect of effectively utilizing surplus capacity such as equipment capacity and floor space resulting from improvements.

4.3 *Sample calculation for Kyocera*

Kyocera Corporation is a company that develops, manufactures, and sells products such as electronic devices and communications equipment. Kyocera has gained much attention for the sublimation of its small group movement in the unique management system called amoeba management.[6] Amoebas are small groups equivalent to the line companies mentioned above.

Kyocera utilizes a unique method to calculate sales of manufacturing divisions. Normally, and in the two cases above, the manufacturing division delivers the product to the sales division at the manufacturing cost, and the balance after deducting sales costs from the difference between the order value (sale price) and the manufacturing cost is evaluated as being profit generated in the sales division [Eq. (29)]. In this case, only the improvement value is calculated as profit in the manufacturing division [Eq. (30)]. This is a calculation method based on the approach of prices being determined by sales and profits being generated in sales.[7]

$$\text{Profit in manufacturing division} = \text{Ongoing manufacturing cost}$$
$$- \text{Actual manufacturing cost,}$$
$$(29)$$

$$\text{Profit in sales division} = \text{Order value} - \text{Ongoing manufacturing cost}$$
$$- \text{Sales cost.} \qquad (30)$$

However, Kyocera's calculations are based on the approach of assuming the price as being determined by the market and lowering manufacturing costs being the only way to generate profit. In addition, the company utilizes a calculation method in which the entire value of orders through the sales division is recognized as sales of the manufacturing division, with the balance obtained by subtracting the manufacturing cost and sales commission from the order value calculated as profit of the manufacturing division.

---

[6]See Miya (2003), Hamada and Monden (1989), Hamada (1989) and Miya, Tani and Kagono (1999) for details on Kyocera's amoeba management.

[7]Miya (2003) refers to this as the "cost invoicing method" (*genka shikiri houshiki*).

The sales division's profits are obtained by deducting sales costs from the sales commission received from the manufacturing division [Eq. (32)].[8]

Profit of manufacturing division

$$= \text{Order value} - \text{Actual manufacturing cost} - \text{Sales commission} \quad (31)$$

$$\text{Profit of sales division} = \text{Sales commission} - \text{Sales costs.} \quad (32)$$

As this method of determining the sale price directly conveys market demand to lower the sale price to the manufacturing division, it is possible to set cost improvement targets based on market prices and targeted profits.

Each amoeba is given authority over the production volume. As amoebas conducting the same type of processing compete for orders, amoebas that implement improvements related to fixed costs utilize the production capacity generated by increasing orders received. In such cases, the improvement value is evaluated using Eq. (10). Also, changing personnel between amoebas is also accepted. In such cases, personnel costs are treated as variable costs, and the improvement value is also evaluated according to the calculation method for variable costs.

With the exception of personnel costs, costs including shared plant costs and headquarters costs are all calculated using actual costs.

Incidentally, Kyocera calculates not only profits but also hourly profitability. Hourly profitability is calculated by subtracting preprocessing costs and costs incurred by the amoeba from amoeba sales, and then dividing this by practical operating time.

Hourly profitability
$$= \frac{(\text{Sales} - \text{Preprocessing costs} - \text{Costs incurred by the amoeba})}{\text{Practical operating time}}.$$
$$(33)$$

Here, practical operating time is obtained using the following equation.

Practical operating time $=$ Actual production volume
$$\times \text{Processing time per work-in-process unit.}$$
$$(34)$$

---

[8]Miya (2003) refers to this as the "built-to-order sales method" (*juchuu-seisan hambai houshiki*).

Therefore, reductions to processing time per work-in-process unit achieved through improvements are evaluated according to Eq. (9) even if sales (production volume) do not increase. However, reductions in equipment time losses are not evaluated despite improvements being related to fixed cost items.

5 Conclusion

This paper outlines a basic framework for evaluating performance with regard to the improvement activities being widely implemented in Japanese firms. It also includes three brief yet characteristic case studies based on this basic framework.

When evaluating improvement performance, it is important to clearly recognize whether the portion reflected in financial performance is being evaluated or whether the value of the improvement proposal itself is being evaluated, and to use these selectively as required. Without doing so could lead to problems such as permitting opportunistic behavior by employees or not properly communicating an improvement to employees despite it being a desirable one.

Keeping the basic framework presented here in mind while considering the three cases studies, each evaluation method employs innovations to appropriately evaluate the value of improvements while taking a stance of evaluating the contribution to financial performance.

Acknowledgments

This work was supporter by MEXT. Grant-in-Aid for Young Scientists (B) (18730238).

References

Cooper, R. (1995). *When Lean Enterprises Collide: Competing Through Confrontation*, Harvard Business School Press.

Factory Management (2000). Special issue: Line-company system that extends ability of workers and manufacturing section steadily, *Factory Management*, pp. 9–77 (in Japanese).

Hamada, K. (1989). Profit management that used amoeba system: a case of Kyocera, *Accounting* 41(2), pp. 46–51 (in Japanese).

Hamada, K. and Monden, Y. (1989). Profit management at Kyocera Corporation: the amoeba system, in *Japanese Management Accounting*, Productivity Press, pp. 197–210.

Miya, H. (2003). *Amoeba Management Theory*, Toyo Keizai (in Japanese).

Miya, H., Tani, T., and Kagono, T. (1999). *The Amoeba Management Changes the Company*, Diamond (in Japanese).

Monden, Y. (1995). *Cost Reduction System: Target Costing and Kaizen Costing*, Productivity Press.

Tani, T. and Miya, H. (1998). Line company system at NEC Saitama, *Journal of Political Economy and Commercial Science*, pp. 17–34 (in Japanese).

Yoshida, E. and Matsuki, S. (2001). Empowerment at Pseudo Mini Profit Center, *Journal of Business and Economics* 47(3), pp. 171–190 (in Japanese).

Part 4

Management Accounting for Supply Chain and Shared Services

Total Productivity Management and the Theory of Constraints: An Integrated Application of Supply Chain Management Methods

Kazuki Hamada

Professor, Institute of Business and Accounting
Kwansei Gakuin University

1 Introduction

It is important in business management to supply customers with what they need in a timely manner. It is necessary to produce and sell optimally, adapting to environmental changes, while always monitoring the environment during execution, and being prepared to change the resource allocation promptly. There are possibilities for the delay of action in the market, and of partial optimization that takes only each operation, department, or internal situation of the company into consideration. Therefore, keeping the holistic relations among companies in view, and managing the flow of products, money and information become important.

Measures for the increase of sales, for the solutions of problems, and for the effective use of assets, etc., can be examined from a wider perspective by putting the interdependent relations among companies in view. Moreover, cost reduction can be attempted by simplifying and standardizing the processing procedures among companies. In addition, if demand information from the customer reaches the manufacturer immediately, a prompt response to the demand by the manufacturer becomes possible.

Supply chain management (SCM) is a typical method for management among companies. SCM manages to oversee the flow of business from the procurement of materials to production, sales, distribution, and service to the consumer as one big chain, and manages to attain the best solution. Manufacturing is the main focus of this chapter and the optimization of the supply chain (SC) as seen from the manufacturer's standpoint is considered.

Moreover, SCM is of two types. One intends to aim at win–win relations of all SC member companies and at the accomplishment of an overall goal. The other manages the SC to achieve an individual company's own goal. The latter is considered in this paper, though the original meaning of SCM is related to the former.

As for SCM, the view that concerned process improvement on the supply side was central till now. However, it is thought that collecting the opinions of customers, improving products and services suitable for their needs as soon as possible, and offering them to customers are important, in recent years. The establishment of a demand chain (DC) that gathers customer information is needed for that. However, appropriate DC alone is insufficient. DC and SC need to be integrated with SCM so that the appropriate, wide meaning (integrated demand SCM) is important (Nishimura, 1999).

The purpose of this paper is to examine the effectiveness and the application method of the Theory of Constraints (TOC) to SCM as mentioned earlier. Concretely, first of all the main indicators (throughput, operating costs, and gross investment) in TOC are explained from the standpoint of SCM, and then development of TOC in a manner corresponding to the corporate strategy is pointed out. How the deployment of TOC main indicators to subordinate ones is necessary in the execution is described, while considering effective methods for deciding measures to achieve the subordinate indicators. The TP (total productivity) management that is researched in Japan and executed in some companies will be focused upon and examined in this paper though the management method by balanced scorecard (BSC) may also be suitable for this purpose.

2   SCM and the Indicators of TOC

The basic goal of SCM is to grasp customer's needs quickly and to offer products which customers want promptly. Therefore, it is especially important that products which customers want are developed and that the speed from the procurement of materials to production, sales, and distribution is increased. TOC is a suitable theory for this speed management and it is based on throughput accounting.

In the throughput accounting, in general, profit is calculated as follows:

$$\text{Profit} = (\text{sales} - \text{direct material costs}) - \text{operating costs}$$
$$= \text{throughput} - \text{operating costs}.$$

The word, "in general," is used because not only direct material costs but also other costs may be included, as costs deducted from sales and the calculation value are called throughput. The operating costs here consist of material costs other than direct material costs, labor costs, overhead costs, etc. These are period costs which are not allocated in products. In SCM the overall SC is considered as a unit; sales are the amount sold in the end to consumers and operating costs are the ones in all SC member companies. However, because this chapter is focused on SCM which intends to increase the profit of one's own company, sales and operating costs are those of the individual company (Hamada, 2000).

In general, direct material inventories are carried forward directly by direct material accounts, though there are various kinds of opinions. And direct material costs deducted from sales are calculated by the multiplication of the direct material costs for each unit by sales volume. Therefore, the amount of deducted direct material costs from sales are fixed, if the direct material costs for each unit does not change, when products that do not sell are produced.

The above is a profit calculation method done by throughput accounting. TOC aims at the increase of throughput, the decrease of operating costs, and a decrease of gross investments based on the method. And TOC interprets throughput as the amount of funds acquired by sales, operating costs as funds used to change inventories into throughput, and gross investments as funds invested in inventories and equipments.

The costs required in the production as it is will increase the total cost only by producing products, because labor costs and factory overhead costs are treated as period costs in the above-mentioned computation. This is different from the usual accounting procedures in which all costs required in producing products are carried forward as the amount of asset and in which only the amount corresponding to sales is treated as the period cost. Therefore, it is necessary that the company quickly perceives the best products to increase the profit, reflects them in the production activity, reduces inventories, shortens the lead time, saves operating costs, and ties material costs to sales in a short time. This is exactly the direction at which SCM aims. It can be said that throughput accounting and TOC are useful theories for SCM in relation to the above.

TOC has three targets as mentioned above, but it is assumed that the increase of throughput is especially important and it lays stress on the development theory concerning the relaxation and the dissolution of bottlenecks to increase the throughput. However, because the increase of sales cannot be expected in an age of low growth and recession, at that time profits need to be earned by efficient use of operating costs and assets in which the overall SC is taken into consideration (Monden, 2001). Therefore, the measures that take not only the increase of throughput, but also those targets into consideration at the same time, are needed.

For the same reason, it is necessary to adopt appropriate measures of bottlenecks for all the three targets. Moreover, it should be understood that an approach called the "Thinking Process" (Noreen *et al.*, 1995; Yazawa, 1999) in TOC is a management method that should be used to achieve these three targets in TOC, though it is impressed on us that it targets only the increase of throughput. When the method of this Thinking Process is applied to SCM, it is especially necessary to focus upon the facts disturbing the flow of products, money, and information among companies.

Moreover it is generally said that TOC is a method for problem discovery and solution generation which stands not as part of a strategic, long-term approach but as a short-term aspect to attain total optimization by improvement. Therefore, most researches focus upon the short-term aspect. This is because TOC deals with all costs except direct material costs as fixed costs. The fixed costs become fewer from a long-term viewpoint. If the period covered is further lengthened, fixed costs are ultimately lost.

However, thinking about the increase of throughput from a long-term perspective by developing the basic idea of TOC is also important and it seems that it is necessary to think about the reduction of operating costs and investments from such a view. Especially, because the relations among companies become important when SCM is considered, a long-term perspective becomes important. Just because the operating costs are fixed in the short-term, does not mean, one may exclude them from the focus of management in the long-term. That is, it should be understood that there is a structural shift in the long-term, though the profit calculation method based on TOC is a computation type which is carried out on each occasion. This is true since cash flow management is not a management approach which lays stress only on the short-term, because the concept of throughput is similar to cash flow.

It is important to consider the strategy that improves the three main indicators of TOC from a strategic and long-term view, in terms of the above. Relating it to SCM is considered in the next section. Therefore, a short-term perspective that focuses on the speed of SCM and a strategic long-term view that looks at structural change will be considered at the same time.

3 Concrete Measures that Improve TOC Main Indicators, and BSC

As mentioned in the previous section, three goals, which are the increase of throughput, the decrease of operating costs, and the decrease of gross investment, have to be considered at the same time from both a short-term and a long-term view.

The increase of throughput is achieved by satisfying customers and increasing sales. Customer satisfaction is achieved by offering what customers hope for, at an appropriate price. The innovation, the quality, the delivery date of products, and the after-sale services are the factors which should be considered in order to bring customer satisfaction. It is also necessary that intra-company processes can deal with challenges promptly and flexibly. To know customer needs and their changes, the establishment of DC is needed. To make DC function efficiently, as a device to make customers send information easily, the establishment of a system to accumulate and analyze information in collaboration with customers is also effective.

Moreover, the increase of throughput is also attained by the reduction of direct material costs. The selection of advantageous buyers is needed for that. Of course, it is necessary to consider the reduction of all costs (total cost of ownership: TCO) which are related to ownership from the view of the overall company, instead of the reduction of direct material costs alone (Kaplan and Cooper, 1998). TCO includes not only the purchase price but also material related costs, appraisal losses, loss from spoilage, and other opportunity costs associated with this material. The cost reduction in the development phase of a new product (target costing) becomes a useful means to reduce the direct material costs too.

The decrease of operating costs are attained by the reduction of labor costs, factory costs, sales costs, and distribution costs in SC, along with general administration costs, and so on. In the companies that produce and sell products such as computers which are short in their life cycle, the appraisal losses concerning remainders and the losses from a disadvantageous clearance sale, etc., are major factors that should be considered. There are companies that try to reduce costs by delivering to customers directly, using joint distribution centers and simplifying the trading system as a part of SCM.

The decrease of gross investments can be achieved by the increase of inventory turnover rates and the effective use of equipment. It also can be achieved by the improvement of development efficiency and the reduction of lead time in production, etc. Some companies try to reduce inventories by sharing the data results and the plans of sales, inventories, and production. Other companies make an effort to reduce equipment, etc., by effective use of outsourcing and shared services.

As mentioned earlier, concrete subordinate goals and measures that should be aimed at improving TOC main indicators cannot help becoming integrated. Moreover, both the financial and non-financial ones will be included among the goal indicators that become the standards of the measures selection. The relation to the overall strategy of a company becomes important if we think about the improvement of those indicators from a long-term perspective. There is a method of BSC as a management approach that coordinates financial and non-financial factors with the strategy, and that integrates them. Because this method is well known, the explanation is omitted here. BSC is a method for aiming at the best solution from the standpoint of all stakeholders and seems to offer a framework that takes into consideration the deployment of TOC main indicators over subordinate ones (Hamada, 2001).

TP management approach that looks like this and that seems to be more effective in the deployment of goals and measures than BSC is explained in the next section. Following that, an application example of the approach in SCM will be considered, in Section 5.

4   Useful TP Management for Goals/Measures Deployment in SCM

TP management is a management method that Professor Masao Akiba designed, and it is useful for matching the vector of an entire company, to extend the constitution of production innovatively and for achieving goals effectively (Akiba, 1994). One basic type is shown in Figure 1. The reason for using the word, "one," is that each company can change this model to the one that is most suitable for them. Five processes of goal setting, goal deployment, measures selection, an execution plan, and results acquisition are centered as shown Figure 1.

There are two types of overall goals in TP management, and they are performance goals and state (constitution) goals. The company's goals are deployed logically and concretely using the hierarchy diagram. The measures that can be constructed are also deployed using it. Leakage is decreased by using it, and the relations between goals and measures become

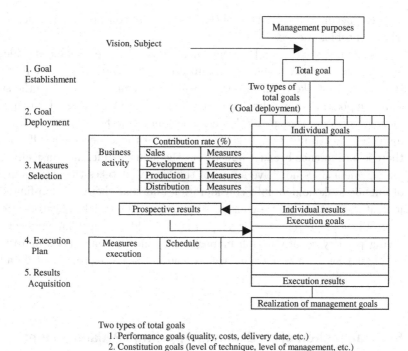

Fig. 1   Five steps in TP management (Akiba, 1994, p. 11)

clear. Moreover, the relations among two or more items become clearer and the entire composition can be understood and viewed at one time, because the relations between goals and measures are deployed by the matrix. This is useful in relating measures easily within the overall view.

The contribution rate in the figure is the rate that the attainment of an individual goal contributes to the attainment of an overall goal. The comprehensive evaluation of the achievement situation every day, every week, and every month becomes possible by using these rates. The influence upon the overall goal of the activity at the job site can also be known at the right time. If a financial goal is given as an overall goal, an assessment of how the daily activities at the site as measured by non-financial factors influence the financial goal will be obtained by the contribution rate.

If TP management is adopted in order to examine the goals and measures that achieve TOC main indicators, the relations among subordinate goals, the causal relations between goals and measures, and their horizontal relations become clearer. And it becomes easier to consider countermeasures when a problem arises.

As mentioned above, TP management aims at the well-balanced achievement of the goals of an entire organization and is a management method that looks a lot like BSC. Moreover, when deploying indicators to the subordinate position is attached great importance, BSC resembles TP management even more, though BSC is a management method that designed the indicators to attain strategic goals, and aims at the achievement. Of course, there is a difference because how to put the focus is different. Basically, TP management does not have a way of thinking that takes the various needs of outside stakeholders into consideration and that there are non-financial indicators that should be considered to achieve financial indicators. However, TP management was developed in the field of industrial engineering, giving priority to production management, and it seems to be more useful than BSC as a framework that executes the development of detailed goals/measures.

5   Examination of an Example Applying TP Management to SCM

The example of the Internet Platform division in Hitachi Ltd. (Shinozaki *et al.*, 2001), which had been reorganized and renamed, is examined as an application experience of SCM. However, this case is one where SCM was not alone, but rather one of the whole strategies and SCM measures were decided from the overall view. The division started the "STEP UP 2000 project," which was introduced by TP management in January, 1999, to deal with the fall in the price of PC (personal computers) and extreme changes of the business environment.

The total goal was "customer value × speed/correspondence loss to changes." The meaning of this was to increase customer value and speed, to lower the correspondence loss to changes. The total goal was divided into three components: "customer value," "speed," and "correspondence loss to changes," as shown in Figure 2, and the improvement goals were set respectively. If those goals were achieved, the increase of sales, the decrease of total costs, and the increase of profit were expected.

Regarding customer value, the increase of product quality, the shortening of delivery dates and the improvement of customer support were chosen as sub-goals, because it is difficult to make the difference in the product

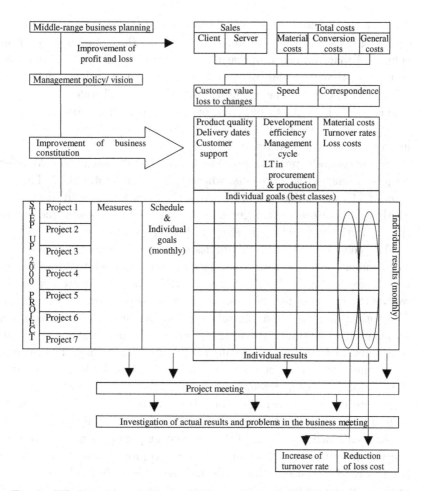

Fig. 2   Whole systematic chart of TP management (Shinozaki *et al.*, p. 58)

spec, the price, and so on. Regarding speed, the increase of development efficiency, the improvement of the management cycle, and the shortening of lead-time in procurement and production were chosen as sub-goals. Regarding the correspondence loss to changes, the decrease of material costs, the increase of inventory turnover rates, and the decrease of "loss costs" were chosen as sub-goals. "Loss costs" mean the costs which were caused when materials and products remained. These goals were set as concrete numerical goals.

If we think about the relation between these goals and the main indicators of TOC, throughput relates chiefly to the columns of customer value and material costs, operating costs relate chiefly to the columns of costs other than material costs, and gross investments relate chiefly to the columns of speed and the inventory turnover rates. Therefore, though this case is not divided like throughput, operating costs, and gross investments, the goals shown in this figure are the ones that need to be considered to improve those goals concretely.

Seven concrete projects are adopted in the division. "TSCM reform project" is one of those projects, where TSCM shows total SCM. The character of "T" was added to SCM because the managers wanted to show that SCM in this instance manages information about products, money, and time collectively, while the former SCM managed only products.

The goals of TSCM in this division are the adequate correspondence to customer needs, the short delivery date, punctual delivery, and the offer of reliable products. The measures to attain these goals are deployed as well as the measures for the goals of other projects. Also, the target values of monthly measures and the schedule are decided. These measures are formulated, while taking the interdependent relations among projects into consideration from the standpoint of the overall company. The measures concerning TSCM are also decided in relation to the whole. Figure 2 shows the relationships being executed according to the goals. As for the individual goals seen in the vertical direction, they will be attained if the measures seen in horizontal direction are executed according to the goals.

As mentioned above, the TP management puts all strategies in a perspective from the overall standpoint of the company, and offers a holistic framework that can examine goals and measures collectively. SCM is one of the strategic goals of the company and the relations among all strategies are important in the decisions made about measures.

6 Concluding Remarks

In this paper, inter-company management, especially SCM is focused, and the goals/measures deployment from the management accounting standpoint is considered. The application of useful TOC for speedy management is examined because it is most important to assess customer needs quickly and to respond to them promptly in SCM. But in TOC, the increase of throughput has been overemphasized up until now, and the examination of diminishing operating costs and gross investments has been sparse. There-fore, three goals of TOC were thought to be equally important and devel-oped. Moreover, the structure in each occasion was thought to be decided by long-term factors though TOC has been referred to as an approach standing on short-term ideas, and as mentioned, the strategy, subordinate goals, and measures must be coordinated.

In this paper, TP management is appraised as a useful method for the goals/measures deployment, and this is considered while showing an execu-tion example about the future. It is mentioned that TP management is a method which can execute the goals/measures deployment while consider-ing complex interrelations, when strategic management methods other than SCM are executed in a company.

The egocentric SCM where the manufacturer is centered has been the focus in this paper. Besides this, there is a whole-intended type of SCM in which the entire SC is considered as a big chain and is managed in this way. This SCM is the original and has been excluded from consideration in this paper. In the case of this type, it is important to devise the method of total SCM and to build the win–win relations among companies.

Though there are few studies where inter-company management is treated in the field of management accounting now, it seems that big results can be expected by executing inter-company management appropriately. Therefore, it can be thought that the research relating to how to use man-agement accounting to manage relationships among companies will be one of the important themes for management accounting in the future.

References

Akiba, M. (1994). *Method of TP Management*, Japan Management Association (in Japanese).

Hamada, K. (2000). Back-flush costing and throughput accounting, in *Text-book of Management Accounting*, 3rd ed., edited by Monden, Y., Zeimu-keiri Kyoukai, Chapter 23, pp. 351–366 (in Japanese).

Hamada, K. (2001). An application of the TOC to SCM/BSC, *Kigyou-kaikei* 53(11), pp. 31–37 (in Japanese).

Japan Management Association (ed.) (2001). *Summary Collection of the Com-memoration Rally in 2001: Examples of Companies Which Win Excellent Prize of TP Management*, Japan Management Association (in Japanese).

Kaplan, R. S. and Cooper, R. (1998). *Cost & Effect*, Harvard Business School Press, Chapter 11, pp. 202–223.

Monden, Y. (2001). Comparisons between the TOC and JIT, *Kigyou-kaikei* 53(11), pp. 22–30 (in Japanese).

Nishimura, Y. (1999). Supply chain management of demand creation type, in *Theory and Strategy in Supply Chains*, edited by Diamond Pub. Co., Diamond Pub. Co., pp. 209–226 (in Japanese).

Noreen, E., Smith, D., and Mackey, T. M. (1995). *The Theory of Constraints and Its Implications for Management Accounting*, The North River Press.

Shinozaki, M., Arai, Y., and Chiba, K. (2001). TP management of the Internet platform division in Hitachi Ltd., in *Technical Examples of TP Management (11)*, edited by Japan Management Association (in Japanese).

Yazawa, H. (1999). Implication of the theory of constraints (TOC) and some problems in management accounting, *Kigyou-kaikei* 51(6), pp. 28–36 (in Japanese).

Allocation of Joint Profit among Supply Chain Companies: Application of Core Theory

Masaaki Imabayashi

Associate Professor, Faculty of Business Administration Mejiro University

1 Introduction

Research papers and books have been published on a variety of supply chain companies since the late 1980s. Research using game theory has been applied to a variety of managerial accounting problems such as allocation of joint profit since the 1980s. As for research applying concepts of solutions of game theory to managerial accounting, we have a series of research on allocation of profit starting with studies by Moriarity (1975, 1976) and on transfer pricing of goods and services (Monden, 1989a,b; and others). These studies often use the theory of the cooperative n-person game. In this game, core is an important concept. It is well known that the concept of core is important as a "necessary condition" for the allocation of common fees and decisions on transfer prices. Moreover, as a concept of the solution necessary to set the amount of allocation, we use the Shapley value and, its application, the general Shapley value. As for an academic paper that proposes and applies the general Shapley value with purchase cost of individual sections as "weight" to the allocation problem of the joint cost, see Gangolly (1981). As for an academic paper that proposes and applies the general Shapley value with the numerical quantity of purchase of individual sections as "weight," see Hamlen *et al.* (1980). As for a study that applies the general Shapley value to the decision on internal transfer price, see Imabayashi (1988). These studies basically apply solutions from game theory to the allocation of joint cost and the allocation of home office cost within a company.

On the other hand, in the supply chain, when companies located on the upper chain sell the goods and services of those located on the lower end of the chain, there are some cases in which scale merit takes place. In other words, in purchasing some goods and services, companies that belong to the supply chain make joint purchases on more favorable cost terms than each company purchasing separately. In interpreting this situation in terms of game theory, we may consider multiple companies comprising the supply chain as players that make a coalition in terms of game theory.

In this case, in order to allocate scale merit to each company, there are two methods. First, the "economized amount" generated by building the supply chain is allocated to each company after the transaction in some way. Second, the adjusted price that automatically allocates the "economized amount" to each company should be set for selling and buying goods and services along the supply chain. As a result, the "economized amount" is allocated to each company.

In the first method, one has to calculate the profit of each term as provisional settlement of the account and allocate the amount to other companies. However, in the second method, once one sets an appropriate price in advance, the "economized amount" is in the end allocated to each company only by making transactions based on the price.

Consequently, based on the second method, this paper proposes a method for finding a provisional price (hereafter, "a provisional price along the supply chain" as a starting point for discussion in case an appropriate price is set by negotiations among companies. As for selling and buying goods and services among multiple companies comprising the supply chain, the "economized amount" generated by building a supply chain is reflected by each company's performance.

In this paper model, assuming that there is one supply company and there are three receiving companies that purchase goods and services provided by the supply company, we propose a method of setting a price to sell the goods and services that the supply company provides to the three companies using the general Shapley value. Moreover, this paper verifies, first, if the price meets the core conditions, a necessary condition of preventing the coalition from breaking up, and, second, if the price meets the "price-numerical quantity condition" (the more a company purchases, the cheaper the per-piece cost becomes) to find out if the price reflects the scale merit.

The structure of this paper is as follows. In Section 2, we will discuss a method of deciding the price for transaction along the supply chain and the necessary conditions. In Section 3, we will talk about the relationship between game theory and the provisional price along the supply chain. In

Section 4, we propose a new model using a two-step game method and a residual contribution quantity comparison method. In Section 5, we show our conclusions.

2 Decision-making Procedure of the Provisional Price for Transaction along the Supply Chain and Necessary Conditions

2.1 *Decision-making procedure of the provisional price for transaction along the supply chain*

In deciding a provisional price for goods and services along the supply chain in our model, following four steps are required.

At the first stage, assuming that we focus on specific goods and services, a supply company sells along the supply chain, and a receiving company buys. In this case, it is necessary to grasp what kind of cost structure the supply side has. In other words, we grasp the amount of generated cost, the characteristic function figure under the whole coalition in an expression of game theory. At the second stage, we assume that each company implements trade individually or by making a partial coalition. Assuming that the supply side sells the goods and services outside the supply chain and the purchase side purchases outside the chain, we find the cost and the profit of each company. In short, we seek the characteristic function figure in an individual or partial coalition in an expression of game theory. At the third stage, based on these characteristic function figures, the economized amount of cost generated by making the supply chain is distributed to the supply company and the receiving company group. At the fourth stage, based on the economized amount, multiple receiving companies decide provisional prices along the supply chain that are different from company to company.

In these ways, we find the provisional prices along the supply chain.

2.2 *Necessary conditions of provisional prices along the supply chain*

In case there is a company that dominates the supply chain across the board, it will decide a provisional price along the supply chain. In case there is no special company that takes leadership, a provisional price along the supply chain will be decided by negotiation. In the latter case, the price that can be calculated in a similar way to this model will function as a price for the starting point of negotiation.

Regardless of the decision-making entity, there are two aspects that the provisional price along the supply chain must meet. The first aspect concerns the purpose of the provisional price along the supply chain. The second aspect concerns the decision-making criteria of the provisional price along the supply chain.

The purpose of the provisional price along the supply chain, the first aspect, is to distribute the scale merit generated by making the supply chain in each company. In our model, it is possible to sell and purchase goods and services outside the supply chain, and both the selling and purchasing prices outside the supply chain are open to the public. In this situation, we set the provisional price along the supply chain in order to allocate the economized amount generated by the scale merit to the supply and receiving companies.

As for the decision-making criteria of a provisional price along the supply chain, the second aspect, we can point out the following two factors. First, a provisional price along the supply chain must consider the cost to the supply company and cover the cost. Second, for the receiving companies, the price of purchasing goods and services from the supply company must be lower than that of purchasing them from outside the supply chain, that is, the market price. In other words, if such conditions cannot be met, there is reason to purchase goods and services along the supply chain.

In order to acquire an answer for the price to meet such necessary conditions, the next section surveys a cooperative n-person game theory, and discusses the decision-making method of a provisional price along the supply chain as the starting point for the supply chain decision-making entity to decide the price.

3   Game Theory and Provisional Price along the Supply Chain

This section discusses the significance of applying the core theory of a cooperative n-person game to decisions on the provisional price along the supply chain and explains a residual contribution quantity comparison method, a general Shapley with the amount of purchased goods as core theory based on Imabayashi (1988).

A comprehensive collaboration in Section n is called N, and partial collaboration ex gratia (including the comprehensive collaboration) is set S.

Suppose the profit that can be acquired by S is $\Psi(S)$; Ψ is called the characteristic function. Also suppose the minimum cost under the collaboration S is cost-type characteristic function $C(S)$. These functions make the monetary amount, the real figures, correspond to the set.

3.1 *The two-stage game*

As mentioned in the previous section, this model aims to present a price that represents a starting point for negotiation. There are two methods as a process for negotiation.

The first method assumes that each of the companies comprising the supply chain becomes a negotiator. A person in charge from each company on an equal footing proceeds with negotiation to decide a provisional price along the supply chain. In terms of the game theory, this method is based on the idea of considering all parties as players.

The second method assumes the following negotiation process. At the first stage, a person in charge of supplying goods and services and people representing the receiving companies negotiate to decide a total average provisional price along the supply chain from the supply company to the receiving companies. This method can find expected attribution profit that belongs to the supply company. In terms of game theory, this method is called a cooperative two-person game. At the second stage, all people representing the receiving companies set a provisional price for each receiving company along the supply chain through negotiation.

Because the partial collaboration S between the supply company and some of the receiving companies is not born in the negotiation process in the second method, there is no need to find such S's cost-type characteristic function $C(S)$.

This chapter adopts the second method. Hereafter, this method is called "two-stage game."

3.2 *Core theory*

Using the cost-type characteristic function, this subsection explains core theory, the most important concept in applying the cooperative n-person game.

The core is a set of vectors of allocation amounts that meets the following three formulas. When a case that each company makes a comprehensive collaboration to make a joint procurement of certain goods and services the most profitable one, allocation vector $E = (E_j)(j = 1, 2, \ldots, n)$ represents how each company allocates the joint procurement price inside the set. There are three necessary conditions to meet the core.

Conditions of individual rationality

$$E_i \leq C(\{i\}), \quad \forall i \in N. \tag{1}$$

Conditions of comprehensive rationality

$$\sum_{i \in N} E_i = C(N). \tag{2}$$

Conditions of collaboration rationality

$$\sum_{i \in S} E_i \leq C(S), \quad \forall S \subseteq N. \tag{3}$$

In case of an allocation amount that is included in the core, there is no incentive for some companies to destroy the comprehensive collaboration of the supply chain. Even if it is possible for member companies to exercise the right to purchase goods and services from companies outside the supply chain, they will continue to make purchases from companies along the supply chain.

3.3 *"Principle of goal congruence" and "principle of fairness"*

In case profits generated by collaboration of multiple companies, as in this model (in this model, profit is the economized amount from the fact that member companies along the supply chain make joint purchase of goods and services manufactured by other members within the same supply chain), are allocated, the principles of goal congruence and fairness are necessary just like the case of evaluating performance of businesses.

In case of the supply chain in our model, having goal congruence means there is compliance between each company's goal and the goal of the supply chain as a whole. In other words, as for the whole supply chain, it is assumed that using goods and services along the supply chain is beneficial for each company comprising the supply chain. Consequently, the price with goal congruence is a price that does not provide a person in charge at the supply company with an incentive to increase profits by selling his/her goods and services outside the supply chain that are supposed to be sold within the chain. On the other hand, the price with goal congruence is a price that does not provide one or more people in charge at the receiving companies with a positive incentive to procure goods and services outside the supply chain either unilaterally or jointly.

The price with the principle of fairness is a price that is set to be effective to motivate a person in charge, at least to avoid a reverse functional result. In other words, it is a situation in which a person in charge of a certain company feels that the price allocated to his company is not unfair in comparison with those of other companies in the same business line. Consequently, the price that satisfies the core is one of the necessary conditions of the principle of fairness.

Basically, the principle of fairness is a human sensory scale that is difficult to express in a quantitative manner. However, at least as a condition other than the core that meets the principle of fairness, we point out the price-quantitative condition. The price-quantitative condition is a condition that demands the price of a company that purchases a larger number of goods and services to be lower than that of another company that purchases less goods and services.

3.4 *General Shapley value*

We will explain a method to find the price by the residual contribution quantity comparison method, a method this chapter proposes to decide a provisional price along the supply chain.

Loehman and Whinston (1974) proposed a general Shapley value. It is also an answer in game theory that Hamlen *et al.* (1980) applied to an issue of cost allocation. Let us explain the relationship between the Shapley value and the general Shapley value. The Shapley value $\phi_i(\Psi)$, an allocation figure of player I under the characteristic functions Ψ, can be shown in the following formula:

$$\phi_i(\Psi) = \sum_{S \subset N} \frac{(n-s)!(s-1)!}{n!} \{\Psi(S) - \Psi(S - \{i\})\}, \quad \forall i \in N$$

$$(s \text{ is an element count of } S). \tag{4}$$

Because of the concept of the residual contribution m_R, formula (4) has been proved in the following formula (Suzuki, 1980, pp. 206–213):

$$\phi(\psi) = \sum_{\substack{R \subset N \\ i \in R}} \frac{1}{r} m_R \quad \left(m_R = \sum_{S \subset R} (-1)^{r-s} \psi(S) \right)$$

$$(r \text{ is an element count of set } R). \tag{5}$$

The residual contribution is also called the carrier or support in the context of game theory.

The answer that the residual contribution m_R in formula (5) divided by each company's "weight" and allocated is the following general Shapley value:

$$\phi(\psi) = \sum_{\substack{R \subset N \\ i \in R}} \left(\frac{w_j}{\sum_{i \in R} w_j} m_R \right), \quad m_R = \sum_{S \subset R} (-1)^{r-s} \psi(S)$$

$$(r \text{ is an element count of set } R). \tag{6}$$

In other words, the Shapley value is to take the number of players as the weight of the general Shapley. In this sense, the Shapley value can be interpreted as a special case of the general Shapley value. The Shapley value that regards only the number of players as weight ignoring each player's size is not an appropriate figure because when we regard companies with a variety of sizes that comprise the supply chain as players, there is normally a substantial difference in size among companies.

The general Shapley value tries to have this residual contribution m_R attribute to each player with some kind of weight. As for a case regarding purchase quantity of goods and services as weight, see Hamlen *et al.* (1980). It is called a residual contribution quantity comparison method. As for an ICP method that regards a price when each player purchases separately as weight, see Gangolly (1981).

Because this chapter tries to propose a price that meets the price-quantity conditions better, we adopted the residual contribution quantity comparison method rather than the ICP method to provide players that purchase a larger amount with a larger residual contribution allocation amount.

4 Two-stage Game Method and Residual Contribution Quantity Comparison Method

4.1 *Numerical figure model*

As shown in Figure 1, using a model of one supply company and three receiving companies, this chapter clarifies a method to find a provisional price along the supply chain using a way of applying a two-stage game method and taking advantage of the residual contribution quantity comparison method on the second stage. The model is as follows.

As for the cost function of the supply company Y's product, the cost is C_Y, the variable cost is v, the fixed fee is F, and the manufacturing quantity is q.

$$C_Y = v \cdot h + F = 0.2 \ (\$\text{thousand/piece}) \times q + 120 \ (\$\text{thousand}). \quad (7)$$

The receiving companies A, B, and C are to purchase $q_A = 100$ (pieces/term), $q_B = 400$ (pieces/term), and $q_C = 100$ (pieces/term) of goods and services from Y. Consequently, Y's prospective active mass (the so-called standard capacity utilization) is 600 (pieces/term).

When A, B, and C jointly procure the total goods and services of the same kind ($q_M = 600$ pieces) outside the supply chain, we assume that the joint procurement price P' is 0.55 (\$thousand/piece). When Y directly offers its own services outside the supply chain, it wishes to set the price at $P'_Y = 0.45$ (\$thousand/piece), lower than the market price in order to maintain competitiveness. It is also possible for the receiving companies A, B, and C to procure Y's services and the same kind of services outside

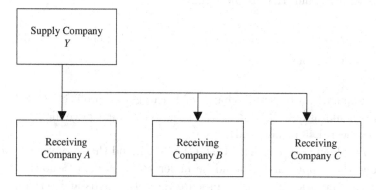

Fig. 1   Our model (one supply company and three receiving companies)

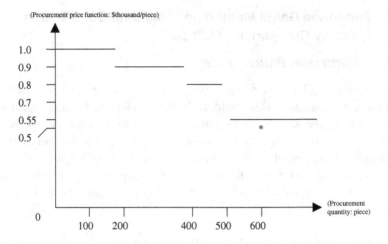

Fig. 2   Procurement price function from outside the supply chain

the supply chain. The procurement price function from outside the supply chain is in a staircase pattern as shown in Figure 2.

4.2 Two-stage games

We will explain the first stage in the two-stage game method.

Suppose the supply company Y sells all its goods and services outside the supply chain. In this case, the supply company's profit π'_Y can be calculated by subtracting the cost C from the profit R'_Y gained by selling outside the supply chain. Here is the formula:

$$\pi'_Y = R'_Y - C = P'_Y \cdot q_M - (v \cdot q_M + F) = 0.45 \times 600 - (0.2 \times 600 + 120)$$
$$= 30 \ (\$\text{thousand}). \tag{8}$$

Consequently, a person in charge of Y can gain a profit of 30 ($thousand) and should ask A, B, and C to set the provisional price along the supply chain over 0.45 ($thousand).

People in charge of set (A, B, C) will demand that the provisional price along the supply chain should be under $P'_{ABC} = 0.55$ ($thousand/piece), that is, the price when they procure the total goods and services outside the supply chain.

Consequently, at the first stage, the total average provisional price along the supply chain $\bar{P}$ is within the following formula:

$$P'_Y < \bar{P} < P'_{ABC}. \tag{9}$$

In other words, $\bar{P}$ is set within the negotiating limit between 0.45 (\$thousand/piece) and 0.55 (\$thousand/piece). Suppose that in this mode, the negotiation was concluded at $\bar{P} = 0.50$ (\$thousand/piece). This figure satisfies the imputation of a cooperation two-person game, a concept of game theory. In this case, the attribution profit for Y is

$$\pi_Y = \bar{P} \cdot h_M - (v \cdot h_{ABC} + F) = 0.50 \times 600 - (0.2 \times 600 + 120)$$
$$= 60 \text{ (\$thousand)}. \tag{10}$$

Consequently, the relationship between $\bar{P}$ and π_Y can be described as

$$\bar{P} = \frac{v \cdot h_{ABC} + F + \pi_Y}{h_{ABC}} = \frac{0.2 \times 600 + 120 + 60}{600}$$
$$= 0.50 \text{ (\$thousand/piece)}. \tag{11}$$

We will now explain the second stage. On the first stage, set (A, B, C) is calculated from Y:

$$C(N) = \bar{P} \cdot q_{ABC} = 0.5 \times (100 + 400 + 100)$$
$$= 300 \text{ (\$thousand/piece)}. \tag{12}$$

They are to procure the total goods and services, but at the second stage, the problem is out of 300 (\$thousand/piece); how much burden each receiving company assumes as responsibility. In other words, P that is predicted on the first stage is the total average provisional price along the supply chain. At the second stage, the question is a provisional price along the supply chain for each receiving company that can be calculated by the following formula:

$$\bar{P} \cdot q_{ABC} = P_A \cdot q_A + P_B \cdot q_B + P_C \cdot q_C. \tag{13}$$

At the second stage, considering the possibility that the receiving companies set A, B, and C procure Y's goods and services and the same kind of services outside the supply chain, it is necessary to find the following data using the procurement price function outside the supply chain as Figure 2 shows. The procurement price from outside P' shows combination of joint purchase by subscript A, B, or C and their combination. From Figure 2, here is the formula:

$$P'_A = 1.0, \quad P'_B = 0.8, \quad P'_C = 1.0, \quad P'_{AB} = 1.0, \quad P'_{AC} = 0.9,$$
$$P'_{BC} = 0.7, \quad P'_{ABC} = 0.55.$$

Consequently, the price that A, B, and C each individually procures goods and services from outside the supply chain $C'(S)$ (provided $A, B, C \in S$) is described in the following formulas:

$$C'(A) = P'_A \cdot h_A = 1 \times 100 = 100,$$
$$C'(B) = P'_B \cdot h_B = 0.8 \times 400 = 320, \qquad (14)$$
$$C'(C) = P'_C \cdot h_C = 1 \times 100 = 100.$$

In case of considering all combination of collaborations, each procurement price C' is described in the following formulas:

$$C'(AB) = P'_{AB}(q_A + q_B) = 0.7 \times (100 + 400) = 350,$$
$$C'(AC) = P'_{AC}(q_A + q_C) = 0.9 \times (100 + 100) = 180,$$
$$C'(BC) = P'_{BC}(q_B + q_C) = 0.7 \times (400 + 100) = 350, \qquad (15)$$
$$C'(ABC) = P'_{ABC}(q_A + q_B + q_C)$$
$$= 0.55 \times (100 + 400) + 100 = 330.$$

Using the above data, we will calculate a provisional transfer price by the residual contribution quantity comparison method.

In accordance with formula (5), calculations of the residual contribution are done for the number of combinations of collaborations. Consequently, in case of three sectors, we will have the following four calculations:

$$m_{AB} = C'(A) + C'(B) - C'(AB) = (100 + 320) - 350 = 70,$$
$$m_{AC} = C'(A) + C'(C) - C'(AC) = (100 + 100) - 180 = 20,$$
$$m_{BC} = C'(B) + C'(C) - C'(BC) = (100 + 320) - 350 = 70, \qquad (16)$$
$$m_{ABC} = \{C'(A) + C'(B) + C'(C) - C'(N)\} - (m_{AB} + m_{AC} + m_{BC})$$
$$= \{(100 + 320 + 100) - 300\} - (70 + 20 + 70) = 60.$$

Obligation fees of $C(N)$ of each A, B, and C calculated by the residual contribution quantity comparison method are described as a, b, and c, respectively.

In accordance with the formula, obligation fees vector is (a, b, c). However, we always have the following formula: $C(N) = a + b + c$. The figure of a, b, or c may be calculated in the following formula:

$$a = C'(A) - \left(m_{AB} \cdot \frac{q_A}{q_A + q_B} + m_{AC} \cdot \frac{q_A}{q_A + q_C} \right.$$
$$\left. + m_{ABC} \cdot \frac{h_A}{h_A + h_B + h_C} \right)$$
$$= 100 - \left\{ 70 \times \frac{100}{(100 + 400)} + 20 \times \frac{100}{(100 + 100)} \right.$$
$$\left. + 60 \times \frac{100}{(100 + 400 + 100)} \right\} = 66,$$

$$b = C'(B) - \left(m_{AB} \cdot \frac{q_B}{q_A + q_B} + m_{BC} \cdot \frac{q_B}{q_B + q_C} \right.$$
$$\left. + m_{ABC} \cdot \frac{h_B}{h_A + h_B + h_C} \right) = 320 \qquad (17)$$
$$- \left\{ 70 \times \frac{400}{(100 + 400)} + 70 \times \frac{400}{(400 + 100)} \right.$$
$$\left. + 60 \times \frac{400}{(100 + 400 + 100)} \right\} = 168,$$

$$c = C'(C) - \left(m_{BC} \cdot \frac{q_C}{q_B + q_C} + m_{AC} \cdot \frac{q_C}{q_A + q_C} \right.$$
$$\left. + m_{ABC} \cdot \frac{h_C}{h_A + h_B + h_C} \right)$$
$$= 100 - \left\{ 70 \times \frac{100}{(100 + 400)} + 20 \times \frac{100}{(100 + 100)} \right.$$
$$\left. + 60 \times \frac{100}{(100 + 400 + 100)} \right\} = 66.$$

Consequently, the provisional price along the supply chain of each receiving company is as follows:

$$P_A = \frac{a}{q_A} = \frac{66}{100} = 0.66 \ (\$thousand/piece),$$
$$P_B = \frac{b}{q_B} = \frac{168}{400} = 0.42 \ (\$thousand/piece), \qquad (18)$$
$$P_C = \frac{a}{q_C} = \frac{66}{100} = 0.66 \ (\$thousand/piece).$$

Moreover, we will verify whether the provisional prices along the supply chain of these receiving companies meet the core conditions.

First, as for the individual rationality, it meets the core conditions as given below:

$$a = 66 \leq C'(A) = 100,$$
$$b = 168 \leq C'(B) = 320, \tag{19}$$
$$c = 66 \leq C'(C) = 100.$$

As for the comprehensive rationality, it meets the core conditions as given below:

$$a + b + c = 66 + 168 + 66 = 300 = C(N). \tag{20}$$

As for the collaboration rationality, it meets the core conditions as given below:

$$a + b = 66 + 168 = 234 \leq C'(AB) = 350,$$
$$a + c = 66 + 66 = 132 \leq C'(AC) = 180, \tag{21}$$
$$b + c = 168 + 66 = 234 \leq C'(BC) = 350.$$

Consequently, the provisional price within this supply chain is an idea that meets the core conditions.

Then, we will verify whether P_A, P_B, and P_C by the residual contribution quantity comparison method meet the price-quantity conditions. In other words, under the condition of

$$h_A = h_C = 100 < h_B = 400 \tag{22}$$

because

$$P_A = P_C = 0.66 > P_B = 0.42 \tag{23}$$

these provisional prices within these supply chains meet the price-quantity conditions. Consequently, it is an idea showing that a receiving company that consumes a large amount of goods and services may purchase them at a lower price.

5 Conclusion

As a method of setting a provisional price along the supply chain, we propose a two-stage game method and a method of using the residual contribution quantity comparison method at the second stage, and make it the initial figure of negotiation.

The answers that meet the core conditions and the price-quantity conditions are shown in the set. On the other hand, a provisional price along the supply chain gained by our method is overspecified. Consequently, even if a provisional price meets the core conditions and the price-quantity conditions, it is possible that a person in charge of a company does not accept this provisional price and a person in charge of another company shows another provisional price. If this provisional price meets the core conditions and the price-quantity conditions, we have to acknowledge that it is a more appropriate price than that of our model.

However, because the residual contribution quantity comparison method has its own clear logic, if we do not acquire the whole consensus, it has defensibility against objection or traverse without logical foundation.

References

Copper, M. C., Lambert, D. M., and Pagh, J. D. (1997). Supply chain management: more than a new name for logistics, *The International Journal of Logistics Management* 8(1).

Gangolly, J. S. (1981). On joint cost allocation: independent cost proportional scheme (ICPS) and its properties, *Journal of Accounting Research* 19(2), pp. 299–312.

Hamlen, S. S., Hamlen, Jr. W. A., and Tschirhart, T. (1980). The use of the generalized Shapley allocation in joint cost allocation, *The Accounting Review* 55(2), pp. 269–287.

Imabayashi, M. (1988). On transfer price accompanying profit-first orientation of internal service supplying section, *Journal of the Japan Industrial Management and Accounting Institute* 48(1), pp. 105–116 (in Japanese).

Kataoka, Y. (1982). About core theory and numerical planning method in common capacity cost allocation, *Journal of the Japan Cost Accounting Association* 258, February/March, pp. 1–14 (in Japanese).

Kataoka, Y. and Seiichi, K. (1984). Common fee allocation and core theory for management of section performance, *Journal of the Japan Industrial Management Association* 35(6), pp. 398–404 (in Japanese).

Loehman, E. and Whinston, A. B. (1974). An axiomatic approach to cost allocation for public investment, *Public Finance Quarterly*, pp. 236–251.

Monden, Y. (1989a). Cumulative opportunity cost scheme for profit allocations, *Journal of Japan Industrial Management Association* 40(4), pp. 211–217 (in Japanese).

Monden, Y. (1989b). *Foundation of Transfer Price and Profit Allocation*, Dobunkan (in Japanese).

Monden, Y. (1991). *Development of Transfer Price and Profit Allocation*, Dobunkan (in Japanese).

Moriarity, S. R. (1975). Another approach to allocating joint costs, *The Accounting Review*, October, pp. 791–795.

Moriarity, S. R. (1976). Another approach to allocating joint cost: a reply, 2, *The Accounting Review*, July, pp. 686–687.

Suzuki, M. (1980). *Introduction to Game Theory*, Kyoritsu Zensho (in Japanese).

How Can Supply Chain Risks Be Reduced by Mutual Cooperation among Partners?

Application of Real Options and Throughput Accounting

Yoshiteru Minagawa

Professor, Faculty of Commerce
Nagoya Gakuin University

1 Introduction

One of the biggest challenges currently faced by many firms is how to satisfy end-consumers with their products and services in the best possible way. A key to resolving this issue properly is enhanced collaboration with other partners. In consequence, choosing the right supply chains to participate in will become increasingly critical for managers. According to Fisher (1997, p. 107) and Ross (1998, p. 12), supply chains perform two different types of functions. First, a supply chain partner has access to customer demand; this information will be shared within the entire supply chain. Second, supply chains facilitate the timely and cost-effective movement of goods throughout the whole supply chain. These functions of supply chains are assigned to and carried out by their partners. The supply chain partners are legally independent entities. In other words, although the supply chain partners enter into an inter-firm link, they simultaneously seek their own specific interests. This leads to a strong likelihood that some partners will engage in a self-benefiting behavior. As a result, the supply chain partners are forced to expose themselves to risks stemming from the opportunistic behavior of others. If such risks that are induced by the non-cooperation of partners are mitigated, all the partners of supply chains can commonly increase their own profits. This study examines managerial accounting practices relevant to the reduction of risks in supply chains.

A key factor to the success of supply chains is developing a trusting relationship among the supply chain partners. A partner's risk taking for the benefit of others affects building trust positively (e.g., Das and Teng, 1998, p. 494).

What should not be overlooked at this point is that supply chain partners are legally separate firms. As stated in Das and Teng, firms never dare to take economically unjustified risks solely for the interests of others (Das and Teng, 1998, p. 504). Accordingly, a reduction in the degree of risk inherent in any transaction is vital to enhanced inter-partner cooperation.

The present study begins by specifying the highest risk that the supply chain partners face. The causes of risks confronted by supply chains vary depending on whether they supply emerging goods or matured ones. Therefore, the study classifies supply chains into two categories: those that fulfill the demand for the goods in the growth stage and those that cater to the demand for goods in the maturity stage of the product life cycle. The study ultimately leads to the best solution to resolve uncertainty for both types of supply chains.

2   The Effects of Real Options on Supply Chains Fulfilling the Demand of Products in the Growth Stage

2.1   *Risks facing emerging goods supply chains*

The growth stage in the product life cycle is characterized by a high rate of product innovation. Consequently, during the growth phase, the tendency to introduce new goods into the market proliferates among industries as a whole. However, when it comes to the subsequent sale of each of the new goods, only a few can achieve growth in demand. For the new goods to be able to subsequently capture increased demand, it is important for them to ultimately become dominant.[1] Dominant products refer to those that meet the needs of potential users (see Utterback and Abernathy, 1975; Hayes and Wheelwright, 1984, p. 223). Therefore, once the new goods become dominant, they can subsequently ensure a rapid growth in demand.

Every technological innovation may lead to the obsolescence of widely diffused technologies. New products require new expertise and assets specialized to their own development and production. It is necessary for supply chains in rapidly growing markets to keep pace with the growth of demand in the whole market; to achieve this, their individual members

---

[1]See, for example, Utterback and Abernathy (1975), Hayes and Wheelwright (1984).

ought to positively invest in assets devoted to innovation. It is important to keep in mind that such innovative investments have the characteristic of a high degree of asset specificity. According to Williamson (1991, p. 281), a highly specific asset is related uniquely to one specific objective: specific assets have limited values in alternative uses. Suppose that the supply chain partners make innovative R&D investments, where large capital is invested in highly specific assets. The partners run high risks of suffering substantial losses if the innovation fails to meet market demands.

Accordingly, the partners of supply chains fulfilling the demand of emerging goods inherently expose themselves to the following categories of uncertainty. To begin with, R&D itself is a challenge to resolve uncertainty. In addition to such uncertainties intrinsic to innovation, only a few emerging goods will be able to become dominant and thereby achieve penetration into the market. Moreover, the partners of emerging goods supply chains ought to inherently invest enormous funds in assets with a specific range of uses.

2.2 *The effects of real options on competitive performance*

The partners of emerging goods supply chains ought to make highly risky and asset-specific investments. However, when the investments fail to create dominant innovation, the partners of the supply chains need to reduce consequential losses as much as possible.

As in the above analysis, a struggle faced by the partners of emerging goods supply chains is how to actively make investments specialized to innovation, simultaneously limiting the downside risk of the innovative investments. To achieve this successfully, a staged investment approach is of critical importance. Multi-stage investments are able to produce management flexibility for making decisions after uncertainty in the marketplace is reduced based on the new information that emerged (Panayi and Trigeorgis, 1998, p. 676). A staged investment approach can therefore capture strategic options to continue or discontinue projects after future cash flow uncertainty has been substantially resolved using the new information that arrives. On the decision date, if a certain stage investment turns out to create an opportunity for growth, managers can decide to proceed with the project in order to increase revenues. However, if a certain phase investment has been proven to be unable to provide future growth, the partners can decide to discontinue the project to avoid further losses. In contrast, with a staged investment approach, a large investment undertaken collectively from scratch results in the amplification of downside risk, should the market conditions turn out to be worse than expected.

It is of utmost importance for the partners of an emerging goods supply chain to limit the downside risks of investments in assets specific to innovation but simultaneously maximize the innovative investments' upside possibilities. A solution to this issue is the application of multi-stage real options.[2]

This study is not the first to consider real option approaches as a managerial practice relevant to strategic alliances. For example, Das and Teng argue that a multi-stage real option approach leads to a reduction in risks, thereby enhancing trust building (Das and Teng, 1998, p. 504). Gerybadze also emphasizes that a multi-stage real option approach effectively reduces risk and increases flexibility, leading to enhanced cooperation among firms (Gerybadze, 1994, pp. 105–109). The present study is based on these studies.[3] These studies, however, which took the initiative, did not provide details of how to implement the multi-stage investments. The discussion below leads to a suggestion of a way for the supply chain partners to undertake phased investments.

How is a multi-stage investment decision successfully made? The first theoretical focus in this study is on improving the inadequacy of a conventional DCF-based investment justification to properly capture the strategic value of multi-stage investments. The DCF-based calculation to investment's value is, first, to fix the prospective scenario of cash flows (Amram and Kulatilaka, 1999, p. 14); second, to forecast expected cash flows, period by period; and third, to discount the forecasts to present value at the return a firm could expect to earn on an alternative investment entailing the same risk. DCF recommends decision-makers invest if an NPV is greater than zero. What recommendations would decision-makers end up getting if they relied on DCF to justify the two-stage investment? Among the specific analyses on which DCF is conceived the resolution toward the decision to launch into two-stage investment includes evaluating the two stages, that is, the initial trial investment project and the subsequent full-scale

---

[2] The discussion about the value of multi-stage real options here is based on Panayi and Trigeorgis (1998, p. 677).

[3] Also, Hurry *et al.* (1992) formulated a conceptual model of Japanese venture capital investments using real options.

investment project, separately and sequentially. According to this analysis, when the initial trial investment project receives a minus NPV, the second-stage investment project disappears before it becomes an agenda for a CEO meeting. That is, the discontinuance of the initial investment automatically leads to discontinuing the two-stage investment as a whole. However, the initial small investment cannot generate large net cash inflows. Another approach is to evaluate the two-stage investment as a stand-alone project collectively. The drawback of this practice is that there is no room for abandoning the second-stage investment even if market conditions turn sour after starting the initial investment. Put in another way, DCF is unable to alter the prospective scenario of cash flow set up at the outset. Consequently, the application of DCF to justifying the two-stage investment project results in a manipulation of the project's strategic value.

Multi-stage investments can facilitate a period of time to devote to accessing new information on the market condition in order to resolve uncertainty. Therefore, multi-stage projects allow the management to alter its future capital investment plans based on new information, in order to expand its upside future potential and limit its losses (Panayi and Trigeorgis, 1998, p. 676). However, the conventional DCF methods cannot appropriately capture the value of this flexibility embedded in multi-stage investments (e.g., Panayi and Trigeorgis, 1998). This limitation of DCF methods can be overcome by using real call options. The real call options method applies the financial call options theory to quantify the value of strategic capital investment projects.

2.3 Applying the financial option theory to real options

A call option is the right to buy stocks by paying a specified exercise price on or before a specified exercise date (Brealey and Myers, 1996, p. 558). The call option holder is not obliged to exercise it. This leads to the ability of call options to hedge risk. If the market price of the stock is lower than the exercise price of the call, the call option holder will not exercise it, thereby enabling him to limit the losses to the expenditures made for acquiring the options. On the other hand, if the market price of the stock is greater than the exercise price, the call option holder will exercise it, thus obtaining a profit for the difference.

For the first time, Black and Scholes (1973) derived a solution for the equilibrium price of a call option. The valuation of a European call option on an underlying stock is discussed as follows (Black and Scholes, 1973)[4]:

$$C = SN(d_1) - Ee^{-rT}N(d_2),$$

where S = the current price of the underlying stock; σ = the volatility of the stock price; $N(d_2)$ = the cumulative standard normal distribution function; E = the exercise price; T = the time to maturity; r = the risk-free interest rate; $d_2 = d_1 - \sigma\sqrt{T}$

$$d_1 = \frac{\ln\left(\frac{S}{E}\right) + \left(r + \frac{1}{2}\sigma^2\right)T}{\sigma\sqrt{T}}.$$

How can multi-stage real options be valued? There are correspondences between the inputs involved in the financial option model and those required to value multi-stage real options. For example, the present value (PV) of expected cash flows from the following stages of multi-stage investments corresponds to the current value of the stock in the financial option. Furthermore, the investment cost required to undertake the following stages of projects is viewed as the exercise price. However, the method to calculate the future value of the project's cash flows is controversial. Of the real assets, there are very few whose future values are directly quantifiable. If a real asset is not traded in the market, its real option valuation requires the identification of the "twin assets" that carry the same risk as the real option project at the time of the completion of the investments (Teisberg, 1995, p. 38). One example of the twin assets is the current value of the stock of the firms that have been operating in the identical category of business.

Using an example based on Brealey and Myers (1996, pp. 590–592), the remainder of this section illustrates the process of adapting the Black–Scholes formula to the quantification of the flexibility in strategic two-stage

---

[4]The Black–Scholes model relies on the following assumptions: (a) the short-term interest rate is constant; (b) the variance rate of the return on the underlying asset is constant; (c) the underlying asset pays no dividends; (d) the option may be exercised only at maturity — it is a European option; (e) there are no transaction costs; (f) the option is contingent on a single underlying risky asset; (g) there are no penalties to short selling. (Black and Scholes, 1973, p. 640; Copeland and Antikarov, 2001, p. 106.)

investment projects. Currently, we are in the year 2006. At present, the management in Corporation X is evaluating a proposed smaller trial investment in a new product α; the trial investment has an expected period of 5 years, from 2006 to 2010, leading to the subsequent creation of the opportunity for the full-scale investment into the new product as the second stage. The decision to launch the full-scale new entry of α must be made after 5 years, in 2011. Both forecasted net cash inflows and net present value (NPV) at a 20% hurdle rate of the initial trial investment are as follows: an investment of $5 million in 2006; $0.60 and $0.50 million in 2007; $0.65 and $0.45 million in 2008; $0.70 and $0.41 million in 2009; $0.75 and $0.36 million in 2010.

However, the DCF-based justification for the initial trial investment on a stand-alone basis depends only on the cash flows from the trial investment itself. Thus, it ends up giving the investment's $32.8 million negative total NPV at a 20% hurdle rate, leading the management to take a decision not to start the initial trial investment. Unfortunately, this judgment results in misguiding Corporation X. That is, although the trial investment yields not only its own cash flows but also a call option to launch the full-scale entry of the new product, the DCF-based justification does not take the subsequent call options into account. The fact that the subsequent call option results from the trial investment makes the DCF-based calculations' outcome diverge greatly from the real value of the trial investment.

The decision to invest in the full-scale entry of the new product will be made in 2011, which is the year after the first-stage investment terminates. The decision is grounded on the following assumptions: (1) the investment required is $50 million (the exercise price); (2) forecasted cash inflows are worth an NPV of $80 million in 2011 and an NPV of $32.15 million ($80 million$/(1.2)^5$) in 2006; (3) the future value of cash flows from the larger, second-stage investment unfolds as Corporation X's stock price with a standard deviation of 31.5% per year, i.e., the stock is "twin security" of the second-stage investment (Trigeorgis and Mason, 1987, p. 15); (4) the annual risk-free rate of interest is 5%; and (5) the hurdle rate is 20%.

Therefore, the problem with the justification of the initial trial investment project can be restated as follows: Does the value of the opportunity for the full-scale investment created through the initial trial investment exceed the investment outlay of the initial trial investment project? (Kemna, 1993, p. 263) Returning to the above example, calculating the value of a call option (acquiring the right to undertake the full-scale investment in the second stage) based on Brealey and Myers (1996, pp. 579–591) results in the following:

$$\text{Standard deviation} \times (\text{time})^{1/2} = 0.315 \times (5)^{1/2} = 0.70;$$
$$\text{Asset value/PV(exercise price)} = 32.15/(50/(1.05)^5) = 0.82;$$
$$\text{Call option value/asset value} = 0.206 \text{ (figure from Appendix Table 6}$$
$$\text{in Brealey and Myers (1996));}$$
$$\text{Call option value } 0.206 \times 32.15 = 6.62.$$

In summary, the total value of the initial trial investment is its own NPV, ¥3.28 million, plus the $6.62 million option attached to it.

2.4 *Integrated multi-stage investments in supply chains*

The practices of multi-stage real options in supply chains might take several forms, including a separated (or decentralized) and an integrated (or centralized) type. The latter will be examined in depth in this study. In separated multi-stage real options in supply chains, individual partners can separately decide to either continue or discontinue their staged investments; each partner possesses the right for multi-stage real options. On the other hand, integrated phased investments in supply chains emphasize the valuation of the combined return from the multi-stage real options of respective partners. Therefore, the integrated type determines how the whole supply chain responds to changing markets. In other words, integrated real options lead to either the continuation or discontinuation of multi-stage investments from the viewpoint of supply chains as a whole.

The justification for multi-stage investments starts with the projection of the expected future cash flows to be earned in each phase of the whole investment. Such projected future cash flows of the respective stages will be reconsidered using new information when it emerges.

Suppose that a certain supply chain is about to value investment projects that can be viewed as a series of sequential stages. To begin with, the supply chain values the first stage. It is important to note that once the first-stage investment has been undertaken, the managers of the supply chain partners can acquire the option to either make the second-stage investment to increase revenues or to cease the investment so as to limit losses. The value of this embedded flexibility must be incorporated into the investment's justification;

without it, the value of multi-stage real options is underestimated. In consequence, the combined strategic NPV of the first-stage investment includes both values: the sum of the traditional NPVs of the expected cash flows of individual partner from the first-stage investment, and the sum of the values that each partner will obtain from the contingent project for the second-stage investment (Trigeorgis, 1998, pp. 121–124).[5]

Let us assume that the combined strategic NPV of the first phase investment indicates a positive result, and therefore the supply chain decides to launch multi-stage investments. As soon as the first-stage investment starts, managers of the supply chain partners begin to have access to new information that is of use in reconsidering the previously projected strategic NPV of the second-stage investment, namely, the traditional NPV of expected cash flows from the second-stage investment + the payoffs from the real option for the third-stage investment. This reconsideration of strategic NPV is made using the information available at a certain time during the first stage. If the finally authorized combined strategic NPV is positive, the supply chain partners decide to proceed to the second-stage of the investment. Here, presume that the partners decided to invest in the second-stage project. Immediately, aiming to resolve the uncertainty surrounding the possibility of generating positive cash flows in the third stage, the partners' managers begin to have access to applicable information. In order to make a multi-stage real option analysis subsequent to the second phase, it is necessary to have access to new information that is conducive to altering the phased investment strategy, followed by a reexamination of the prior projected strategic NPV of a certain stage using the new information, and finally arrive at a decision on whether to continue or discontinue investments according to the authorized combined strategic NPV.

In applying this valuation approach, how to motivate all partners to invest in order to improve supply chain performance needs to be determined. One solution is the allocation of the total supply chain profit among partners according to the proportion of their respective investments. The total supply chain profit is the revenues earned from selling final products less the cost of goods sold, investments, and resource costs of activities incurred by the partners.

---

[5] "Strategic NPV" is based on Trigeorgis (1998, pp. 121–124). According to Trigeorgis, strategic NPV includes both value components: the traditional NPV of expected cash flows and the real option value of strategic flexibility (Trigeorgis, 1998, pp. 121–124).

3   The Management of Supply Chains Fulfilling the Demand of Matured Goods

3.1   *Critical success factors*

Every product has a limited life. All goods that are launched onto the market, after going through the growth stage, move into the maturity stage, and then decline. Among what affects the product life cycle is the life cycle of the technology embedded in the product. That is, a product becomes saturated as the technology matures.

Goods located in the maturity stage are simultaneously in the maturity stage of the technology life cycle. Therefore, matured goods have little potential for product innovation. Due to this, there is almost no room for competition in terms of product uniqueness. This implies that among matured goods being offered by individual firms, consumers do not perceive any distinction in terms of functional uniqueness. With such a characteristic inherent in matured goods, a key success factor is quick response to market demand. Goods in the maturity stage are technologically standardized and therefore undifferentiated. If matured goods supply chains charge their customers a high price, they automatically lose customer loyalty. In the competition among matured goods supply chains, the best solution is to focus on satisfying demand efficiently at the lowest cost.

From the above discussions, the success of matured goods supply chains rests upon shrinkage in lead times, defined as time elapsed from the date the order is placed to the date the customers receive the products ordered. The curtailment of lead times in turn brings about lowered inventory costs.

3.2   *Transfer pricing in the supply chains fulfilling the demand of matured goods*

This section illustrates the relevance of throughput accounting to the measurement of performance in matured goods supply chains. A key factor to the survival of the manufacturers of undifferentiated goods is their ability to distribute the right goods to customers at the right time. Ensuring such customer satisfaction requires reduction in lead times.

Among the influential advocators of throughput accounting are Galloway and Waldron (1988a, b; 1989a, b), who advance the following propositions: the growth of profits is affected by shortening lead times

(Galloway and Waldron, 1988a, pp. 34–35).[6] The curtailment of lead times in turn depends directly on diminishing inventory.

The reason why a low inventory reduces lead times is that as the queue of inventory at a certain workstation becomes increasingly longer, the average queuing time increases, thereby resulting in longer lead times (Kilger, 2000, p. 203). This means that as Kilger (2000, p. 212) demonstrated, the effect of lead times' contraction resides in the generation of additional sales. As a result, profitability grows with decreasing inventory.

An increase in inventory often causes dysfunction in many managerial functions. This leads Galloway and Waldron to state that any decision-making that induces increased inventories is adverse (Galloway and Waldron, 1989a, p. 33). Hence, accounting practices should not encourage the build-up of inventory. According to throughput accounting, an inventory is valued, at best, at material costs until the time of sales, when an inventory's intrinsic value is realized. This notion of throughput accounting contrasts markedly with that of conventional absorption costing. Absorption costing defines costs as being attached to a product in proportion to the progress of manufacturing: in absorption costing, the amount of product costs increases with the degree of the completion of manufacturing products.

Throughput accounting profit is a function of the cost of goods sold calculated solely at direct material costs, throughput contribution, and operating expenses. In throughput accounting, inventoriable costs include only direct material costs. As a result, the cost of goods sold is valued solely at direct material costs. Other costs, namely, all the manufacturing costs incurred, other than the direct material costs, plus Selling, General, and administrative expenses, are defined as operating costs. Operating costs are defined as period costs; period costs are always expensed in the same period in which they are incurred. Revenue minus the cost of goods sold at direct material costs is throughput contribution. Throughput accounting profit is defined as throughput contribution minus operating costs.

An increase in throughput accounting profits, as discussed above, hinges upon the augmentation of throughput contribution. Increased throughput contribution is engendered by the curtailment of lead times. The reduction in lead times results in the successful response to customer needs. Improving on delivery time, in turn, boosts additional sales (Kilger, 2000, p. 212).

---

[6]See also Noreen *et al.* (1995), Dugdale and Jones (1998) for throughput accounting.

If a firm, however, fails to quickly respond to market changes, it is likely that the firm will encounter a decrease in throughput contribution, thereby jeopardizing the recovery of its operating expenses. Throughput accounting aids managers to ascertain whether they will be able to achieve quick response to demand changes.

For matured goods suppliers, the proper delivery of the appropriate goods at the right time is the key to survival. Accordingly, throughput accounting is relevant to successfully managing matured goods supply chains. Included among supply chain management tools is transfer pricing for transactions between the supply chain partners. Transactions between partners are different from pure arm's length transactions, and may have a separate transfer pricing policy.

With regard to transfer pricing for supply chains, this study expands a throughput accounting ratio, namely, throughput contribution ÷ operating cost, to propose the following:

> transfer prices which will be applied to a selling partner's sales for the entirety of the following year to a buying partner = (this year's annual throughput contribution that the selling partner has earned through its sales to the buying partner) ÷ (this year's annual amount of the selling partner's operating costs that has been driven by its sales to the buying partner) × (the selling partner's standard unit average operating costs for the following year's planned annual volume of transactions with the buying partner) + (the selling partner's standard unit direct material cost for the following year's planned annual volume of transactions with the buying partner).

This transfer pricing model needs to determine the selling partner's standard unit average operating costs, as well as the unit direct material costs for the following year's planned annual amount of transactions with the buying partner. These two standard costs are part of the proposed transfer price, and hence they affect the following year's profits of the partners. With regard to how the two standard costs are predetermined, negotiations between related partners are regarded as the norm. However, this means that the transfer price cannot be determined soon after supply chains begin. Rather, a market price is used as a transfer price during the first year after supply chains are established.

Here, performance measurement in supply chains requires the respective supply chain partners to separate the operating costs incurred with the inter-partner transactions from those resulting from arm's length transactions. In order for supply chain partners to identify their operating costs driven by inter-partner transactions, it is important to use activity-based costing.[7] Activity-based costing assigns the operating costs to activities ranging from the procurement of materials, to the delivery of goods to customers.

The remainder of this section examines how the transfer pricing outlined above can help to properly manage supply chains. The analysis focuses on the impact of both throughput contribution and operating costs of the partners on the transfer prices, holding other variables constant. Under the proposed transfer pricing, the more the selling partners raise the excess of their throughput contribution over the operating costs they incurred, the higher do the following year's transfer prices become. For the selling partners, maintaining the higher transfer price influences the growth of their revenues favorably. Furthermore, an increase in any partner's throughput contribution depends mainly on the curtailment of lead times. Hence, the value of proposed transfer pricing lies in the creation of an optimal relationship between the lead times and the profits of supply chain partners. The proposed transfer pricing model prompts the whole supply chain to cooperate in shortening the lead times. The reason for this is as follows. Transfer pricing hinges largely on the throughput contribution of the selling partners. Among the most important drivers of the enhanced throughput contribution of selling partners is shortened lead time. Here, what should not be overlooked is the fact that the negative effect of prolonged lead times in a certain part of a supply chain is likely to easily spread throughout the whole membership. Thus, any partner's profits depends on whether or not each of the partners can reduce their lead times into a managerially acceptable level. This in turn creates incentives for all members to cooperate in preventing deteriorations in lead times from happening to any of the supply chain partners.

4 Conclusion

A key to supply chain success is to establish cooperative partnerships in which trusting partners are willing to take risks for the benefit of others

---

[7]See Demmy and Talbott (1998) for an integration of throughput accounting and ABC.

(Das and Teng, 1998). However, partners never take economically unjustified risks only in the interest of others (Das and Teng, 1998). This means
that the reduction in the degree of risk inherent in any transaction is critical
to enhanced inter-firm cooperation. The causes of the highest risk encoun-
tered by the supply chain partners vary depending on whether they supply
emerging goods or matured ones. This study classifies supply chains into
two categories: those that fulfill the demand for the goods in the growth
stage, and those that fulfill the demand in the maturity stage of the product
life cycle. This study proposed the managerial techniques that reduce risk
involved in the whole supply chain by applying real options and throughput
accounting.

References

Amram, M. and Kulatilaka, N. (1999). *Real Options: Managing Strategic Investment in an Uncertain World*, Harvard Business School Press.
Black, F. and Scholes, M. (1973). The pricing of options and corporate liabilities,
Journal of Political Economy, 81, pp. 637–659.
Boon, S. D. and Holmes, J. G. (1991). The dynamics of interpersonal trust: resolv-
ing uncertainty in the face of risk, in *Cooperation and Prosocial Behavior*,
edited by Hinde, R. A. and Groebel, J., Cambridge University Press, pp. 190–
211.
Brealey, R. A. and Myers, S. C. (1996). *Principles of Corporate Finance*, 5th ed.,
McGraw-Hill.
Copeland, T. and Antikarov, V. (2001). *Real Options*, Texere.
Das, T. K. and Teng, B. S. (1998). Between trust and control: developing confi-
dence in partner cooperation in alliances, *Academy of Management Review*,
23(3), pp. 491–512.
Demmy, S. and Talbott, J. (1998). Improve internal reporting with ABC and
TOC, *Management Accounting*, November, pp. 18–24.
Dixit, A. K. and Pindyck, R. S. (1995). The options approach to capital invest-
ment, *Harvard Business Review*, May–June, pp. 105–115.
Dugdale, D. and Jones, T. C. (1998). Throughput accounting: transforming prac-
tices? *British Accounting Review*, 30, pp. 203–220.
Fisher, M. L. (1997). What is the right supply chain for your product? *Harvard
Business Review*, March–April, pp. 105–116.
Galloway, D. and Waldron, D. (1988a). Throughput accounting: the need for
a new language for manufacturing, *Management Accounting*, November,
pp. 34–35.
Galloway, D. and Waldron, D. (1988b). Throughput accounting — Part 2: ranking
products profitably, *Management Accounting*, December, pp. 34–35.
Galloway, D. and Waldron, D. (1989a). Throughput accounting — Part 3: a better
way to control labour costs, *Management Accounting*, January, pp. 32–33.

Galloway, D. and Waldron, D. (1989b). Throughput accounting — Part 4: moving on to complex products, *Management Accounting*, February, pp. 40–41.

Gerybadze, A. (1994). *Strategic Alliances and Process Redesign: Effective Management and Restructuring of Cooperative Projects and Networks*, Walter de Gruyter.

Hayes, R. H. and Wheelwright, S. C. (1984). *Restoring Our Competitive Edge: Competing through Manufacturing*, John Wiley & Sons, Inc.

Hurry, D., Miller, A. T., and Bowman, E. H. (1992). Calls on high-technology: Japanese exploration of venture capital investments in the United States, *Strategic Management Journal*, 13, pp. 85–101.

Kemna, A. G. Z. (1993). Case studies on real options, *Financial Management*, Autumn, pp. 259–270.

Kester, W. C. (1984). Today's options for tomorrow's growth, *Harvard Business Review*, March–April, pp. 153–160.

Kilger, C. (2000). Definition of a supply chain project, in *Supply Chain Management and Advanced Planning*, edited by Stadtler, H. and Kilger, C., Springer, pp. 197–216.

Noreen, E., Smith, D., and Mackey, J. T. (1995). *The Theory of Constrains and its Application to Management Accounting*, North River Press.

Panayi, S. and Trigeorgis, L. (1998). Multi-stage real options: the cases of information technology infrastructure and international bank expansion, *The Quarterly Review of Economics and Finance*, 38, Special Issue, pp. 675–692.

Ross, D. F. (1998). *Competing Through Supply Chain Management: Creating Market-Winning Strategies Through Supply Chain Partnerships*, Chapman & Hall.

Teisberg, E. O. (1995). Methods for evaluating capital investment decisions under uncertainty, in *Real Options in Capital Investment: Models, Strategies, and Applications*, edited by Trigeorgis, L., Praeger, pp. 31–45.

Trigeorgis, L. (1998). *Real Options: Managing Flexibility and Strategy in Resource Allocation*, The MIT Press.

Trigeorgis, L. and Mason S. (1987). Valuing managerial flexibility, *Midland Corporate Finance Journal*, Spring, 14–21.

Utterback, J. M. and Abernathy, W. J. (1975). A dynamic model of process and product innovation, *Omega*, 3(6), pp. 639–656.

Williamson, O. E. (1991). Comparative economic organization: the analysis of discrete structural alternatives, *Administrative Science Quarterly*, 36, pp. 269–296.

Characteristics of Japanese Shared Service Centers

Tomoaki Sonoda

Professor, Faculty of Business and Commerce
Keio University

1   Shared Services of Japanese Companies

It was around 1999 when Japanese companies started shared services. This author has interviewed approximately 60 Japanese companies regarding shared services. The first stage of shared services, the introductory stage, has finished in Japan. Shared services have recently become widely used management methods in Japanese companies. Japanese shared services have been moving toward the second stage, the priority of which is the effective operation of the SSC (shared service center).

During the first stage, Japanese companies were not aware of shared services, so they needed to define them and clarify the basic strengths and weaknesses of each type of the SSC. In the first stage, cost reduction perspectives were emphasized. The mission of most shared service centers was to sell their services to companies outside their groups, but very few shared service subsidiaries succeeded in this outsourcing business.

Japanese shared services are currently in the second stage — the main concern of which is the effective operation of the SSC. Some shared service centers make balanced scorecards for themselves, and some contract with their clients using service level agreements. Others measure times of activities or adopt activity based costing to identify performance of their activities.

Beyond the accounting field, other problems are the quality of the activities and the poor motivation levels of SSC employees. Particularly, shared service subsidiaries' goals conflict with their group companies', because successfully reducing SSC costs will bring the prices down in the following year. This contradiction causes a decline in the SSC employee motivation, and it has remained an unresolved issue from the first stage.

The group management perspective is emphasized as the objective for establishing SSCs, even though cost reduction is still important. Changes in the group organizational structure through the establishment of the holding company organized a number of shared service subsidiaries. It is important how the corporate group positions administrative activities. Cooperation between some shared service centers is an emerging new trend in Japan.

2   Definition and Objectives of Shared Services

2.1   *Definition of shared services*

Shared services are management methods for administrative functions from the viewpoint of corporate group management, which (1) centralize administrative functions of the parent company and group companies, (2) reexamine them, and (3) standardize them. Reengineering, activity based management, and benchmarking are the methods used to reexamine activities.

2.2   *Objectives of shared services*

Through the centralization, reexamination, and standardization of administrative functions in establishing SSCs, companies can complete a number of objectives (non-accounting objectives), that is, speed up the creation of consolidated financial statements, offer effective employee training, enhance the quality of administrative activities, reinforce internal control, and improve SSC employee motivation.

The accomplishment of these objectives leads to the achievement of the accounting objective: cost reduction in SSCs. The accomplishment of non-accounting and accounting objectives (cost reduction) improves intra-group customer satisfaction. When the SSC wants to consolidate additional profits, it needs to add outsource business models based on this process. Figure 1 shows the relationships between objectives of shared services.

2.3   *General effectiveness of shared services*

Shared services have five general advantages. Figure 2 shows seven types of shared service centers. They have their own merits, but they have these five general advantages in common.

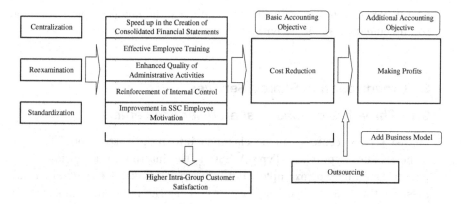

Fig. 1   Relationships between shared services objectives

Type A: Internal organization of the parent company

   A-1 Cost center type

   A-2 Profit center type

Type B: Shared service subsidiary

   B-1 Profit center type (administrative function company)

   B-2 Cost center type (administrative function company)

   B-3 Profit center type (business company)

Type C: Centralization of several corporate group activities

   C-1 Not making new subsidiary (cost center or profit center type)

   C-2 Making new subsidiary (profit center type)

Fig. 2   Seven types of shared service centers

(1) restructuring of the administrative functions from the viewpoint of the group management;

(2) centralization of administrative functions decreases fixed costs;

(3) centralization of economic scales cuts fixed costs per activity;

(4) redundant and non-value added activities are dropped through reexamination;

(5) customized activities at each organization are standardized.

These five merits of shared services enhance corporate value. Companies can reduce costs by restructuring the administrative department, and invest the money in the core business. Labor hours are reduced by the discontinuation of non-value added activities and the standardization of activities.

Companies use these surplus hours to enhance the quality of activities and to implement strategic activities.

3   Organization of Shared Services

3.1   *Three basic types of shared service centers*

Shared service centers can be classified into basic three types: Type A, Type B, and Type C. A Type A SSC is the internal organization of the parent company. For example, Ube Industries, Osaka Gas, Sapporo Holdings, Suntory, and Tokyo Gas have an SSC as the internal organization in their head offices.

Type B is a shared service subsidiary. For example, Asahi Management Service, Isupport, Konica Minolta Business Expert, NTT Business Associe, JP Business Service, Pioneer Shared Services Japan, Sumitomo Shoji Financial Management, and Teijin Creative Staff are shared service subsidiaries.

A Type C SSC centralizes several corporate groups' activities. A Type C SSC is very rare in Japan at present. Human Resource Management Service & Consulting is a typical Type C company.

Type A and Type B provide their services only to group companies to which the SSC belongs. In contrast, Type C provides its services to more than one corporate group.

3.2   *Seven types of shared service centers from the viewpoint of responsibility accounting*

The above three basic types of SSC can be subdivided into seven types from the viewpoint of responsibility accounting, as shown in Figure 2.

Both Type A and Type B have the cost center type and the profit center type. As for shared service subsidiaries, there are two profit center types: Type B-1 and Type B-3. Type B-1 is viewed as a profit center because it is an independent company, but group companies consider it as a cost center from a consolidated viewpoint because it provides its services only to the group companies. Type B-3 is a profit center both from a company and consolidated viewpoint because it sells its services outside its group.

Type A-2 and Type B-2 are unique patterns that are contrary to the principles of responsibility accounting. Type A-2 is a profit center though it is established in the head office of the parent company. Type B-2 is a cost center though it is a subsidiary.

4 Problems with Type A SSC

4.1 *Pricing policies of Type A-1*

Type A-1 is the SSC, which is the internal organization of the parent company, and a cost center. Type A-1 provides its services to (1) internal divisions in the same parent company, and (2) group companies. It does not set a price on services to divisions because they belong to the same company.

Type A-1 has two pricing patterns for group companies. First, it sets a price equal to the costs incurred in the SSC and chooses a cost basis pricing policy. Second, the SSC can set a price to pursue profits and chooses profit basis pricing policy. The second policy has three patterns:

(1) costs incurred in the SSC plus profit;
(2) market price; and
(3) costs incurred in the group companies before they outsource functions to the SSC.

4.2 *Combination of the cost center and the profit center*

When Type A does not set a price on services for internal divisions, and chooses the profit basis pricing policy for group companies' transactions, it means the SSC has two responsibility centers at the same time (Figure 3). The former is the cost center, and the latter is the profit center.

In this case, it is desirable that the SSC divides its performance calculation segment on management accounting into part of the cost center and part of the profit center. But most Japanese Type A SSCs have kept a segment mix of responsibility centers.

Type A SSC	
Cost center	Profit center
To provide services to the internal divisions	To provide services to group companies

Fig. 3 Type A: Combination of cost center and profit center in one SSC

Type A SSC	
Profit center	Profit center
To provide services to the internal divisions	To provide services to group companies

Fig. 4   Responsibility center after the chargeback system

A chargeback system is the other solution in this situation. With the chargeback system, the SSC can set a price on its services to the internal divisions even though it is a virtual price without cash transfer. The chargeback system can also choose two pricing policies: cost basis and profit basis. If the SSC chooses profit basis for its pricing policy, the segment mix of responsibility centers can be integrated into the profit center (Figure 4).

5   Problems with Shared Service Subsidiaries

5.1   *Shared service subsidiaries as administrative function companies*

When shared service subsidiaries sell their services to the companies outside their groups, revenues and profits are added to the consolidated financial statements (Type B-3). However, many Japanese shared service subsidiaries sell their services only to the group companies (Type B-1). In the latter case, shared service subsidiaries are administrative function companies, the characteristics of which are explained in Sonoda (2006b).

5.2   *Discrepancy between independent and consolidated responsibility centers of the shared service subsidiary*

The shared service subsidiary as the administrative function company can be defined as the cost center from the viewpoint of consolidated financial statements because it does not contribute to an increase in consolidated revenues and profits. On the other hand, the shared service subsidiary is the profit center from the viewpoint of the independent company. This discrepancy between independent and consolidated responsibility centers makes it difficult to manage Type B-1. Figure 5 shows the present discrepancy condition of Type B-1 and three solutions.

	Independent	Consolidated	Solution
Present	P	C	–
Solution 1	C	C	SSC in the parent company
Solution 2	C	C	Shared service subsidiary as cost center
Solution 3	P	P	Sell services to companies outside groups

(C means cost centers, P means profit centers)

Fig. 5　Discrepancy between independent and consolidated responsibility centers of the shared service subsidiary

5.3　*Three solutions to the discrepancy regarding responsibility centers*

5.3.1　*Solution 1*

A shared service subsidiary is absorbed into its parent company, which positions the SSC as the cost center of both independent and consolidated organizations. Solution 1 changes the shared service subsidiary into the internal organization of the parent company (internal functional administrative department or the SSC of Type A).

5.3.2　*Solution 2*

A shared service subsidiary is positioned as the cost center even though it is an independent company. The shared service subsidiary becomes the cost center of both independent and consolidated organizations. It means the SSC is positioned in Type B-2. Sonoda (2006b) introduces two shared service subsidiaries, as for solution 2: Teijin Creative Staff (TCS) and Sumitomo Shoji Financial Management (SFM).

5.3.3　*Solution 3*

A shared service subsidiary sells its services to the companies outside its group. Because the shared service subsidiary adds profits to consolidated income statements, it becomes the profit center of both independent and consolidated organizations. It also means the SSC is positioned in Type B-3. This is the best solution because the organization will not change and a shared service subsidiary will have a chance to expand itself. But solution 3 is physically quite difficult and there are very few shared service subsidiaries that belong to Type B-3 in Japan. NTT Business Associe and Isupport are shared service subsidiaries classified as Type B-3.

6 Management Accounting Tools Used in SSC

6.1 *Effective management of shared service subsidiaries*

In spite of the above three solutions, many shared service subsidiaries are still profit centers without selling services to companies outside their group. They have to manage themselves effectively to simultaneously reduce costs and improve the quality of activities. Some shared service subsidiaries make use of activity based management and balanced scorecards.

6.2 *Activity based management and improvement in activities*

Some shared service subsidiaries calculate their activity costs. There are two ways to choose cost drivers. Some use activity based costing and choose more than one cost driver. Some shared service subsidiaries use only working times of each activity as the cost driver to calculate activity costs. Some measure only working times and do not calculate activity costs.

Some select target activities to improve, whose costs are bigger or whose working times are longer. They improve their activities and reduce their costs by activity based management thinking.

It is characteristic for Japanese companies to benchmark the wide spectrum of shared service topics: the methods of cost reduction, how to improve and standardize activities, ERP systems for SSC, services lineup, how to calculate and price their services, etc.

6.3 *Balanced scorecard*

Some Japanese shared service companies make their own balanced scorecard. It is an effective tool to manage an administrative function company like a shared service company. The balanced scorecard simultaneously facilitates cost reduction and improvement in the quality of activities, even though they are trade-off related. Moreover, the balanced scorecard will clarify that customers of the shared service company are not external customers but internal customers, for example, its parent company and group companies. Some shared service companies came up with various ideas for their balanced scorecard. For example, Pioneer Shared Services Japan adds a parent company perspective to its balanced scorecard as the fifth perspective.

The balanced scorecard for the shared service company has some defects. First, the shared service company executes administrative activities for group companies. These functions have little relationship with group strategy. Second, it is difficult for the shared service company to choose financial measures except costs, because group companies do not want them to make large profits. Third, overestimating customers' perspectives may be harmful to the shared service company. If a shared service company processes its group companies' activities in standardized ways, their degree of customer satisfaction may drop, even though the standardization of activities is a shared service company's mission.

7   Conclusion

This paper has explained the characteristics of Japanese companies' shared services. It has provided a definition and the objectives of shared services, three basic SSC organizations, seven types of SSC (responsibility center viewpoint), problems of Type A and Type B, and activity based costing (management) and balanced scorecard used in SSC.

The motivation of SSC employees, service level agreements (SLA), and how to spread shared services to group companies are unresolved issues of Japanese shared services. It is anticipated that management accounting will contribute to solving these problems.

References

Kigyo Kenkyukai (ed.) (2003). *Casebook of Shared Services*, Kigyo Kenkyukai (in Japanese).

Kigyo Kenkyukai (ed.) (2005). *New Casebook of Shared Services*, Kigyo Kenkyukai (in Japanese).

Sonoda, T. (2006a). *Management Accounting for Shared Services*, Chuo Keizai Sha (in Japanese).

Sonoda, T. (2006b). Management of the shared services subsidiaries as cost centers, in *Value-Based Management of the Rising Sun*, edited by Monden, Y., Miyamoto, K., Hamada, K., Lee, G., and Asada, T., World Scientific Publishing.

Business Model of Convenience Stores Based on a Charge Base of Royalty

Focusing on Seven-Eleven Japan Co., Ltd.

Noriko Hoshi

Associate Professor, Faculty of Business Administration
Hakuoh University

1 Introduction

More than ten years have passed since the collapse of the bubble economy in Japan. While the manufacturing as well as the retail industry are almost slowing down, the convenience store industry is making smooth progress in business. Most convenience stores are connected by some type of franchise system and are spreading all over the country.

In a franchise system, the franchiser and the franchisee make a contract and share the work in order to achieve co-existence and co-prosperity. The franchisees use the same logos, sell the same products and services and take business guidance from their franchisers. In return, the franchisees pay royalties to their franchisers. The reference used to calculate the royalty is gross profit on sales.

The types of industry adopting the franchise system are: retail industry (convenience stores, medical/cosmetics, clothes/shoes, etc.), service industry (cleaning, DPE/printing, barbering/beauty, etc.), and confection/food industry (confectionary, hamburger shops, coffee shops, restaurants, Japanese style bars called *izakaya*, etc.). Among these, convenience stores have the highest percentage in use of "gross profit on sales" as a standard for calculating royalty. Gross profit on sales is the amount after which the cost of goods sold has been subtracted from the sales amount.

In most franchise systems, when the "sales volume" is used as a standard for calculating royalties, the franchiser must take responsibility only for the sales amount. However, when the "gross profit on sales" is used, the franchiser must take responsibility not only for the enlargement of the sales amount but also for the cost cutting of goods sold.

If so, how did convenience store franchisers manage to take responsibility for both "sales amount" and "cost of goods sold" and still make progress during the period of recession? The purpose of this paper is to make this point much clearer by focusing on Seven-Eleven Japan Co., Ltd. which has shown especially excellent business performance compared to other convenience store franchisers.

This paper is organized as follows. First, the structure and present state of the franchise system is examined. Second, the calculation standard as well as the system of calculation is explained. Last, the management way used to expand the sales amount and lower the cost of goods sold is considered.

2   Structure and Present State of Franchise System

2.1   *Structure of franchise system*

According to the definition given by the Japanese Franchise Association (JFA), a franchise is

> The continuous relationship between a business (franchiser) which makes a contract with another business (franchisee) in order to provide authorization to carry out its business activities, selling of the products etc., based on the identical image by allowing and offering them to make use of their trademark, service mark, trade name, and other signs which could be the symbol of the business as well as their business techniques. In return, the franchisees invest the necessary amount of capital to carry out the business under the guidance and support from their franchisers while paying value for them as collateral.

Franchisees invest their own capital, pay a membership fee, make a contract with their franchiser and carry out the business using their franchiser's trademark and sign. Franchisers are compensated for their support and management guidance by their franchisees.

Since the same trademarks and names are used, franchisees may resemble a franchiser's branch. However, both franchisers and franchisees are independent enterprises. They are a "coalition of enterprises," each trying to make profits by sharing their works.

Trademarks, techniques, management supports, and so on offered by the franchiser are called "packages" and the fee franchisees pay as collateral is termed "royalty."

2.2 General situation of convenience stores[1]

2.2.1 Sales amount and the number of stores

According to the research conducted by JFA, the sales volume for the entire convenience store industry is ¥7217.9 billion and the number of stores is 39,877, showing respectively 1.1% and 2.5% growth compared to the year before. Compared with the numbers in 1998, a significant growth could be seen both in the sales amount and the number of stores (30.6% and 28.4%, respectively). Figure 1 below shows the transition of growth from 1998 to 2005. Growth rate in 1998 is regarded as 100.

2.2.2 Commodity composition

As seen in Figure 2, commodity composition can be divided into four groups: daily delivered foods, processed foods, non-foods, and services. In 2006, the composition ratio of daily delivered foods was 35.5%, processed

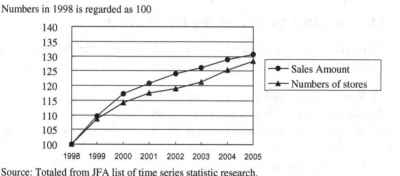

Numbers in 1998 is regarded as 100

Source: Totaled from JFA list of time series statistic research.

Fig. 1   Transition of sales amount and number of stores

---

[1]Data from investigation conducted by JFA is used for the general situation of convenience stores.

Commodity category	Content examples
Daily Delivery foods	Rice based meal (sushi, bento, rice balls), breads, cooked breads, pre-cooked meals, pickled vegetables, fruits, processed meat, milk, milk based drinks, daily products, pastes, cakes, salads, desserts, etc.
Processed foods	Confectionary, soft drinks, alcohol beverages, seasonings, non-essentials, salt, sugar, cooking oil, frozen foods, ice creams, instant goods, etc.
Non-foods	Magazines, publications, newspapers, clothes, stationeries, toys, general goods, cigarettes, cleansers, cosmetics, medical goods, stamps, revenue stamps, etc.
Services	Copy machine, facsimile, home delivery service, merchandise coupon, various tickets, D.P.E., cleaning service, etc.

Note: Services do not include sales amount by deputy receipt of any fees for the following public services: power rates, gas rates, TV license fee, telephone rates, and water rates.

Source: Extracted from JFA monthly report on statistic investigation on convenience stores (July, 2006).

Fig. 2 Commodity composition in convenience stores

foods, 32.8%, non-foods, 26.3%, and services, 5.4%. Compared with the ratio in 1998, no striking difference can be found in the ratio of daily delivered foods. Services made a small advance from 3.7% to 5.4% while the ratio of processed food showed a decline.

3 Royalty of Franchise System

3.1 *Standard for calculating the royalties*

Below are the methods for setting the standard for calculating the royalties that the franchisees pay to the franchisers:

(1) Rate corresponding to the sales amount
(2) Rate corresponding to the gross profit
(3) Rate corresponding to the gross profit on sales (gross profit + amount of loss)
(4) Fixed amount system, etc.

According to "Fact finding report on business management of franchise chain" (2002) announced by the Ministry of Economy Trade and Industry, the method most often used to set the standard for calculating the royalties in the retail industry is the "rate corresponding to the sales amount" (36.3%), followed by the "rate corresponding to the gross profit" and "rate corresponding to the gross profit on sales" (both are 20%). The "fixed amount system" is 16.3%. The amount of loss mentioned in (3) is the expense shared by franchisers for discarding packed lunches and purchasing dead stocks.

According to "Japanese franchise chain 2006" (Shogyokai, 2006), 16 companies out of 122 in the retail industry (13.1%) have used "gross profit" or "gross profit on sales" as the standard for calculating the royalties, and most of them were convenience store companies (13 companies). For convenience store franchisers, using "gross profit on sales" as a calculation standard means that they must not only offer the business guidance in order to promote sales volume, but also take responsibility for the cost of goods sold and support store management to increase gross profit on sales.

Although JFA regards "the gross profit on sales," a standard for calculating the royalties, as the sum of "the amount of gross profit" and "the amount of loss," while distinguishing "gross profit" from "gross profit on sales," "gross profit" generally means the same as "gross profit on sales." Therefore, in this paper, "gross profit" and "gross profit on sales" will not be distinguished and only the term "gross profit on sales" will be used.

3.2 *Gross profit on sales enlargement plan*

When the royalties are calculated by the rate corresponding to the gross profit on sales, the fixed rate will be used because the rate will be determined when the contract is made. If the rate is fixed, it goes without saying that for the franchisers, the amount of the royalties could be raised by increasing the gross profit on sales. Gross profit on sales can be defined as follows:

$$\text{Gross profit on sales} = \text{Gross margin ratio} \times \text{Volume of sales}$$
$$= (1 - \text{Cost of goods sold ratio})$$
$$\times \text{Volume of sales} \qquad (1)$$

Therefore, even if the sales volume is fixed, the gross profit on sales will be enlarged with the storewide growth of the gross margin ratio.

To raise the gross margin ratio of the whole of stores, the cost of goods sold ratio should be kept low. Then to raise the gross margin ratio of the whole of stores, (1) the franchisers should work out a way to lower the cost of goods sold ratio on each item and (2) the franchisers should suggest the mixture of items that could raise the gross margin ratio of the whole of stores. In other words, it is important to increase the proportion of the commodities with a lower cost of goods sold ratio (or with a higher gross margin ratio) in the total sales volume of the whole of stores.

$$\begin{aligned}
\text{Gross profit on sales} &= \text{Return on capital} \times \text{Total capital} \\
&= \text{Gross margin ratio} \\
&\quad \times \text{Turnover ratio of total capital} \\
&\quad \times \text{Total capital} \qquad\qquad (2)
\end{aligned}$$

In addition, according to the above formula, gross profit on sales could also be improved if the turnover ratio of total capital increases, even in the event that the invested capital of the store is consistent. The capital invested in the store includes the goods in stock as working capital, so gross profit on sales will be enlarged with the increase of the inventory turnover ratio (= sales volume ÷ amount of goods in stock).

As long as there is no change in the business scale, there should not be any striking difference of fiscal-year quantity of goods in stock. However, if the amount is significant, inventory turnover ratio decrease, meaning that the business is inefficient. In other words, the number of days for which merchandise is overstocked, will be longer. To reduce the number of days for which excess merchandise is stocked, convenience store companies have established an original delivery system. This logistic system will be explained in the next section.

4 Factors to Raise the Gross Profit on Sales

As mentioned above, to raise the gross profit on sales, the volume of sales must be promoted while the cost of goods sold must be lowered. In other words, the cost of goods sold ratio must be lowered. This issue has been addressed for a long time not only by convenience stores but also by other retail industries such as supermarkets. However, this rapid growth in the convenience store industry indicates that they must have utilized a different management from the other industries. In this paper, the author will be examining this difference.

4.1 *Improvement in sales amount*

4.1.1 *Utilization of information systems*

As can be seen from the size of the stores, the assortment of goods in convenience stores is far more limited than that in supermarkets. The reason why convenience stores were able to make progress in sales with a limited assortment of goods could be that they have adopted a different management style. They collect only products of marketable goods while removing dead stock immediately. They only collect the items strongly in demand, rather than keeping a wide variety.

To do the above, it is important to collect information based on reliable data and select and cut off items based on this research. The first device that convenience stores adopted to gather information was POS (point of sales) register, which a record of who bought what, when, how many, etc. at the point of purchase. The accumulated sales data allows convenience stores to select items in high demand. Sales selection varies depending on the location and environment around the store. Franchisees that are fully aware of the location and environment around their stores are responsible for placing orders with due consideration to the various conditions.

Currently, other than POS register, devices such as SC (store computer), DOT (dynamic order terminal), POT (portable order terminal) and GOT (graphic order terminal) are also used as a part of this information system. SC is a computer for store administration that accumulates and analyzes the information from a POS register, allowing users to obtain real time data for marketing and stocking goods and collecting a variety of information required for placing orders. DOT, POT, and GOT are terminal units for placing orders which enable users to place an order while checking the information on goods (Seven-Eleven website, Lawson website).

4.1.2 *Reform of logistics*

In addition to making an effective use of information systems, logistic systems play an important role in assorting items. Stores are required to collect various items to respond to consumers' changing demand. In order to display these various items within a store, franchisees must reduce the quantity of each item, to ensure space for as many different items as possible.

However, the biggest risk of displaying only small quantities of items is the possibility of running out of stock. If this happens often, then the store will lose customers. The joint delivery system has been adopted and is being carried out to prevent this stock shortage. Items are no longer delivered from the chain wholesaler of each manufacturer. All goods are warehoused in one delivery center and only the required number of goods are delivered. In short, under this system they deliver "various items in small amounts" frequently. This is the so-called "Just-in-time delivery," developed by TOYOTA. This system enables convenience store companies to deliver the necessary items to their stores only when needed and reduces the risk to excess inventory as well as stock shortage.

Since this system lightens inventories, management efficiency will also be improved. In other words, the system improves inventory turnover ratio (= sales volume ÷ inventory).

The indicator shows the efficiency of acquiring the sales volume and turnover frequency of inventory into cash in a certain period. The joint delivery system reduces the volume of the denominator (inventory), so that the management efficiency will be improved.

To achieve this, the quantity of each item displayed on the shelves should be reduced so that the inventory turnover ratio of item will be improved. Then, even if the sales amount of the concerned item is constant, the capital profit ratio of the item will be improved. This increases return on investment in the whole of stores, and the gross profit on sales of the entire store increases even if the amount of capital invested is constant.

Further, Seven-Eleven manages their joint delivery system by temperature zones while Lawson and Circle K Sunkus use deal-temperature system vehicles.

4.2   Reduction in cost of goods sold

4.2.1   Reduction in ratio of cost to sales of bento and pre-cooked meals

The items that account for a high percentage of the sales amount in the convenience stores are Japanese-type fast foods such as *bento* (prepared boxed food), rice balls, pre-cooked meals, sandwiches, and so on. The sales composition rate of Seven-Eleven in 2005 is as follows. Fast foods (rice meals, pre-cooked meals, breads, salads, etc.) is 29.3%; daily delivered foods (milk-based drinks, milk, desserts, breads, etc.) is 13.1%; processed foods (soft drinks, confectionaries, instant noodles, etc.) is 30.1%; and non-foods (magazines, cosmetics, household goods, etc.) is 27.5% (data from Seven-Eleven Web page). Rice balls, bento, and pre-cooked meals are items that have a higher profit margin than processed goods and household goods (Tanaka, 2006). The growth in sales of these fast foods should lower the ratio of cost to sales for the whole of stores and raise the gross profit on sales.

Currently, Seven-Eleven deals with about 80 companies that make bento and pre-cooked meals. Those 80 companies act as factories for Seven-Eleven, only making items for Seven-Eleven. They form a team to develop new products and jointly purchase raw materials with lower costs. They even have a committee to study hygiene management and environment conservation (Yamaguchi and Yanagawa, 2006).

Joint purchase of raw materials may enable them to utilize the advantage of scale to cut down the purchase price. The team of 80 companies allows them to hire a labor force to develop new products, which a smaller number of companies would find difficulty to accomplish due to smaller cash flow. Joint product development will also allow them to produce items that will increase customer satisfaction while contributing to the sales growth. Moreover, those 80 companies have provided the training to each company to keep the same product quality so that consumers can expect the same taste of rice balls (Yamaguchi and Yanagawa, 2006), bento, and pre-cooked meals no matter where they are purchased. This brings a sense of security and satisfaction to the consumers.

Furthermore, joint operations also greatly contribute to the reduction of expenses for hygiene management and for environmental protection, utilizing the advantage of scale. These efforts allow franchisees to purchase rice balls, bento, and pre-cooked meals with a high return on sales.

4.2.2   *Reduction in cost of goods sold by developing original items*

The POS system shows not only the information of the goods consumers demand, but also the sales volume of items that convenience stores developed. Sales of the original items developed with manufactures accounted for 52%–53% of the entire daily sales of each Seven-Eleven store in 2004 (approximately ¥647,000 per day per store) (Yamaguchi and Yanagawa, 2006). Besides rice balls, bento, and pre-cooked meals, Seven-Eleven has developed various original items such as processed foods (soft drinks, ice creams, instant noodles), "dynamic foods" (jelly beverage), nonessentials (coffee beans), and others (frozen noodles, liquors, confectioneries, women's cosmetics, oxygen cans, sanitary supplies, women's undergarments, stationary, men's undergarments, pet food, smoking-related products).

Products sold under the original brand (trademark) of the wholesale store (group) are generally called "private brands." However, Seven-Eleven uniformly uses the expression "original products" instead of "private brands." These original products are created through "joint development" (team merchandising) with manufactures (Figure 3). As mentioned above,

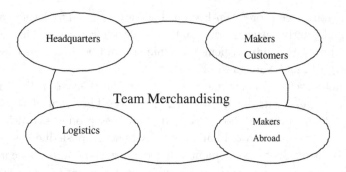

Source: http://www.sej.co.jp/oshiete/kaibou04.html
(Seven-Eleven Japan Co., LTD. website).

Fig. 3   Team merchandising of Seven-Eleven Japan Co., Ltd.

the POS system can provide an enormous amount of data. Utilizing this system, Seven-Eleven proposes a new product to the manufactures. Then the manufactures follow the proposal to develop new products (Yamaguchi and Yanagawa, 2006). Seven-Eleven and the manufactures repeatedly examine the samples to complete the original products, which are solely sold by Seven-Eleven stores. From selection of material to planning and securing of supply channels to manufacture original products, domestic and overseas manufactures logistic centers are involved in the joint development of their original products.

Selling original products works as an "introduction of the products with high gross margin ratio" (Yanagawa, 2006). This is because the original products are attractive for customers. In other words, they are tasty, easy to use, of high quality, in short, good products that meet the customer needs and become a factor of raising sales volume. These products can increase the gross profit on sales by "small profits with quick returns," even if they do not have high earning rates.

First, let us consider the formula shown earlier:

$$\text{Gross profit on sales} = \text{Gross margin ratio}$$
$$\times \text{Turnover ratio of total capital}$$
$$\times \text{Total capital} \qquad (3)$$

This "small profits with quick returns" measurement attaches a great deal of importance to products with a high "turnover ratio on stock," in other words, a "high marketing speed" (sales amount during a certain period), even if the product has a low gross margin ratio, which is on the right side of the formula above.

Second, since all of these original products are sold in Seven-Eleven, economy of scale can be utilized to keep the purchase price low. For national brands, on the other hand, purchasing price is the same as other retail industries. Seven-Eleven has a sales volume of a certain national brand of (500 ml) coke that is 3.2 times greater than that of the total sales volume of four other companies combined (AEON, Ito-Yokado, Daiei, Seiyu). However, there is no difference in purchase price between Seven-Eleven and the other four (Nikkei October 23, 2006). There is no economy of scale for the national brands. By selling original products, increases in sales amount and reductions in cost of goods sold will be achieved at the same time.

5 Conclusion

Convenience stores have increased their profits because of their assortment of goods which cannot be achieved by other retail industries such as supermarkets. Development of original products is essential to keep this unique assortment. Original products can increase the sales volume while reducing the cost of goods sold by utilizing economy of scale. Hence, original products could be considered indispensable for increasing the gross profit on sales, which is a standard for calculating the royalties.

To support the development of original products, information systems are required. Logistic systems are also important to arrange the necessary amount of goods only when needed.

The franchise system itself also plays an important role for convenience stores. In the restaurant industry, companies adopting the franchise system have a lower rate of return on investment compared to non-franchise system companies. An experimental study (Komoto, 2006) shows that the main reason lies in their low rate of return on sales. In the convenience store industry, which is the retail industry, since most companies have adopted the franchise system, we are not able to compare franchise companies with non-franchise ones. However, the constant growth during the recession would indicate they have been making the best use of the franchise system. In particular, franchisees are responsible for the placement of orders and store operation while franchisers give management guidance to their franchisees and work on plans to develop products and reduce their purchasing costs. By sharing tasks with each other and successfully fulfilling their own roles to conduct business jointly, they have been able to increase the sales amount and share the gained profit together.

However, convenience stores which have been showing constant growth are recently facing a sluggish increase in their sales amount. One large-scale supermarket has recently opened near the author's house. In less than six months, a convenience store located not more than 100 m away from this supermarket closed. It can be assumed that the closure was due to the decrease in sales of bento, rice balls, and pre-cooked meals, which are the key commodities of convenience stores. The recently opened supermarket offers a discount on these specific commodities on an everyday basis during certain store hours. Bento price are reduced earlier in the day for lunch and in the evening for dinner. Bento, rice balls, and pre-cooked meals are made within the store, so they are fresh and placed in a display case during a fixed time period. Sushi is also available, which cannot be found in convenience stores. Though the business hours of the supermarket are shorter, from 9 a.m. to 12 p.m., consumers can buy bento during this period of time. In the convenience store in question, which was open 24 hours a day, the items of which sales was not affected by the newly opened supermarket were only rice balls and sandwich-like foods for breakfast. The competitive edge of convenience stores, which capitalize on the convenience of an assortment of goods, is starting to collapse due to the appearance of these supermarkets.

As another example to illustrate this collapse of competitive edge, Seven-Eleven was forced to discount the price of their seasonings. This has been implemented by other convenience stores as well. Additionally, Seven-Eleven offered a 15% discount on some of the plastic bottled beverages last year. Then, this year, they decided to sell their original 500 ml plastic bottled beverages at a lower price. Among other convenience stores, some started to open stores and stock goods for female customers. As just described, convenience stores may appear in various forms in the future, and will keep changing to maintain their competitive edge in the retail industry.

In this paper, one theory that could be used as the basis for the convenience store business model was considered without conducting interview surveys. As a challenge in the future, the author would like to empirically verify this theory based on interview surveys and keep an eye on the future trends of convenience stores.

References

Bradach, J. F. (1998). *Franchise Organizations*, Harvard Business School Press translated by Kono, S. *et al.* (2006) *Bunshindo.*

Higuchi, M. (2004). *Current State and Issues of Franchise Service*, Sibaura Institute of Technology: Report of Humanity System 38(1), pp. 89–92 (in Japanese).

Hoshi, N. (2006). Management of franchise chains and multi-divisional organization: a comparative study on royalty and corporate cost, *Value-Based Management of the Rising Sun*, pp. 103–116.

Komoto, K. (1999). Positive analysis of franchise contract, *Japanese Economy Research* No. 38, pp. 1–24 (in Japanese).

Komoto, K. (2006). Management analysis of franchise business, *Management Analysis Study* No. 22, pp. 18–25 (in Japanese).

Ministry of Economy Trade and Industry (2002). *Fact Finding Report on Business Management of Franchise Chain* (in Japanese).

Rothschild, M. (2006). Shareholders pay for ROA: then why are we still living in a margin only world? *Strategic Finance*, November, pp. 27–31.

Shogyokai (2006). *Franchise Chain 2006*, February, *Separate Volume* (in Japanese).

Takaku, R. (2005). Discussions on attribution and allocation of the profits derived from use of intangibles in transfer pricing taxation, *Zeidai Ronso (The Journal of National Tax College)*, No. 49, pp. 1–105 (in Japanese).

Tanaka, Y. (2006). *Secrets of the Winning Company, Seven-Eleven*, Nihon Keizai Shimbun, Inc. (in Japanese).

Yamaguchi, H. and Yanagawa, T. (2006). Case 3 Seven-Eleven franchise business, *Corporate Strategies of Modern Enterprises*, Hakuoh University Institute of Business Research, ed., Hakuoh University, pp. 37–52 (in Japanese).

Yanagawa, T. (2006). New industry creation focusing on finding-out, business model and corporate interfacing power, Case 2 Seven-Eleven Japan, *Hakuoh University Journal*, 20(2), pp. 165–197 (in Japanese).

Materials

Websites

http://www.circleksunkus.jp/member/support/index.html (Circle K Sunkus Co., Ltd. website).

http://jfa.jfa-fc.or.jp/qa_1.html (Corporate juridical person, Japan Franchise Association website).

JFA list of time series statistic research.

JFA monthly report on statistic research on convenience stores (July, 2006).

http://www.lawson.co.jp/company/index.html (Lawson Co., Ltd. website).

http://www.sej.co.jp/faq/shohin.html (Seven-Eleven Japan Co., Ltd. website).

Newspaper article

Daily Nikkei, "Management Viewpoint, Destination of ¥6 billion distribution union, M&A, to grow attraction," October 23, 2006, p. 9 (in Japanese).

Part 5

Process Management

Chain Effects among Objectives under Management by Objectives

Noboru Ogura

Professor, Graduate School of Business Sciences
University of Tsukuba

Susumu Nibuya

Graduate School of Business Sciences
University of Tsukuba

1 Introduction

Management by Objectives (MBO) refers to a management control system advocated in 1954 by P. F. Drucker. MBO was introduced into Japan in the early 1960s. In the 40 years that have since elapsed, different studies have reported that over 60% of the listed corporations on the stock exchange markets in Japan have introduced MBO systems. Thus, the MBO system is, like budgeting, one of the most prevalent management control systems in Japan. Unlike other management control systems, MBO involves the application of a function that can break down the company-wide strategy and organization goal of a corporation to the level of individual workers. For the purposes of this paper, this function is called "chain effects among objectives." Chain effects among objectives are essential for the management control system of a corporation. MBO will become more instrumental in implementing corporate strategy when it is organically combined and operated with other management control systems.

This paper explores MBO's chain effects among objectives for Japanese corporations and focuses on identifying those factors that have an impact on chain effects among objectives. The results have revealed that the concern and the involvement of top management have a great impact on chain effects among objectives and that target workers' satisfaction with their MBO and chain effects among objectives are related in such a way that will bring about synergistic effects.

2　Chain Effects among Objectives under the MBO System

Most Japanese corporations have adopted different management control systems concurrently according to their corporate goals (Hayashi, 2005). In principle, MBO is characterized as targeting and controlling individual members of an organization, unlike many other management control systems that target and control the lower units of an organization, such as divisions, departments, and offices.

In this paper, MBO's chain effects among objectives refer to the condition in which the goal of a corporation is broken down to consider low-ranking individual workers and the ways in which the corporate goal will be achieved when workers achieve their individual goals. Today, corporate management environments are constantly changing. Corporations are urged to prepare a strategy that can accurately cope with rapidly changing environments and which can carry out this strategy without delay. Under these circumstances, MBO's chain effects among objectives will play an extremely important role.

Since any management control system is a means to achieve the goal of a corporation, the corporation should naturally measure the effects of the system after it has been introduced. As Okuno (2004) pointed out, however, most Japanese corporations have hardly considered measuring the effects of their MBO systems in order to use them to improve corporate performance. While there have been different studies conducted on MBO in recent years, such as those by Takahashi (2001) and Yanagisawa and Furukawa (2003), these studies have focused on MBO systems as personal ratings systems and have accordingly evaluated the extent of feelings of satisfaction and fairness among target workers. Until today, the author has found no other studies that have identified evidence-based MBO's chain effects among objectives.

3　Circumstances of the Introduction of MBO into Japanese Corporations

A series of studies about MBO systems in Japanese corporations were conducted by the Institute of Labor Administration in 1987, 1989, 1991, 1993, 1995, 1997, and 2001. These studies have revealed that the number of corporations operating MBO has increased dramatically since the late 1990s.

Some 40 years have passed since MBO was introduced into Japan. To determine what is behind the recent, rapid increase in the introduction of

MBO systems, The Sanno Institute of Management (2000) prepared and sent questionnaires to 2496 listed corporations and major non-listed corporations selected at random. Answers were obtained from 447 corporations. The questionnaires revealed that 79.9% of the corporations had introduced MBO and that 61.4% of those corporations had introduced MBO from 1991 onward. Answers to multiple-choice questionnaires also revealed that 61.9% of the corporations chose as their main purpose for introducing MBO the implementation of "result-based rewards" and "performance management." This percentage was the highest among the purposes given for the introduction of MBO. Furthermore, the questionnaires indicated that among the corporations that introduced MBO from 1976 onward, the ratio of corporations that aimed at "thorough implementation of result-based rewards" increased in relation to a later period of introduction.

The study also indicated that the number of Japanese corporations introducing MBO increased in a period when corporations were building momentum to introduce result-based rewards. Result-based rewards basically promote the personnel management of individual workers; workers who achieve more will be rewarded more, and workers who achieve less will be rewarded less. In such a case, it is considered to be difficult to make a fair and objective evaluation on target workers' performances while keeping worker's agreement. Corporations suffering in the post-bubble economy were apparently drawn again to MBO systems as a means to transform themselves into corporations with result-based personnel appraisal. Such corporations regarded MBO as the method that ensured target workers' satisfaction with their performance appraisals, as well as creating feelings of fairness among them, while making objective measurements of their performances for a specific period. It could be said that from the late 1990s until today, MBO systems have been introduced by Japanese corporations mostly as a personal rating system that can thoroughly implement result-based rewards and clarify evaluation standards (Okuno, 2004).

Considering this historical background, currently operating MBO systems are weak as management control systems and have apparently demonstrated inadequate chain effects among objectives.

4 Defining Study Purposes and Setting Hypotheses

One of the purposes of this paper is to discern MBO's function of chain effects among the objectives of Japanese corporations in the recognition that those effects belong to the primary function of the MBO system as a means of management. The other purpose of this paper is to identify evidence-based factors that have an impact on chain effects among objectives. As long as the current MBO's chain effects among objectives remain unsatisfactory and no solution is found to improve or enhance them, the original function of MBO will remain irretrievable. This paper attempts to identify those factors that have an impact on chain effects among objectives in the hope that such a finding will lead to reinforcing the MBO function as a management control system. There are adverse assertions, on the other hand, that solely focusing on and enhancing chain effects among objectives is not enough. For example, in a case in which chain effects among objectives are overemphasized, workers will be at the risk of merely following orders without taking the initiative to set their own goals. Since most MBO systems adopted nowadays tend to reflect their evaluation results in personal ratings, assigning workload-based goals to target workers would be instrumental in influencing chain effects among objectives. On the other hand, these MBO systems are unlikely to boost satisfaction among target workers. Conversely, in a case where the target workers' own goal setting, self-control, and self-evaluation are overemphasized to primarily enhance their satisfaction, the force required to mobilize target workers to achieve the corporate goal is unlikely to have momentum, and will likely develop no chain effects among objectives (Okuno, 2004). In response to such assertions, this paper also analyzes factors that affect target workers' satisfaction with MBO. A comprehensive discussion of both assertions will be made.

The following three hypotheses have been established to further the study:

Hypothesis 1: Top management's concern and involvement in MBO will better clarify the positioning and the purpose of the introduction of MBO systems and promote an appropriate MBO operation.

Ivancevich (1972), Rodgers and Hunter (1991), and other researchers have reported that top management's concern and involvement in MBO improved the effects of MBO. This paper attempts to establish that top management's involvement will play an important role in chain effects among objectives and that such involvement will clarify the positioning and purposes of MBO in corporate management and lead the MBO operation in an appropriate direction.

Hypothesis 2: In the case that MBO's institutional purpose is sharing the organization goal among target workers and in which the planning office is involved in an appropriate MBO operation, chain effects among objectives will be enhanced.

In general, the purpose is to introduce a management control system that defines the institutional system and that will effect results accordingly. If the main purpose of a management control system is *sharing the organization goal*, then *involvement of the planning office* (which usually provides long-term corporate plans and policies) will become indispensable. Furthermore, if such a management control system is designed to cooperate with other management control systems and is operated by the planning office, chain effects among objectives of the corporation will be enhanced.

Hypothesis 3: The function of chain effects among objectives and satisfaction of target workers are not in a trade-off relationship, but instead interact to bring about synergistic effects.

Those chain effects among objectives that endure presume that target workers are satisfied with the MBO system and that they act on their own initiative in the MBO operation. When an MBO system divides the organization goal into segmented roles for target workers who feel that contributing to the corporation is rewarding, both chain effects among objectives and satisfaction of target workers will exhibit synergism.

To examine these hypotheses, questionnaires were sent to the planning offices of 2171 corporations listed on the First and Second Sections of the Tokyo Stock Exchange during the period August to September 2005. Two-hundred ten corporations responded to the questionnaires (response rate: 9.67%). Of these, 159 corporations answered yes when asked if they had implemented MBO.

In past studies, many MBO-related questionnaires were sent to the personnel offices of corporations to inquire about their MBO systems as personnel appraisal systems. In fact, as described later in this paper, among the different corporate sections that responded to the questionnaires, personnel offices comprised the majority of sections in control of their MBO systems. Since this paper focuses on the function of MBO as a management control system, answers to the questionnaires have been examined in such a way as to measure evaluations from the standpoint of the planning office.

5 Results of Data Analysis

To ascertain the extent to which MBO's chain effects among objectives have been achieved, the following question was prepared: *"Has your company introduced an MBO system so that your personal goal is linked to the corporate goal or the department goal and that when you achieve your personal goal, the corporate goal or the department goal is also achieved?"* The answer *linked closely* has been assigned five points, the answer *linked rather closely* four points, the answer *neither off nor on* three points, the answer *linked not so closely* two points, and the answer *not linked closely* has been assigned one point.

To ascertain satisfaction of target workers the question was devised to determine whether they were satisfied with the MBO system in operation after taking MBO's purposes, operation, evaluation results reflecting methods, etc., into consideration. The answer *quite satisfied* has been assigned five points, the answer *rather satisfied* four points, the answer *neither off nor on* three points, the answer *rather dissatisfied* two points, and the answer *dissatisfied* has been assigned one point. Similarly, five-stage Likert scales were applied to other criteria.

First, before calculating Spearman's rank correlation coefficients, correlation analysis on the items' chain effects among objectives, circumstances of MBO introduction, basic policy, and variables referring to MBO operating conditions was performed. Likewise, a correlation analysis of satisfaction of target workers was performed. Finally, a comparison between chain effects among objectives and the results of the analysis of satisfaction of the target workers was made. The variables *circumstance of introduction* and *basic policy* (with the exception of *top management's concern and involvement*) are part of a nominal scale. The relations among these variables, *chain effects among objectives* and *satisfaction of target workers*, were analyzed using *t*-testing.

5.1 *Distribution of answers regarding MBO's chain effects among objectives*

The first step is to ascertain answers to MBO's chain effects among objectives and satisfaction of target workers, which is the main theme of this study. Figure 1 shows the distribution of these answers.

The average of chain effects among objectives scores 3.39 (standard deviation: 1.005). The answer *linked rather closely* is largest in number, followed

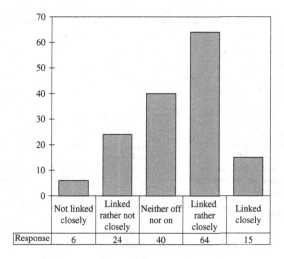

| Response | 6 | 24 | 40 | 64 | 15 |

Fig. 1   Distribution of answers regarding MBO's chain effects among objectives

by the answer *neither off nor on*. The standard deviation is beyond 1, indicating a broad distribution of answers. The distribution supports the fact that MBO's chain effects among objectives for Japanese corporations are satisfactory.

5.2   *Variables affecting chain effects among objectives and satisfaction of target workers*

Among 35 variables listed in the questionnaires that purportedly impact MBO results, the variables that indicate a correlation significant to chain effects among objectives number 12, including *A. Top management's concern and involvement, B. Involvement of the planning office, C. Purpose of introduction,* and *D. Well-informed company-wide strategy.* Fifteen variables indicated a correlation significant to satisfaction of target workers. Of these, 11 variables are common to the variables that have an impact on chain effects among objectives. Figure 2 lists the results of the *t*-testing and correlation analysis.

In addition, the analysis of individual variables with eigenvalues of the correlation matrix has identified no major factors that can satisfy a 45% cumulative of four variables whose eigenvalues are beyond 1. In other words, each of the individual variables is understood to be separate.

	Chain effects among objectives		Satisfaction of target workers	
Controlling sections	*p* < 0.001		*p* < 0.01	
Purposes of MBO	*p* < 0.001		*p* < 0.01	
Linkage with long-term planning	*p* < 0.01		*p* < 0.001	
Linkage with budgeting	–		*p* < 0.01	
Top management's concern and involvement	0.441	**	0.422	**
Well-informed company-wide strategy	0.350	**	0.229	**
Well-informed target of office	0.380	**	0.422	**
Linkage with budgeting in goal setting	0.292	**	0.298	**
Goal settings other than short-term result	0.187		0.278	**
Opening of superior's target to the public	0.211	**	0.207	**
Multipronged use of MBO sheets	0.238	**	0.242	**
Progress management in MBO	0.143		0.209	**
Giving of dissemination and authority	0.344	**	0.305	**
Execution of interview by the middle period	0.258	**	0.156	
Proper change of target	0.209		0.312	**
The superior's advice	0.238	**	0.304	**

**1% significant difference.

Fig. 2   *t*-Testing and correlation analysis

5.3   *Analysis in combinations of multiple variables*

Next, the differences when different items are combined will be determined. *Top management's concern and involvement* scores 0.441 to chain effects among objectives and 0.422 to satisfaction of target workers, indicating relatively high correlations compared with other items. It suggests that top management's greater concern and involvement in MBO will help to clarify the purposes of MBO introduction and promote the involvement of the planning office that supports top management. This section will focus on analyzing these items.

With regard to the 157 valid answers to questions regarding top management's concern and involvement, 80 answers (nearly one half) point to the item *top management's concern and involvement are large.* The analysis described below classified 77 answers into one group prior to comparison. The grouped answers include *top management's concern and involvement are rather large, neither off nor on, top management's concern and involvement are rather small,* and *top management's concern and involvement are small.*

5.3.1   *Top management's concern and involvement in MBO and controlling sections*

Corporations that responded to the questionnaires were classified into a group of corporations that answered *top management's concern and involvement are large* (large) and a combined group of corporations that answered *top management's concern and involvement are rather large and ... are rather small* (small). Those sections controlling MBO were divided into personnel offices only and involvement of the planning offices. These two classes of variables allowed the creation of four subclasses in combination (cross tabulations), among which the averages of chain effects among objectives and satisfaction of target workers were compared before the results were examined in analysis of variance (F-testing).

As listed in Figure 3, corporations in which top management's concern and involvement in MBO are large and in which their planning offices are involved rank highest in terms of chain effects among objectives and satisfaction of target workers. Corporations in which top management's concern in MBO is small and whose MBO is controlled by their personnel offices alone, however, rank lowest in terms of chain effects among objectives. F-testing also indicated a significant p value of 0.000.

5.3.2 *Top management's concern and involvement and purpose of introduction*

As mentioned earlier, four subclasses were created: top management's concern is *large* (i.e., corporations which answered that top management's concern and involvement are large); top management's concern is *small* (combined group of corporations whose top management's concern and involvement are rather large and ... are small); and categories relating to the purpose of introduction: *sharing the organization goal* or *other purposes*. These four subclasses were used to make a comparison among the averages of chain effects among objectives and satisfaction of target workers before the results were examined in analysis of variance (F-testing).

Top management's concern and involvement	Controlling sections	Chain effect among objectives			Satisfaction of target workers		
		Response	Average	S.D.	Response	Average	S.D.
Large	Planning offices	35	3.94	0.873	37	3.62	0.681
Large	Personnel offices	42	3.64	0.850	43	3.47	0.667
Small	Planning offices	18	3.39	0.850	18	3.17	0.383
Small	Personnel offices	52	2.85	0.998	57	2.89	0.817
Total		147	3.40	1.005	155	3.26	0.763
		F-value 11.555		p-value 0.000	F-value 9.635		p-value 0.000

Fig. 3 Top management's concern and involvement, controlling sections

Top management's concern and involvement	Purposes of introduction	Chain effect among objectives			Satisfaction of target workers		
		Response	Average	S.D.	Response	Average	S.D.
Large	Sharing the organization goal	36	3.94	0.681	36	3.58	0.692
Large	Other purposes	40	3.65	0.834	42	3.50	0.672
Small	Sharing the organization goal	21	3.48	0.873	21	3.29	0.463
Small	Other purposes	50	2.76	0.960	55	2.84	0.788
Total		147	3.39	1.011	154	3.25	0.763
		F-value 13.955 p-value 0.000			F-value 10.991 p-value 0.000		

Fig. 4   Top management's concern and involvement, purposes of introduction

As listed in Figure 4, corporations whose top management's concern and involvement are large and whose purpose of introduction lies in sharing the organization goal rank highest in terms of both chain effects among objectives and satisfactions of target workers. Corporations whose top management's concern is small and whose purpose of introduction is the enhancement of target worker's satisfaction rank lowest. F-testing also indicated a significant p value of 0.000.

5.3.3   *Purpose of MBO introduction and controlling sections*

In the end, the author combined purposes of introduction and controlling sections to ascertain MBO's chain effects among objectives and satisfaction of target workers. Figure 5 lists the results.

The results revealed that corporations in which the personnel office alone controls MBO to enhance satisfaction of target workers with their

Controlling sections	Purposes of introduction	Chain effect among objectives			Satisfaction of target workers		
		Response	Average	S.D.	Response	Average	S.D.
Planning offices	Sharing the organization goal	37	3.73	0.932	37	3.51	0.607
Planning offices	Other purposes	16	3.81	0.834	17	3.41	0.712
Personnel offices	Sharing the organization goal	20	3.85	0.875	20	3.40	0.681
Personnel offices	Other purposes	74	3.03	0.979	81	3.07	0.818
Total		147	3.40	1.005	155	3.26	0.763
		F-value 7.964 p-value 0.000			F-value 3.584 p-value 0.015		

Fig. 5   Controlling sections, purposes of introduction

evaluation rank lowest in terms of chain effects among objectives. Other combinations also indicated little difference in results from chain effects among objectives. Although both the MBO controlling section alone and the purpose of introduction alone can be variables that have an impact on chain effects among objectives and on satisfaction of target workers, their combinations showed no difference in the results.

6 General Discussion

This paper has set three hypotheses. Each of the three hypotheses will be examined based on the data analysis above.

6.1 *Examining Hypothesis 1*

Of the 12 variables that had impacts on chain effects among objectives, *top management's concern and involvement* indicated the greatest correlation coefficient. In addition, analyses using variables in combinations were performed. However, the combinations of the variables *controlling sections* and *purpose of introduction* reveal no difference, unlike the combination of the variables *top management's concern and involvement* and *controlling sections* or the combination of the variables *top management's concern and involvement* and *purpose of introduction*, which have made significant differences. In actual corporate activities, top management's influence is overwhelming; there are not a few cases where corporations improved performances dramatically when their management was merely replaced. Current MBO systems have targeted a broad range of persons, from general workers to the management and division managers. Their evaluation results are reflected in personal ratings. Therefore, when top management is greatly concerned with and involved in the MBO system, other management and ordinary workers will naturally come to have a greater concern for MBO.

In total, 12 variables affected chain effects among objectives. The results of the discussions mentioned above indicate that *top management's concern and involvement* is the prerequisite for other items. In other words, the first hypothesis — that "top management's concern and involvement in MBO will better clarify the positioning and the purpose of the introduction of MBO systems and promote an appropriate MBO operation" — is nearly proved to be true.

6.2 *Examining Hypothesis 2*

As described earlier, the combinations of *controlling sections* and *purpose of introduction* indicated no difference, unlike the combination of *top management's concern and involvement* and *controlling sections* and the combination of *top management's concern and involvement* and *purpose of introduction*, which show remarkable differences. Examinations reveal that corporations whose purpose of introduction lies in sharing the organization goal rank highest in terms of chain effects among objectives and that corporations whose planning office is involved in MBO rank higher in terms of chain effects among objectives. However, this does not mean that corporations whose purpose of MBO introduction lies in sharing the organization goal and whose planning office is involved in MBO will rank highest in terms of chain effects among objectives. Only when the variable *top management's concern and involvement* is added will MBO's chain effects among objectives be enhanced. In other words, this study's second hypothesis — that when MBO's institutional purpose is sharing the organization goal among target workers and in which the planning office is involved in an appropriate MBO operation, chain effects among objectives will be enhanced — could not be proved.

6.3 *Examining Hypothesis 3*

Spearman's rank correlation coefficient of chain effects among objectives and satisfaction of target workers scores a significant 0.443 at a 1% level. The author also identified variables that had impacts on chain effects among objectives or on satisfaction of target workers. The circumstances of introduction and basic policy have four variables in common, while the circumstances of MBO operation have seven variables in common. In other words, when a measure is taken to enhance chain effects among objectives, satisfaction of target workers will also be enhanced. The opposite effect is also true. Satisfaction of target workers who feel that contributing to the company is rewarding will be enhanced more when the organization goal is broken down to the level of individual workers and when respective portions of the organization goal are allocated to them. As a result, chain effects among objectives of the corporation will also be enhanced. Lasting chain effects among objectives cannot be expected as long as satisfaction of target workers is disregarded. Rather, to enhance chain effects among objectives, satisfaction of target workers also needs to be enhanced. In other words, this study's third hypothesis is proved; namely, that the "the function of objective chain effects and satisfaction of target workers are not in a trade-off relationship, but instead interact to bring about synergistic effects."

6.4 *Summary of results*

Figure 6 shows the results of discussing this study.

When top management is concerned with and actively involved in MBO, the positioning of MBO in corporate management will be enhanced, maintaining top management's concern and involvement at a high level. Participation will also involve a planning office that supports top management, and this office will naturally try to link the MBO system with other management control systems in operation. In this case, the purpose of introducing MBO is clearly defined as sharing the organization goal with target workers and the design of an institutional system that will be operated accordingly. This will lead to an enhancement in satisfaction with the MBO system among target workers and in chain effects among objectives.

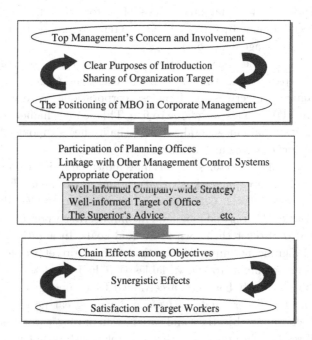

Fig. 6   Chain effects among objectives and satisfaction of target workers

Even when chain effects among objectives are enhanced, satisfaction of target workers is not in a trade-off relationship but in a relationship that will bring about synergistic effects. In other words, maintaining enduring chain effects among objectives is indispensable for target workers' satisfaction and initiative in working on MBO.

7   Conclusion

Recognizing that chain effects among objectives are the primary function of the MBO system as a management control system, this paper aims to ascertain MBO's chain effects among objectives for Japanese corporations. The motive behind this study lies in the observation that MBO systems, which have been introduced by a rapidly growing number of Japanese corporations in recent years, are mostly used as tools for personnel appraisal and that Japanese corporations have apparently failed to take full advantage of chain effects among objectives.

The other purpose of this paper is to identify evidence-based factors that have an impact on chain effects among objectives for Japanese corporations. The author believes that an analysis of factors that have an impact on chain effects among objectives will lead to reinforcing functions of the MBO system as a management control system.

Answers to the questionnaires, which aimed to ascertain the first purpose explained in this section, reveal that current MBO's chain effects among objectives for Japanese corporations score 3.39 (standard deviation: 1.005) on a scale of one to five. This score is higher than expected and indicates that, in general, MBO's chain effects among objectives for Japanese corporations are satisfactory.

Of a total of 35 variables, 12 variables indicated a significant correlation, including *A. Top management's concern and involvement, B. Involvement of the Planning offices, C. Purpose of introduction,* and *D. Well-informed company-wide strategy* and long- and medium-term corporate goals to target workers who also set their own individual goals. In addition, 15 variables indicated significant impacts on satisfaction of target workers. Of these, 11 items are common to the variables that had impacts on chain effects among objectives. It has been ascertained that, among other factors, top management's concern and involvement have a great impact and that the chain effect among objectives and satisfaction of target workers are not in a trade-off relationship but are rather in a relationship that will bring about synergistic effects.

This paper has identified variables that have impacts on chain effects among objectives. However, the paper has not detailed the mechanism used to enhance MBO's chain effects among objectives nor the method for achieving a given result. Thus, additional case studies are necessary to uncover patterns of involvement in MBO by top management and planning offices and methods for cooperating with other management control systems. The author hopes that such studies will result in building MBO models that are well-suited to Japanese corporations.

References

Hayashi, S. (2005). Strategy communication by integrating management systems: the interaction of long-term planning, budgets and MBO, *Accounting Progress*, No. 6, pp. 86–102 (in Japanese).

Ivancevich, J. M. (1972). A longitudinal assessment of management by objectives, *Administrative Science Quarterly* 19(1), pp. 563–574.

Okuno, A. (2004). *Contingency Approach in Research of Management by Objectives*, Hakuto-syobo (in Japanese).

Rodgers, R. and Hunter, J. E. (1991). Impact of management by objectives on organizational productivity, *Journal of Applied Psychology* 76(2), pp. 322–336.

Takahashi, K. (2001). Fairness of personnel evaluation in employment organization, *Organizational Science* 34(4), pp. 26–38 (in Japanese).

The Sanno Institute of Management (2000). *Fact-Finding of Management by Objectives — The Present Conditions and a Future Problem about MBO* (in Japanese).

Yanagisawa, S. and Furukawa, H. (2003). Features of goal setting in MBO-relation to individual characteristic and effect of goal setting, *The Japanese Association of Industrial/Organizational Psychology*, The 19th rally thesis collection, pp. 188–191 (in Japanese).

The Framework of Business Process Management and Dell Computers

Gunyung Lee

Professor, Faculty of Economics
Niigata University

Naoya Yamaguchi

Associate Professor, Faculty of Economics
Niigata University

1 Introduction

Today, information networks using IT and the Internet are spreading on a global scale. Corporate activities both inside and outside corporations have been conducted in broad areas simultaneously beyond the limits of time and space. This era is called the "IT era." In the IT era, it is said that successful corporations possess not "material assets" but "information assets." In other words, information assets are becoming the means to a competitive advantage, while new managerial techniques are required to manage these assets.

On the other hand, because of environmental adaptation to cutthroat competition, leadership in commercial deals has shifted from suppliers to buyers and consumers. Consequently, suppliers' appropriate responses to satisfy buyers and consumers become one of the primary means to lead to competitive advantage. Gradually, in order to respond to the power of customers (buyers and consumers), it becomes necessary for suppliers to customize their services in accordance with consumers' desires and to provide customers with products and services that will bring solutions for the customers. Because of these changes of responses to customers, cooperation among departments becomes crucial and it is necessary to manage processes across the organization to promote cooperation swiftly.

Taking Dell as a case study, this paper focuses on and examines how to build business processes both inside and outside the corporation and how to manage it under the competitive environment in the IT era. We take up Dell because it provides us with an appropriate case how Business Process Management (BPM) across the organization utilizing IT effectively may lead to competitive advantage. First, this paper surveys Dell's business model. Then, it analyzes process management to support the model from the perspectives of "process management inside the corporation" and "process strategy outside the corporation."

2   Business Process Management in the IT Era

2.1   *Necessity and possibility of business process management in the IT era*

Because everything is on the move today, it is increasingly difficult to predict what will happen in the near future. Moreover, the development of information without the limit of time and global business transaction beyond the limit of space alter the corporate environment from various aspects. Because of such an environmental change, it is necessary for corporations to match the input of environmental changes with corporate output swiftly. In particular, because the traditional response focusing on functions easily brings about imbalance among functions and accumulation of information and materials due to walls between functions, there is a need for a swift response to the environmental changes from the process management perspective. In the information era, the ultimate source for competitive advantage is to compress time and distance of the supply chain between corporations and buyers or customers, as well as to provide products and services efficiently (Dell, 2000, p. 9). Such a movement essentially requires BPM. In the information era, the necessity and possibility of the BPM advance simultaneously.

2.2   *Features of the process*

This paper considers that the process has configurationality depending on the level of management subjects. This paper also regards the process as "something composed of various interdependent groups of activities toward creation of customer values that may be distinguished clearly between input and output of the process." The categorization and extent of the process, as well as its definition and the minimum measurement unit are different depending on the authors; this paper considers the process as the minimum measurement unit. This is because, in a competitive environment, full of opaqueness and changes, improvements of processes and evaluation by the process unit are effective for the whole optimization by flexibly connecting activities within the process. On the other hand, the management area of the process is not limited to a corporation, but it extends outside the corporation. This means that corporations are interdependent and it is necessary to reflect their own ideas by making an active commitment in other corporations' processes.

2.3 *Business process management*

Business Process Management means the "break up of traditional walls both within and outside corporations, the sharing of information and resources, the combining and connecting of transactions, the grasping of the flow as a process, and the management of it." This paper divides Business Process Management into two: a process management within the corporation across walls of functions and departments within the corporation and a process strategy outside the corporation beyond walls among corporations.

Process management within a corporation breaks up walls within a corporation and seeks optimization and integration of the "value chain" and "management chain," while the process strategy outside a corporation means to break up walls between corporations, build process networks, and seek choice, concentration, and cooperation among processes.

3 Business Model of Dell Inc.

3.1 *Direct model of Dell Inc.*

Dell Inc. primarily makes products that become the core of infrastructure computing[1] such as PCs, servers, and storage systems. Recently, Dell Inc. has entered in earnest into the "digital home solution" business such as small and light projectors, wide liquid crystal display TVs, and PDAs.[2] Dell's basic strategies are not to commit itself in fields where the burden for

---

[1] They are "products and services for building infrastructure that utilize IT and the Internet for business to a maximum extent."

[2] www1.jp.dell.com/content/topics/

research and development is heavy, to take advantage of widely used technologies developed by other corporations, to focus its managerial resources
onto the development of hardware and sales, to carry out customer support
to emphasize customers' satisfaction experiments, and to establish a competitive advantage based on its price competitive power.[3] Dell's business
model is called a "direct model" comprised of direct sales, make-to-order,
and customer support.

3.2   *Direct sales*

Direct sales consist of two factors: "direct relationship with customers"
and "products and services targeting specific customer segments" (Kraemer
et al., 2000, p. 8). By building a "direct relationship with customers"
without sales corporations, Dell eliminates margins for sales corporations in order to increase its cost competitiveness and makes it possible to respond to customers' detailed needs by utilizing information
acquired through the direct sales for product development and marketing
(Kraemer *et al.*, 2000, p. 8).

3.3   *Make-to-order*

Make-to-order makes it possible to respond to customers' detailed product
needs through product mass customization. In particular, because PC products consist of standardized parts, containing characteristics of standardization and modulization, mass customization becomes possible (Kraemer
et al., 2000, p. 6). Dell eliminates necessity of maintaining parts and completed products and avoids cost and risk that accompany inventory holdings
by connecting make-to-order with direct sales. In the PC industry where
technological invention rapidly banalizes parts and products, this method
is particularly useful. Moreover, because Dell orders parts after accepting
product orders, it can sell products with the latest technology at premier
prices. Because Dell starts production after receiving payment from customers, it is not necessary to have floating capital and it maintains capital
cost at a lower level.

---

[3] *Nihon Keizai Shinbun* (Newspaper), June 19, 2003 (in Japanese).

3.4 *Customer support*

Based on the customer data acquired at the time of order, Dell provides detailed customer support such as after sales service and additional orders. Adopting the direct sales method, Dell may acquire customers' purchase data directly. Consequently, it accumulates the data as a product and customer database and realizes accurate customer support through established support system for each customer segment.

Figure 1 depicts Dell's business model. In the case of Japan, after taking orders from customers directly over the telephone and the Internet and receiving confirmation of payment, the order data will be transferred to factories in Malaysia and China as well as to commodity distribution corporations within and outside Japan that are consigned for transport operation (Ui, 2002, p. 121). FedEx is responsible for the management of the whole transport business from two factories in Asia to Japan and the logistic center in Japan. Seibu Transportation (for corporation customers) and Sagawa Express (for individual customers) are responsible for transportation from two domestic distribution centers in the Kanto and Kansai regions to customers (Ui, 2002, pp. 151–158). Depending on each order, a domestic logistics center combines the product with peripheral goods such

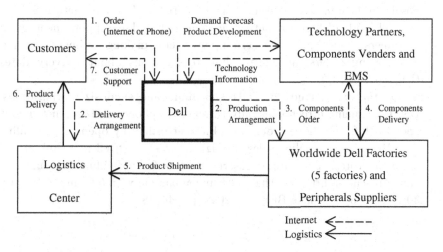

Source: Nikkei Business (2002), Weekly Toyo Keizai (2002), Nikkei Business (2001) and www.dell.com/html/jp/press/about/

Fig. 1   Dell's business model

as printers and monitors that are procured in Japan and delivered to a customer.[4]

Customer segments of Japan Dell (the official corporation name is "Dell Inc.") are composed of consumers (individual customer), big- and medium-size corporations, SOHO/medium- and small-size corporations, global corporations, government, and other public offices/educational institutions/medical institutions.[5] As for the big- and medium-size corporations that comprise most of the sales, Dell carries out consulting sales by sending its employees to the corporations.

After they sign a business deal, Dell offers services of product information and additional orders at the "premier page" provided for each customer at Dell's website. In the US, more than 27,000 "premier pages" exist that are customized for each customer. Through this page, it is possible to make automatic orders without paperwork, customize product specification, confirm order records and order status, and to take advantage of service tools provided for the customer's exclusive use (Saunders, 2002, p. 130). As for dealing with major customers, external and internal sales representatives make a joint "account team" to carry out business negotiations. The external sales representatives explain Dell's direct model, conduct research into customers' needs, and make system proposals in face-to-face meetings. The internal sales representatives provide all kinds of first contact services such as making appointments with customers, consultation concerning products, making estimates, taking and placing orders, and responding to questions about delivery dates (Ui, 2002, p. 132).

On the other hand, for SOHO/medium- and small-size corporations, Dell implements direct sales only through telephones and Internet, but it tries to shift telephone orders into Internet orders by opening an "online store" that makes online sales through Internet or "Dell real site" at PC discount stores. The rate of Internet orders for individual customers in Japan reaches a little less than 80% in comparison with 50% in the US and 30% in Europe (Nikkei Business, 2002, pp. 44–48).

---

[4] www.dell.com/html/jp/press/publicity/ccc.htm.

[5] As for the direct sales method for each customer segment, see the following: www.dell.com/html/jp/press/about/model/dsale.htm

4 Process Management Inside Corporations

Business Process Management deals with business process and it is necessary to maintain the most appropriate balance between the "management chain" to run the management cycle in the functional organization and the "value chain" of the business process. In an organization focusing on functions, the functions manage business operations and managers naturally consume resources per business transaction, and focus on management and strict adaptation of standard.

Consequently, because employees are eager to observe functional standard and save sources, their relations with suppliers and customers are not optimized. It is necessary to manage the process that breaks up walls among the functions in Figure 2 and optimizes the whole value chain by connecting A. The IT innovation makes the possibility greater. On the other hand, in BPM, it is necessary to realize harmony among processes and to fulfill the link B in Figure 2. In other words, it is necessary to establish a system to reorganize and integrate the whole process in an organizational, integral, and continual manner. To put it differently, it is important to consider how to compose a Plan-Do-Check-Action (PDCA) cycle of repetitive management chain that is continuous management system like that in Figure 2. After all, BPM is a management technique to eliminate stagnation among processes, to increase process productivity, and to improve corporate values.

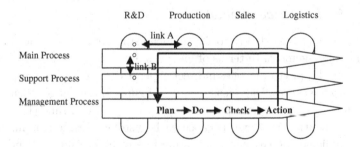

Fig. 2   Change from function-based management to process-based management

4.1 *Dell's management of value chain*

Dell adopts a make-to-order system. After taking orders and receiving payment from customers, Dell employs an SCM system, placing orders for parts necessary for requested specification, assembling parts, and delivering the product in as few as three to four days. In the assembly process, workers touch a PC around 18 times. It takes about five hours including inspection before delivery (Saunders, 2002, pp. 26, 42). At a Dell factory, two employees make a team that engages in production, packaging, and delivery. Dell has a system in which the team's productivity becomes an incentive (Dell, 2000, p. 187). Dell consigns production of print basal plates with electronic components to the EMS (Electronic Manufacturing Service) and makes the final assembly of all the products for itself. Dell does not consign the assembly operation to EMS because Dell believes that it is more efficient than EMS (Nikkei Business, 2002, pp. 44–48).

What makes this possible is "Six Sigma activity" called BPI (Business Process Improvement). The BPI is a program to review daily business transactions and to improve cross functional process for the purpose of advancing "customer's satisfaction" by a project team beyond departments and countries.[6] Concretely, BPI is an activity in which all the employees take up business problems, the quality control department summarizes the problems and decides appropriate themes, and a project team consisting of selective employees from each department carries out improvement (Ui, 2002, p. 179). In Dell, several projects always emerge across the organization and their performances reflect compensation assessment (Ui, 2002, p. 180).

4.2 *Performance evaluation*

Dell examines basic figures of its financial statements every month for corporate management. In terms of income statement, Dell considers margins, average sales price, and sales indirect expenses as the most appropriate performance measures. Dell measures these figures and manages them depending on customer segment, product, and country in real time (Dell, 1998, p. 81). As mentioned above, because each customer segment is managed as a self-sufficient department, Dell's method of managing cost and profit is similar to Mission Costing.

In order to measure cash flow from the balance sheet, Dell examines the average age of inventory, the accounts receivable, and the accounts payable (Saunders, 2002, p. 81). Because, in principle, Dell begins production only

---

[6]www.dell.com/html/jp/press/about/dellkk/injapan.htm

Fiscal-year Ended	Feb 3, 2006	Jan 28, 2005	Jan 30, 2004	Jan 31, 2003	Feb 1, 2002
Days of sales outstanding	29	27	27	28	29
Days of supply in inventory	4	4	3	3	4
Days in accounts payable	77	73	70	68	69
Cash conversion cycle	−44	−42	−40	−37	−36

Source:–Dell Fiscal 2006 in Review.

Fig. 3   Dell's cash conversion cycle, fiscal year from 2002 to 2006

after taking orders and confirming payment, collection of sales always precedes. In such a system, a cash circulation cycle is minus 44 days in the fiscal year of 2005 (Figure 3). In contrast, other competing corporations without the "direct model" cannot help carrying out sales on credit for the purpose of supporting distributing agents, their cash circulation cycles become substantial plus. Because Dell does not maintain parts inventory and has suppliers deliver them just before the assembly, the age of inventory is prominently shorter than other competing corporations. In fiscal year 2005, the average age of inventory was four. As Figure 3 shows, the short age of inventory also has an important positive effect on the cash circulation cycle. As mentioned above, the short age of inventory is especially effective in IT-related industries in which technology invention is remarkable and rapidly decreases parts prices. Suppose other competing corporations' age of inventory is 20. Once Intel releases a new type of chip, Dell may deliver a new product 16 days earlier than its competitive corporations.

Dell also reflects the achievement rates of the goal of customers' satisfaction to its employees' bonus that is calculated according to the following formula: the rate of sales achievement × the rate of profit achievement × the rate of customer satisfaction achievement. Dell has made all the employees become aware of the degree of customer satisfaction by reflecting it to bonuses for those who do not directly deal with customers in the sections of personnel, accounting, and information systems (Ui, 2002, pp. 178–179).

Moreover, Dell has a performance plan like MBO (Management By Objectives). Employees set a concrete annual goal that may be evaluated in figures. Twice a year, they have meetings with their direct bosses and senior members above the bosses in which their pay rise for the following year is decided by the degree of achievement of their set goals (Ui, 2002, pp. 187–188). Since the fiscal year 2004, Dell has introduced a new personnel system of examining the degree of employees' satisfaction and of reflecting the results to the managers' bonuses. Individual and team achievements and the degree of customer and employee satisfaction become important factors to decide the bonus (Nikkei Business, 2004, p. 12).

5 Business Process Strategy Outside Corporations

In today's competitive environment with increasing uncertainty and severity, it is necessary to make a strategic policy of maintaining and expanding competitive advantage while decreasing risk generated by environmental changes. In other words, it is necessary to invest limited corporate resources to identify and foster a process that may become a core competence, and to utilize resources outside the corporation when necessary for processes other than the core competence. This is because taking advantage of other corporations' assets rather than making or buying new assets necessary to respond to environmental changes may decrease economic risk and improve "corporate flexibility" that can respond to environmental changes at short notice.

However, in order to improve corporate flexibility, the basic assumption is to build an inter-corporate process network that smoothly connects processes across multiple corporations as well as information sharing through IT. In other words, it is necessary to have a business process strategy that responds to environmental changes around corporations, breaks up walls between corporations both at home and abroad, builds process networks, and carries out selection, concentration, and cooperation of processes. The business process strategy mobilizes process assets, increases operating leverage (the percentage change in operating income/the percentage change in sales volume), and improves corporate values. In the business process strategy, as Figure 4 shows, a corporation secures its competitive advantage by

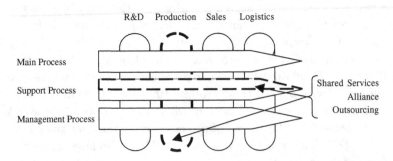

Fig. 4   Change from process management organization to process collaboration

a collaboration strategy of seeking processes other than the process that becomes a core competence from outside the corporation.

5.1   *Collaboration of Dell's business process*

Dell's process collaboration strategy is to strengthen collaboration by shifting vertical integration of the supply chain into a "virtual integration." In other words, it is a strategy that "outsourcing and collaboration take care of capital-intensive and labor-intensive services while Dell concentrates its sources on the most competitive field" (Saunders, 2002, p. 75). For example, Dell consigns a labor-intensive telephone marketing service to a third party such as companies in India. As for capital-intensive services, Dell establishes partnership relationship with suppliers. Dell concentrates its corporate resources on the solution of customers' needs (Saunders, 2002, pp. 75–76). On the other hand, in its relationship with suppliers, Dell simplifies the relationship and decreases the number of suppliers. Less than 40 suppliers provide approximately 90% of parts, which has great effect on cutting cost and increasing speed to provide products for the market (Dell, 2002, p. 274). Moreover, Dell makes "supplier report card" in order to evaluate suppliers' performance. Using this card, Dell examines to what extent each supplier satisfies a variety of demands and compares it with other suppliers that may provide similar products. By doing so, Dell may urge its partners to make improvements (Dell, 2000, p. 280).

Because the primary profit source for Dell is its sales to large corporations, Dell covers its weak points as hardware manufacturers such as fields of servers and storages in which corporate clients may request for certain software services by collaborating with major corporations in these fields. For example, in the storage field, Dell collaborates with EMC in the US. In Linux, Dell collaborates with the Redhat and Oracle in the US. Dell's collaboration strategy is that it has its own consulting section while it establishes strategic collaboration so that it can "commodify solutions" and "turn black boxes into white boxes" (Shukan Toyo Keizai, 2002, pp. 82–92). By doing this, Dell may customize its clients' needs and provide what they demand by providing a variety of service menu and price information depending on clients' individual needs and combining each of them as parts or module (Noguchi, 2001, p. 160).

Dell implements sales and production through information sharing with partners, the so-called "virtual integration." This integration regards its partners as Dell members, carries out business together, and shares information real time (Dell, 1998, pp. 73–84). Because Dell and its partners have common goals of "mutual profits," "mutual growth," and "building of continuous reliable relationships," they achieve effective performance as if they were one integrated corporation (Ui, 2002, p. 121).

Dell continuously acquires information from its clients, and let not only other sections in Dell but also from suppliers access immediately a variety of acquired client information. Moreover, Dell may access its suppliers' database directly. For example, as for basic parts such as circuit boards, Dell is directly linked to the suppliers' manufacturing database. If there is anything wrong with the parts, Dell may grasp the situation before the parts arrive at Dell's factory (Saunders, 2002, p. 66). Seeking information sharing, Dell establishes a law that "the accumulated amount of information is inversely proportional to the cost of inventory" (Saunders, 2002, pp. 58–60). In other words, if Dell may accurately grasp information about what clients demand, the smaller the inventory Dell should have in order to satisfy their needs. Dell considers it necessary to strengthen communication with suppliers in order to speed up the inventory turnover. For this purpose, Dell uses a website (Valuechain.dell.com) for the suppliers. They share any information about issues between Dell and its suppliers (Saunders, 2002, pp. 85–86).

In addition, in Dell's supply chain, based on the "virtual integration" shown in Figure 5, they can share information by adding chains. They reduce time and cost by rationalizing business operations along with their customers.

For example, as customers become sensitive to not only the price of PC itself but also to TCO (total cost of ownership)[7] including collateral costs,

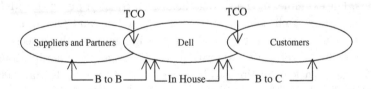

Fig. 5   Dell's virtual integration and supply chain management

---

[7]It is a total retention cost consisting of an inherent computer-related cost plus a cost for maintenance and operation.

Dell makes a proposal to reduce TCO by installing package software and customers' own software and providing service to attach tags, and shares merits of reducing the cost (Hioki and Yorulmaz, 1998, pp. 100–103). Dell provides its integration service concerning the TCO on its website: "custom factory integration" (Ui, 2002, pp. 21–23). Moreover, Dell's customer support plays a role of IT management department of a customer corporation. For example, a "user name" and a "password" are necessary to login on the "premier page," but by giving to each section power of setting the access level of the "premier page," related departments of the customer corporation may enter a decision of specifications, estimates, taking orders, and management of delivery date depending on different access levels. Consequently, the "premier page" may function as an integrating tool of diversified business operations of the customer corporation (Ui, 2002, pp. 138–139).

6 Conclusion

Today's IT innovation promotes the possibility and necessity of restructuring the business process. This paper discusses the restructuring of the business process in the IT era by dividing it into two. In other words, this paper discusses the integration and optimization of the "value chain" and the "management chain" from a perspective of "process management within the corporation" and how to implement process collaboration by establishing a business process network from a "process strategy outside the corporation."

On the other hand, this paper also states that Dell carries out its process management within the corporation by cross-functional activities (Six Sigma Activity) that emphasize the speed of decision-making and implements business process collaboration through virtual integration with its partners. As Dell's self-designation that "Dell is an Internet corporation that deals with the IT space" shows, Dell provides us a good case of telling the current trend of the Business Process Management.

References

DellComputer — It won alone in a shrinking market, *Nikkei Business*, June 10, 2002, pp. 44–48 (in Japanese).

Dell, M. (interviewed by Joan Magretta) (1998). The power of virtual integration: an interview with Dell Computer's Michael Dell, *Harvard Business Review*, March–April, pp. 73–84.

Dell, M. (2000). *Direct from Dell: Strategies that Revolutionized an Industry*, Harperbusiness (Translation in Japanese by Kokuryou, J.).

Dell's Homepage (www.dell.com/).

Economic and Social Research Institute, Cabinet Office, Government of Japan (2001). *Corporate Management Revolution by Information Technology* (in Japanese).

Get more than 50% employee satisfaction — U.S. Dell evaluates its managers by employee satisfaction, *Nikkei Business*, March 1, 2004, p. 12 (in Japanese).

Hioki, K. and Yorulmaz, T. (1998). Dell Computer — Three development stages and five key success factors, *Diamond Harvard Business*, June–July, pp. 100–103 (in Japanese).

Kraemer, K. L., Dedrick, J., and Yamashiro, S. (2000). Refining and extending the business model with information technology: Dell Computer Corporation, *The Information Society* 16, pp. 5–21.

Noguchi, H. (1998). *Extra Production Revolution-BTO*, Japan Management Association Management Center (in Japanese).

Quick Delivery of PC to striken 80 companies, *Nikkei Business*, October 22, 2001, pp. 130–134 (in Japanese).

Saunders, R. (2002). *Be Direct!: Business the Dell Way*, Capstone *Ltd.* (Translation in Japanese by Kim, T.).

Simons, R. (1995). *Levers of Control*, Harvard Business School Press.

Special issue: Dell Computer — its impetuous penetration in Japan, *Weekly Toyo Keizai*, August 31, 2002, pp. 82–92 (in Japanese).

Ui, H. (2002). *How Dell Computer Can Attract Its Customers?*, Diamond Inc. (in Japanese).

Business Process Reforms through Strategic Use of IT

Noriyuki Imai

Vice President, Toyota Financial Services Corporation

1   Introduction: Significance of Business Process Reforms in the Automotive Industry

Economic and social globalization progressed rapidly toward the end of the 20th century. Information technologies advanced substantially in the same period, such as Internet technology, which brought forth an epoch-making network-based society. At present, in the very early 21st century, corporations in the automotive industry are facing fierce competition worldwide for survival. To outpace the competition, it is essential for a business entity to achieve growth on a global basis. However, rushing solely for increased business size is not effective at all for healthy growth of the business entity. For a firm to be an excellent company sided by various stakeholders in the business entity, it is of vital importance for the business entity to achieve efficiency as well as growth. How is it possible to attain both growth and efficiency at the same time, and how can it be done to come out ahead of the severe global competition present these days? These are key issues faced by the most critical strategy for the automotive business in the early 21st century.

Since the mid-1990s, the Toyota group reviewed in this chapter has strategically made the most use of IT, and has actively promoted business process reforms for simultaneous achievement of both growth and efficiency. The result is the present enhanced corporate competitiveness and strong business structure of the group. This chapter outlines the developments of the group's achievement and presents desirable principles for future business process reforms.

2   Characteristic Elements of Business Process Reforms

Before describing the business process reforms carried out in the Toyota group, this chapter presents major common aspects and differences of business process reforms between the average Japanese company and the Toyota group, as suggested by the results of a survey on business process management carried out by the Japanese Association of Management Accounting.

Five principal common points were found: (1) growing globalization (localization) of production and sales principally in Asia, North America, and Europe; (2) the keenest competition in price; (3) cost competence and new-product development ability as aspects to be improved mainly for enhancement of overall competitiveness; (4) business operation speedup (efficiency gains) set as the most significant purpose of IT investment in the past five years and coming five years; and (5) advances in management and evaluation through global networking, considered as an influential factor for IT investment in business processes in the coming five years. The survey results reveal several facts observed in many Japanese industrial circles. Faced with fierce price competition, other companies are positively addressing business operation speedup (efficiency gains), which necessitates IT investment, for gaining improved cost competence in the future. They are also promoting global networking by way of IT investment, as well as globalization (localization) of production and sales. These situations similarly exist in the Toyota group.

In contrast, two major differences are present concerning business process reforms between the average Japanese company and the Toyota group: (1) Many Japanese companies are content with simple improvement or partial reforms of their business processes, while in most cases at the Toyota group, the reforms that are carried out are sweeping; and (2) business process management at many Japanese firms is carried out independently from function to function, while in the Toyota group, most projects aim to promote cross-department cooperation and activities.

3   Medium- to Long-Term Vision

The Toyota group follows what are known as its Guiding Principles, a set of universal management concepts that have been in place since the company's foundation. In line with the guiding principles, the group constantly envisions, and shares within the group, the ideal form it wants to achieve in the next 10 years. In this way, Toyota continuously promotes its robust and powerful management consistently within the group.

At present, the Toyota group has implemented Global Vision 2010, which identifies concrete images of global business and operation for the 2010s. The basic theme of the vision is "Innovation into the Future — A Passion to Create a Better Society." This vision describes four categories of innovation to be achieved: the Arrival of a Revitalized, Recycling-Based Society; the Coming Age of ITS and the Ubiquitous Network Society; the Promotion of Motorization on a Global Scale; and the Advent of a Mature Society. Also advocated in the vision is a paradigm change necessary for innovation to emerge. The paradigm change sets seven goals: technology development; product development; transnational management; group strategic management; new ways of working; creating a balanced global structure; and focusing on stakeholders and efficient use of capital (Figure 1).

Among the four innovation categories and seven paradigm-change goals, the global growth strategy "the Promotion of Motorization on a Global Scale" is particularly important in terms of corporate strategy. The Toyota group aims to ensure a stable global market share of about 15% in automobile sales in the 2010s as envisioned in Global Vision 2010. Business strategies being positively pursued to fulfill this aim include development of next-generation technologies such as hybrid power and fuel cells; development and launch of a number of new products under a multi-brand strategy; discovery and development of capable suppliers on a global basis; enhancement of production capacity in various regions of the world including North America, China, and emerging nations; and strengthening of sales networks in every region/country of the world.

In addition to pursuing these growth strategies, the Toyota group is also working energetically to improve the overall efficiency of its global automotive business and to reform business processes and innovate the corporate organization structure for additionally enhanced cost competence. In particular, business process reforms have been promoted strenuously over the medium term, making full, strategic use of IT. These reforms have expanded across all business functions of the entire Toyota group and have been pursued in close relation with IT investment, always keeping in mind standardization, efficiency gains, and cost reduction of the group's global business processes.

Four Future Innovation Categories (Expected Society for the First Half of the 21st Century and a New Corporate Image to Pursue)

I. Toward the Arrival of a Revitalized, Recycling-Based Society
Global movement occurs toward a revitalized society. There will be a growing demand to shift from an age of mass production and mass consumption/disposal to a recycling-based society through reduction, reuse, and recycling of resources. In this situation, Toyota will strive to become a leader and driving force by implementing the most advanced environmental technologies in global regeneration.

II. Toward the Coming Age of ITs and the Ubiquitous Network Society
Telecommunication technology and automobile IT technologies advance. Information services accessible while driving improve dramatically. Driving safety increases, being coordinated with the traffic infrastructure. Against this backdrop, Toyota is striving to become a leader in creating automobiles and an automobile-based society in which people can live in ease, safety, and comfort.

III. Toward the Promotion of Motorization on a Global Scale
Increasing motorization occurs in emerging markets, including China. People all over the world will benefit from the mobility the car enables. Toyota will promote the appeal of cars throughout the world and strengthen the Toyota brand image. It is envisioned that Toyota's efforts will bear the fruit of a global market share of about 15% in the very early 2010s.

IV. Toward the Advent of a Mature Society
Society will move toward greater respect for people from other nations and cultures. In international companies, people from different nations and ethnic groups will work together to achieve common goals. Toyota aims to be a truly global company that earns the respect and support of people all over the world.

Paradigm Change

To attain our vision, we must adopt a new corporate structure paradigm and improved business practices that will enable us to address challenging issues, such as advanced technology development in diverse areas, construction of a corporate organization structure outpacing global cost competition, global business management, product development precisely responding to market demands, efficient regional business operations, and building of market-oriented sales systems.

1. Technology/Product Development
(1) Technology development
(2) Product development

2. Management
(1) Transnational management
(2) Group strategic management
(3) New ways of working

3. Profit Structures
(1) Create a balanced global structure
(2) Focus on stakeholders and efficient use of capital

Fig. 1   Medium- to long-term vision at Toyota

4 Development of Business Process Reforms

Since the mid-1990s, the Toyota group has built a platform for promoting full-scale reforms of its business processes, as described below.

In the period from the mid- to late 1990s, each Toyota group company quickly provided itself with computerized infrastructure. They began making fully advanced use of personal computers, achieved revolutionary popularization of e-mail, and shifted to self-processing of various internal applications. Using the above-mentioned infrastructure in the early 2000s, Toyota group companies fully rebuilt major tools for global standardization and efficiency gains in their business processes.

In the technology development and production technology areas, Toyota established an innovative product development method made possible by a newly developed design system and has achieved a substantial (several tens of percent) lead-time reduction in the new model development. The Toyota group also developed a novel parts information system. This system is used for unified management of parts information throughout the world. In this system environment, parts information is accessible from every part of the globe all the year round on a 24-hour basis. The required working hours for the new model development have also been reduced significantly through radical revision of the design process.

In the area of parts procurement, the Toyota group has developed a new procurement system. This system is intended to standardize the parts procurement process on a global basis and unify and share information on quality, cost, and delivery dates. It serves as a platform for achieving optimal parts procurement on a global basis.

Completed in the area of supply chain is a series of standardized business processes covering vehicle order placement, vehicle production, parts procurement, and vehicle logistics. The Toyota group established these business processes simultaneously with the full-scale implementation of the global strategic vehicle project targeting emerging countries. The purpose of the standardized business processes is to dramatically increase mutual supply of vehicles and parts among all the regions and countries of the world. These processes have been introduced gradually concerning vehicle families produced outside Japan. In Japan, supply-chain processes were fully revised in order to build an organizational structure for substantial lead-time reduction, spanning from order placement by customers to delivery of vehicles to customers, and for prompt reply to customers regarding delivery dates and meeting deadlines.

In the area of service parts, Toyota has made uncompromising efforts to eliminate *muri, muda,* and *mura* (beyond capability, no value added, and unevenness) and rebuilt the basic system in the warehousing process of the Parts Center. The result is a marked reduction in service parts supply lead-time, and major efficiency gains in business processes.

Regarding sales, Toyota created a standard dealer system and installed it at virtually all dealers in Japan. This system aims to streamline and quicken business processes followed by auto dealers and to undertake early implementation of the headquarters' marketing measures at dealers.

In the quality assurance area, the quality-related information acquisition and analysis system was reconstructed to quickly detect and settle quality issues. In particular, the Toyota group has succeeded in reducing the lead-time required by the headquarters in Japan to collect quality-related information from overseas (it was a substantial, several tens of percent reduction).

In the management area, the Toyota group developed and introduced the Process KPI system to build a framework designed for information sharing, problem finding, and self-directing improvement/emergence within group-wide cross-department processes.

Furthermore, the group significantly improved the IT infrastructure and enhanced its processing capacity in parallel with these efforts aimed at business process reforms in order to accommodate increased data communication and processing volumes on a global basis. Thus, Toyota has pursued substantial improvements in capacity, quality, flexibility, and disaster management capability of the overall system.

All business functions of the entire Toyota group, as explained above, have made full, strategic use of IT to strenuously provide basic tools for promoting standardization and efficiency gains in the group's business processes on a global scale.

5   Present Situation of Business Process Reforms

Now, as of the mid-2000s, the Toyota group is sharing tools that make strategic use of IT group-wide on a global scale, as explained in the preceding section. The group's entire business processes extend like capillaries or peripheral nerves throughout the world. Toyota takes the following measures to improve the productivity of its group-wide business processes.

The newly developed design system is being increasingly coordinated with other related systems and its scope of application is gradually expanding to cover product development processes of all vehicle families. Moreover, the new design system is contributing to additional, substantial lead-time and cost reductions in the development of new models.

Use of the new procurement system is spreading to many countries throughout the world and is making an important contribution to the global standardization of the parts procurement process and to the optimal procurement of parts on a global scale.

By carrying out mutual supply of vehicles and parts in the global strategic vehicle project targeting emerging countries, the standardized supply chain system is gaining a foothold and is spreading to advanced and other countries.

Regarding the standard dealer system, the Toyota group has installed it throughout the world, notably in China and other Asian countries, and is making the most use of it for streamlining and quickening business processes within dealers in every region or country.

Having been applied throughout the world, the quality-related information acquisition and analysis system has increasingly demonstrated its effectiveness in early detection and resolution of quality issues.

For the present in the mid-2000s, as explained above, the Toyota group is transferring newly developed basic systems and business processes throughout the group's global auto business networks. Tenacious efforts have been constantly made by the group to make the most use of these basic systems and business processes and allow them to take root.

6   Future Directions of Business Process Reforms

The Toyota group intends to go further toward the 2010s in its business process reforms, as stated below. The reforms aim to enlarge the group's global business size (to a stable share of about 15% of the global auto sales market). The increased market share is expected to augment the volume of business activities in technology development, product development, parts procurement, global production, and global sales. Through these business process reforms, Toyota will meet the challenge of handling increased work volume with limited resources, especially limited human resources.

The technology development and production technology areas have two goals. One is to carry out product development within an equally short time in whatever region of the world and the other is to build advanced, synchronous processes of product development among distant locations.

In the area of parts procurement, Toyota aims to attain an increased level of optimal procurement even involving sub-suppliers on a global scale.

In the area of supply chain, the group intends to additionally reduce the order cycle time on a global basis.

Two objectives are set with regard to sales. One is to carry out additional standardization of business processes on a regional basis, and the other is to attain an increased level of CRM by utilizing customer data.

In the quality assurance area, increased quality satisfaction is pursued, making strategic use of IT for sophisticated communications with customers.

In the management area, a management cockpit will be constructed in a form that assembles KPI information in both financial and nonfinancial aspects. The goal is to improve risk management by using feed-forward indicators for visualizing business conditions.

Furthermore, the Toyota group will make full, strategic use of IT in all business functions of the entire group. These business process reforms will be radically carried out in close relation with IT investment. By doing so, Toyota aims to standardize, increase the efficiency in, and reduce the cost of the group's global business processes, and will strive to achieve growth and efficiency simultaneously.

7 Summary: Desirable Principles of Business Process Reforms

Automotive companies including the Toyota group are faced with sharp competition because of globalization. This trend is expected to be increasingly intensive in the future. To survive under such a situation in the auto industry, an automotive company must enhance its core competence, on the one hand, and achieve steady growth in the global market, on the other.

An extremely important requirement for achieving global growth is standardizing and ensuring efficiency gains in global business processes by way of reforms. Business processes should first be standardized and streamlined on the company's home ground (Japan, in the case of the Toyota group) of global business operations and then transferred to other countries on a global scale. This could be a model method for promoting global standardization and efficiency gains.

To promote business process reforms as described above, the four principles shown below are highly significant.

(1) on-site cross-department cooperation in line with business processes;
(2) understanding of and emphasis on relations and interactions within each business process and among business processes;
(3) building company-wide awareness regarding concepts such as *genchi genbutsu* (first-hand experience), *nitsume* (thorough discussions), *suri-awase* (coordination/integration), *fukabori* (thorough investigation), *kaizen* (improvement), and *sohatsu* (emergence); and
(4) Pursuit of total optimization based on systematic thinking.

The most important thing in the on-site cross-department cooperation in (1) is to retain all the improvements and reforms from segmented departmental optimization resulting from making much of inter-department barriers. (Note that such optimization is commonly seen in the business process reform scene.) In many cases, the core business processes of a company penetrate its corporate structure, spreading across many departments and functions, although some differences are present among different industry categories. Simply improving or innovating a segment of such a business process would produce only limited effects. What is worse, the improvement or innovation could cause a mismatch or friction between the target segment and other parts of business processes. Improvement or innovation efforts will be successful in carrying out a significant, large-scale activity only when cooperation exists across the entire organization (divisions and departments) involved in a business process and among all the on-site members working on the business process. Setting up a limited-time project team apart from the ordinary form of the existing organization is one possible measure for ensuring cross-department cooperation. The Toyota group has an established corporate culture or climate that allows on-site work to be carried out through cross-department cooperation with Toyota Production System (TPS) used as fundamental thinking. Consequently, once staff members share awareness of the need for, or objective of, a business process reform, relevant activities progress autonomously. However, even the Toyota group, when undertaking a large-scale business process reform, may form a time-limited team (which could be a virtual team) under the title of, for example, xxx Project or xxx Working Group. Organizing a team in this way is intended to strengthen the drive to carry out the business process reform through cross-department cooperation.

The need for understanding of and emphasis on relations and interactions in (2) is necessary for various reasons. Corporate business processes are never linear or static. Indeed, they interact constantly and repeatedly with one another, intertwining in various complex relations. Furthermore, the complex relations and interactions constantly change over time (with progress in business). Therefore, when reviewing and promoting standardization and efficiency gains in a business process, it is vitally important to have a thorough understanding of and give full consideration to the actual relations and interactions that are present.

Building company-wide awareness regarding concepts such as *genchi genbutsu*, *nitsume*, *suriawase*, *fukabori*, *kaizen*, and *sohatsu* in (3) deserves an explanation. As stated above, actual corporate business processes are highly complex. Standardization or efficiency gains in business processes should be achieved by the on-site staff most familiar with the actual state of the target business processes. When proceeding with the task, it is extremely important for them to ascertain this complexity on a first-hand basis and have thorough discussions and coordination among themselves. Furthermore, the staff should not immediately consider that the existing business process is basically right when standardizing (or systematizing) it. Rather, they should visualize the entire process and thoroughly identify *muri*, *muda*, and *mura* in the process from scratch. The factors involved in *muri*, *muda*, and *mura* should be fully investigated. It is essential to carry out standardization once effective and fundamental improvements have been achieved and measures have been taken for full efficiency gains after the aforementioned investigation. The extent and depth that staff members working on a business process site can perform regarding concepts like *genchi genbutsu*, *nitsume*, *suriawase*, *fukabori*, and *kaizen* depends on the awareness of each member. Accordingly, to achieve business reforms, it is strongly important that the executives and the managers exercise leadership to build relevant awareness in the staff members undertaking business process reforms.

Business process reforms promoted according to principles (1)–(3) must, as a result, produce total optimization of the company as indicated in (4). From another perspective, principles (1)–(3) must be implemented by pursuing total optimization based on systematic thinking.

Success in business process reforms depends largely on the degree to which the desirable principles in business process reforms are formed and take root as a climate in the management structure of a company or a corporate group.

References

Imai, N. (2004). Management system by process KPI to support emerging and evolving organization, *Meijo Ronso* 5(1), pp. 53–63 (in Japanese).

Johnson, H. T. and Bröms, A. (2000), *Profit Beyond Measure — Extraordinary Results through Attention to Work and People*, The Free Press.

Kawada, M. (2003). *The Toyota System and Management Accounting*, Chuo Keizaisha (in Japanese).

Kimura, S. (2003). *Patterns of Relations and Management Accounting*, Zeimukeiri Kyokai (in Japanese).

How to Measure the Effect of Investments in Various IT Tools on Each Department

Yoshiyuki Nagasaka

Professor, Faculty of Business Administration
Konan University

1 Introduction

The optimum design and continuous improvement of a business model for dominant competitions are very important for increasing the value of an enterprise. Advances in IT (Information Technology) have encouraged the creation of new business models where patents protect the rights of the inventors of such business models. However, the effectiveness of each business model cannot be determined by the amount of investment alone.

It is necessary to know a certain relation between an IT investment and the value of a business model. For example, business models and IT investments, the degrees of maturity of IT and a business model, the value of the intellectual assets of a business model patent (the cost for the patent and the effect), and the correlation between a competitive environment and corporate performance should be investigated.

Thus, to evaluate how an IT investment fits the design of each business model, it is necessary to estimate how each IT investment could affect each one. When conducting such measurements, it should be noted that a specific IT tool will affect multiple processes and may result in cost reduction or added value in various departments simultaneously.

This paper proposes a new measurement method that applies an input/output model to evaluate the effects of a specific IT investment on each department separately, and also the synergy effect among various departments.

2   IT and Business Models

Generally, a business model is said to be a profit engine within the business (Magretta, 2002). Both core processes and management processes are important elements for supporting a business model. IT innovations are emphasized over other environmental changes since IT influences all business processes of the business model, either directly or indirectly. Consequently, it is vital to clarify the relationship between IT and business processes (Ishikawa, 2001).

On the other hand, a business model patent may attract attention as a means to guarantee a business model. A patent is given for the technical idea that uses natural law. Furthermore, invention, novelty, and inventive steps should be involved in a patent. Historically, the target of a patent has been limited to tangible items; however, it is now possible to extend patents to software and business models. Although not all business models can be patented, some — including unique IT systems — can be protected by patents. Figure 1 shows a schematic drawing of the category representing business models.

The sale arrangement for an airline ticket is a typical example in the US of a patented business model. A customer registers the point of a departure place, a destination, and a desired price with the broker. Then, the airline that wishes to sell vacancies even at a discounted price shows the selling price based on the customer's information, and registers it with the broker's computer. The seller side subsequently accepts the request of the buyer side through Internet. This is a new business technique called a "reverse auction." This system's novelty is that it is Internet-based.

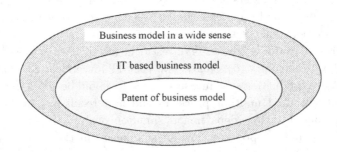

Fig. 1   Category of business models

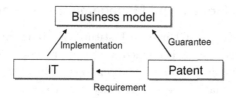

Fig. 2   Relations between a business model, IT, and a patent

Figure 2 shows mutual relations between a business model, IT, and a patent. Attempting to protect a business model by patenting it, it is necessary to begin the patent acquisition process in the initial stages of constructing the business model in question. In other words, it is important to clarify the requirements and specifications of IT in order to construct the business model.

This creates a strong link between the business model and its related IT. Figure 3 summarizes the objectives of IT investment in Japanese companies based on a company survey conducted in 2003 (Nagasaka *et al.*, 2006). The results show that the objectives for the next five years are different from the previous ones. This suggests that the trend of business models is changing.

Objective of IT investment	Last 5 years	Next 5 years
Reduction of inventory cost	51 (9.6%)	57 (10.5%)
Reduction of procurement cost	27 (5.1%)	68 (12.5%)
Reduction of personnel cost	61 (11.5%)	38 (7.0%)
Speed-up of operation	156 (29.4%)	106 (19.5%)
Improvement of marketing and sales force	81 (15.3%)	78 (14.3%)
Improvement of development capability of new product or service	30 (5.6%)	21 (3.9%)
Strengthening of relationships or incrimination of business partners	20 (3.8%)	23 (4.2%)
Improvement of customer satisfaction	39 (7.3%)	90 (16.5%)
New entry into different business areas	3 (0.6%)	10 (1.8%)
Organizational reformation	58 (10.9%)	48 (8.8%)
Others	5 (0.9%)	5 (0.9%)

Fig. 3   Objectives of IT investment in Japanese companies (Nagasaka *et al.*, 2006)

3 Business Models and Management Accounting

According to CIMA (Chartered Institute of Management Accountants), management accounting is defined as: "The process of identification, measurement, accumulation, analysis, preparation, interpretation and communication of information used by management to plan, evaluate and control within an entity and to assure appropriate use of and accountability for its resources. Management accounting also comprises the preparation of financial reports for non-management groups such as shareholders, creditors, regulatory agencies and tax authorities." For the framework of a management accounting system, the processes of business management are considered based on developing strategy, management control and operational control. (Anthony and Govindarajan, 1998). Management accounting is also important for designing and operating a business model.

At the stage of designing a business model (devising a strategy for a business model patent), it is necessary to evaluate its competitive superiority, its effect on the IT budget, investment planning, profit planning, and investment planning in regard to patents. Then, at the stage of implementing the business model, the IT maturity index and the degree to which instrumentation for a business model has been achieved should be as high as possible. Furthermore, at the stage of improving the business model, cost management is important. It is important to pay attention to patent maintenance costs, IT costs, and management expenses. Cost management involves all of the related business processes.

The structure of business processes differs depending on the characteristics of the business model in question. For example, each IT tool may be related to multiple processes and be effective for reducing costs and creating value. It is necessary to quantitatively estimate how each IT tool affects a business process, and a careful estimation makes it possible to evaluate the consistency of the IT investment for the structure of a business model. For example, regarding procurement processes, transaction and quality costs are problems in addition to parts and materials costs. Suppose that some IT tools are installed and transaction costs decrease drastically. However, it does not make sense if quality costs rise due to the frequent occurrence of quality problems. There may arise a case where some processes can reduce costs which others increase costs adversely by adopting a new IT tool. We must evaluate those interactions.

According to a research on 2,800 companies in Japan by Gartner, Inc, in August 2002, the rate of enterprises that employed quantitative techniques to measure the IT cost effect was only 4.2%. Furthermore, the rate of enterprises that require a method to measure the effect of IT-induced costs but have not yet reached such a development step for this is 55% (Kobayashi, 2003).

Matsushima proposed a new framework after having pointed out many problems in the economic efficiency assessment of the IT investment pair effect (Matsushima, 1999).

There have already been several investment valuation methods suggested for IT. One is a method of IT portfolio management that deals with the stock market. This method is based on investment forecasting, and the IT property is managed by calculating risk, yield, and profit (META group, 2005). META Group research indicates that chief information officers who embrace IT portfolio management (PfM) have exemplary records of continuous IT efficiency improvement, with some enterprises able to reduce costs by up to 30% while improving the effectiveness through enterprise-wide asset deployment and management. Economic Value Source (EVS) is a method to determine the value of IT from four viewpoints: sales growth, productivity gains, shortening of the cycle time, and risk reduction (META group, 2005). In the same way, in October 2003, Nihon Unisys Ltd. developed the IM-FIT (Investment Management Framework for IT) model as a method for evaluating the IT investment effect using an IT portfolio.

In addition, recognizing that a company's department is one of its value-creation sectors, a method to grasp sales by an IT department using EVA (Economic Value Added) has been proposed. In this case, an IT department is considered the same as a beneficiary paying service for an outside company (Stern Stewart & Co., 2006).

Hubbard (2006) developed AIE (Applied Information Economics) as a practical application of scientific and mathematical methods for the IT investment process (Hubbard research, 2006). In this method, intangible assets elements such as the degree of customer satisfaction and strategic alliances are regarded as measurement units. Mathematics studies, portfolio theory, and statistics are applied to calculate the value of information.

On the other hand, JMA (Japan Management Association) suggested a model for management change procedures to calculate reasonable IT investment scales from the perspective of the investment finance condition of a scheme, its effect, and the forecasting model (Sasaki and Omori, 2002). This model consists of the following three sub-models: (1) A distinction model to judge the condition of a scheme in regard to management or performance of IT investment; (2) a guide table for selecting profit targets due to IT investment and an individual expectation category; and (3) a forecasting model that roughly estimates the average level of investment on the basis of an IT investment expectation-effect category.

However, more discussion is required that focuses on the design of a business model (a structure) and its connection to IT investment. In particular, there is a need to develop an evaluation method for the interaction effect between multiple business processes.

4   A Method to Evaluate the Effect of Investments in Various IT Tools in Each Department

As mentioned already, it is necessary to estimate quantitatively which IT tool affects each business process in order to evaluate the design of a business model. One IT tool is related to multiple processes, and we recognize that it is sometimes effective in reducing costs and creating new value by an unpredictable process. Thus, this paper proposes a method to evaluate the mutual effect of multiple processes by applying input–output (I/O) analysis.

Input–output analysis is sometimes expressed as inter-industry analysis. Inter-industry means that more than one industry is affected. In I/O or inter-industry analysis, there is a one-to-one correspondence between processes and products. Industrial manufacturing each day is affected by recent demands by consumers and this somewhat affects the wages and salaries of employees working in each industry. Economic activity is not limited to individual enterprises, but relates to between-industries activity or between industry and the household economy. The result of such economic transactions in one year is represented in an input–output table, the Inter-industry Relations Table.

Similarly, an IT tool may affect more than one process (or department), and there may be more than one process (or department) that produces follow-on effects. Figure 4 shows a proposed IT cost–effect evaluation table, which considers the mutual interaction.

In Figure 4, department i makes investment c_i for an IT tool, then not only itself but also another department, j, can be affected by the IT tool. This effect is shown as x_{ij} in Figure 4. In addition, other effects may be created in external transactions such as B to B (business-to-business) and B to C (business-to-customer). This is shown as e_i. Furthermore, $X(= \Sigma x_{ij} + e_i)$ is the total effect created by the investment i.

Department	Effect (internal)				Effect (external)	Total effect	Investment
	1	2 ---------- j ----------		n			
1	x_{11}	x_{12} -----------------------		x_{1n}	e_1	$\Sigma x_{1j}+e_1$	I_1
2	x_{21}	x_{22} -----------------------		x_{2n}	e_2	$\Sigma x_{2j}+e_2$	I_2
i			x_{ij}		e_i	$\Sigma x_{ij}+e_i$	I_i
n	x_{n1}	x_{n2} -----------------------		x_{nn}	e_n	$\Sigma x_{nj}+e_6$	I_n
Output	Σx_{i1}	Σx_{i2} ---------- Σx_{ij} -------		Σx_{in}			
Cost	c_1	c_2 ---------- c_i -------		c_n			
Output - Cost	$\Sigma x_{i1}-c_1$	$\Sigma x_{i2}-c_2$ ------- $\Sigma x_{ij}-c_i$ -----		$\Sigma x_{in}-c_n$			

Fig. 4   IT cost–effect evaluation table

On the other hand, department j can be affected by utilizing several IT tools in which not only department j, but also other departments, invest. It is represented as Σx_{ij} in the columns of Figure 4.

IT investments are considered as input and their effects are output. Thus, this table can be considered as a type of I/O table. The profit in each department can be found using p_i $(= \Sigma x_{ij} - c_i)$ in the columns of Figure 4.

Conventionally, each department makes a plan to install a specific IT tool. The cost allocation for the tool is simple: it is the amount of invested money, namely, I_i is c_i in Figure 4 for conventional cases. However, the mutual effects, including the effect of the transaction processes between companies, are also important today in practice. The IT costs should be allocated depending on their actual effects. The effects of the transaction processes between companies may be the same for all departments.

Therefore, Figure 4 can be expressed as follows:

$$X_i - \sum_{j=1}^{n} a_{ij} X_j = e_i \quad (i = 1, \ldots, n), \tag{1}$$

where

X_i: a total effect created by the investment I_i $(=\Sigma x_{ij} + e_i)$;
a_{ij}: an input coefficient $(=x_{ij}/X_i)$;
e_i: other effects created at external transactions due to investment I_i.

Thus, the relation between internal and external effects is expressed as a matrix as follows:

$$X - aX = e \tag{2}$$

$$[E - a]X = e \tag{3}$$

X: n-dimensional column vector of which the element is X_i;
a: n-dimensional square matrix of which the element is a_{ij};
e: n-dimensional column vector of which the element is e_i;
E: unit matrix.

An input coefficient matrix a shows the characteristics of the entire IT investment. The synergy effect among various departments generated by the IT investments can then be analyzed and the tracing of pervasive effects becomes possible. In addition, a standard value of the input coefficient matrix may be found in accordance with the characteristics of the IT tool in question. Furthermore, it is possible to evaluate the synergy effects.

Let us suppose the case of an investment of EDI (Electronic data interchange) in a manufacturing company. The procurement department may draw up a draft of the investment, outlining the expected improvements to transaction processes in the procurement department itself. Moreover, the design department, the pre-production department and the accounting department may also estimate some effects by using the same EDI system. If the actual b_{ij} value is not good enough in comparison to the expected one, managers should clarify why and devise a solution.

Figure 5 shows an example of the IT cost–effect table. In this example, for a manufacturing company, several IT tools such as 3D-CAD (three-dimensional computer aided designing), PDM (product data management), EDI, APS (advanced production planning system), CAM (computer aided manufacturing), CAT (computer aided testing), EOS (electronic ordering system), and ERP (enterprise resource planning) are installed following the proposals of the design, procurement, manufacturing, sales, and accounting departments.

The first row of Figure 5 shows that the design department installs a 3D-CAD and a PDM system, then itself generates an effect of ¥400,000

| Department | IT tool | Effect (internal) | | | | | | Effect (external) | | Total | IT |
		Design	Procurement	Manufacturing	Sales	Accounting	Sub-total	BtoB	BtoC		investment
Design	3D-CAD	250	80	100	0	0	430	120	0	550	300
	PDM	150	40	100	0	0	290	80	0	370	250
Procurement	EDI	50	100	50	20	30	250	250	50	550	200
	APS	80	30	150	30	0	290	130	20	440	275
Manufacturing	CAM	80	0	150	0	0	230	20	0	250	250
	CAT	40	20	100	20	0	180	30	0	210	125
Sales	EOS	50	50	50	300	20	470	50	350	870	200
Accounting	ERP	80	100	100	0	400	680	50	0	730	600
Sub-total		780	420	800	370	450	2,820	730	420	3,970	2,200
IT cost		550	200	650	200	600	2,200				
Sub-total − IT cost		230	220	150	170	-150	620				

Fig. 5 Example of IT cost–effect evaluation table (¥1,000/month)

per month. In addition, the 3D-CAD and PDM systems generate an extra ¥120,000 per month in the procurement department, ¥200,000 per month at the manufacturing department, and ¥200,000 per month from B to B transaction processes. Clearly, the pervasive effects are not small.

The total positive effect generated by the 3D-CAD tool is regarded as ¥550,000 per month compared with the cost of ¥300,000 per month. The rows demonstrate the effect and cost generated by each IT tool. Figure 6 shows which IT tool is effective by visualizing the rows of Figure 5. Such a graph is useful for understanding internal and external effects with respect to investments.

On the other hand, the design department can generate an extra ¥50,000 per month using EDI installed by the procurement department, ¥200,000 due to APS, CAM, and CAT installed by the manufacturing department, ¥50,000 due to EOS installed by the sales department, and ¥80,000 owing thanks to ERP installed by the accounting department. The total positive effect generated by the design department is considered to be ¥780,000 per month compared with the cost of ¥550,000 per month if the allocated IT cost is equal to the costs of IT tools installed by the design department itself. This can be seen in the first column. Figure 7 shows which department produces more output by visualizing the columns of Figure 5. Such a graph is useful for recognizing that department's abilities.

The mutual effects among the departments are summarized in Figures 8 and 9, based on Figure 5. An input coefficient matrix is calculated from

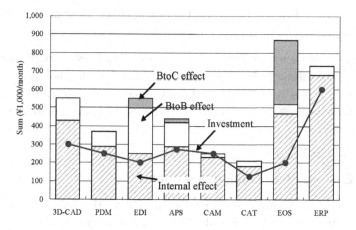

Fig. 6   Graph of the cost and the effect of each IT tool

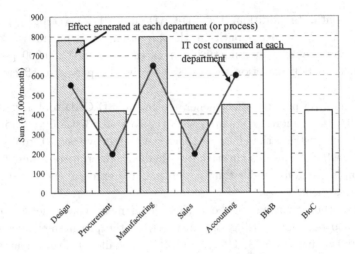

Fig. 7   Graph of the cost and the effect in each department

Department	Effect (internal)						Effect (external)	Total
	Design	Procurement	Manufacturing	Sales	Accounting	Sub-total		
Design	400	120	200	0	0	720	200	920
Procurement	50	100	50	20	30	250	300	550
Manufacturing	200	50	400	50	0	700	200	900
Sales	50	50	50	300	20	470	400	870
Accounting	80	100	100	0	400	680	50	730
Sub-total	780	420	800	370	450	2,820	1,150	3,970
Added value	140	130	100	500	280	1,150		
Total	920	550	900	870	730	3,970		

Fig. 8   Mutual effect among multiple departments

Figure 8 as shown in Figure 10: the design and accounting departments contribute relatively large outputs. In addition, EOS and 3D-CAD generate strong positive effects in external processes such as B to B and B to C transactions. Synergy effects can thus be analyzed quantitatively using these figures.

5   Evaluation of Business Model

We need the two measures, such as the IT maturity level and the business excellence level, to finally evaluate a business model. A schematic drawing of the evaluation is shown in Figure 11.

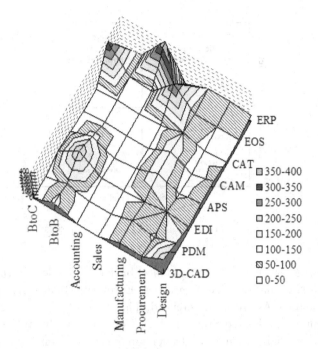

Fig. 9   Contour line presentation of Figure 8

	Design	Procurement	Manufacturing	Sales	Accounting
Design	0.4348	0.2182	0.2222	0.0000	0.0000
Procurement	0.0543	0.1818	0.0556	0.0230	0.0411
Manufacturing	0.2174	0.0909	0.4444	0.0575	0.0000
Sales	0.0543	0.0909	0.0556	0.3448	0.0274
Accounting	0.0870	0.1818	0.1111	0.0000	0.5479

Fig. 10   Input coefficient obtained in Figure 8

COBIT is an IT governance framework developed by ISACA (Information Systems Audit and Control Association, 2006) and a supporting toolset that allows managers to bridge the gap between control requirements, technical issues, and business risks. COBIT enables clear policy development and good practice for IT control throughout organizations. It is useful for evaluating the IT maturity level as follows: Level 5: Optimized; Level 4: Managed; Level 3: Defined; Level 2: Repeatable; Level 1: Initial; Level 0: Non-existent.

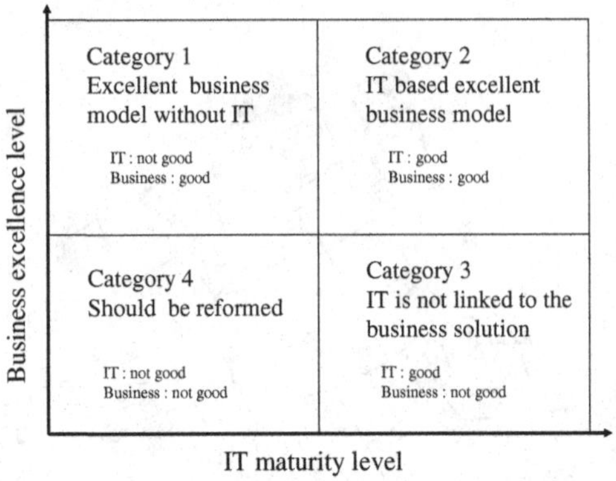

Category 1 Excellent business model without IT IT : not good Business : good	Category 2 IT based excellent business model IT : good Business : good
Category 4 Should be reformed IT : not good Business : not good	Category 3 IT is not linked to the business solution IT : good Business : not good

(vertical axis: Business excellence level; horizontal axis: IT maturity level)

Fig. 11   Evaluation of business models

On the other hand, to evaluate business excellence, the Malcolm Baldrige National Quality Award, the European Quality Award, and the Japan Quality Award are referenced. The Baldrige Award is given by the President of the United States to businesses that apply and are judged to be outstanding in seven areas: leadership; strategic planning; customer and market focus; measurement, analysis, and knowledge management; human resource focus; process management; and results.

The IT maturity level and business excellence level are both important. Namely, IT investments should be successfully linked to multiple business processes, with the business model assessed as in Figure 11. However, to improve the business model, it is important to analyze the relation between IT investments and the effects of multiple processes.

6   Conclusion and Summary

To evaluate how an IT investment fits the design of each business model, it is necessary to estimate how each IT investment could affect each one. While conducting such measurements, it should be noted that a specific IT tool will affect multiple processes and may result in cost reductions or added-value in various departments simultaneously.

This paper proposed a new measurement method that applies an input/output model, and evaluated the effects of a specific IT investment on each department separately as well as the synergy effect among various departments. Thus, since IT is generally related a lot to business models, it is important to not only assess the final structure and effects of a business model but also the relation between IT investments and business models.

References

Anthony, R. N. and Govindarajan, V. (1998). *Management Control Systems*, 9th ed., Irwin/McGraw Hill.

Hubbardresearch (2006) (http://www.hubbardresearch.com/).

Information Systems Audit and Control Association (2006). (http://www.isaca. org/).

Ishikawa, H. (2001). Effect and limitation of business model, *Office Automation*, 22(1), pp. 45–51 (in Japanese).

Kobayashi, H. (2003). Summary about measurement of IT investment effect, *@IT*, May, ITmedia Inc. (in Japanese).

Magretta, J. (2002). The proper definition of business model, *DIAMOND Harvard Business Review*, August, pp. 123–132 (in Japanese).

Matsushima, K. (1999). *Strategic IT Investment Management*, Hakutou Co., October (in Japanese).

MetaGroup (2005). (http://www.itworldcanada.com/Pages/Docbase/MetaGroup. asp,30,August).

Nagasaka, Y. and Sakate, K. (2005). Investigation of process management in Japanese companies, Accounting, Chuokeizai Co, 57(5), pp. 33–41 (in Japanese).

Nagasaka, Y., Sakate, K., and Kimura, A. (2006). IT and process innovation in Japanese enterprise, *Value-Based Management of the Rising Sun*, edited by Monden, Y. *et al.*, Chapter 30.

Sasaki, T. and Ohmori, T. (2002). Investigation about IT investment effect and evaluation, *JMA Management Review*, May, pp. 42–47 (in Japanese).

Stern Stewart & Co. (2006) (http://www.sternstewart.com).

Index

rolling budgeting, 86
royalties, 203

section system, 41
segment information, 29
sequential managerial
  decision-making process, 108
seven types of shared service centers,
  194
shadow price, 108
Shapley value, 161, 162, 167, 168
shared service subsidiary, 196, 198
shared services, 193, 194
shareholder's equity, 31
short-term incentives, 63
short-term performance, 62
similar scale of business, 14
SSC (shared service center), 193
stakeholders' evaluation, 114
standardization, 251, 253–256, 258
stock subscription right, 31
stock swap, 4
stock transfer, 4
stock transfer income, 17
strategic expenditures, 27
Sumitomo Electric Industries, 140
sunk costs, 107
supply and demand relationship of
  "resources", 57
supply chain management (SCM),
  149
survey, 263
surviving company, 28
Suzuki, 168
system architecture, 123
systematic thinking, 257, 258

Tanaka, 86
target costing, 117–121
target worker satisfaction, 219, 221,
  222, 228, 232
tax-reduction, 94
taxation postponement, 13
team merchandising, 211
Theory of Constraints (TOC), 110,
  150

three targets in TOC, 152
throughput, 151
throughput accounting, 150, 186
time of the improvement, 135
TOB (take over bids, tender offer), 31
top management's concern and
  involvement, 222, 224–232
total cost of ownership (TCO), 153,
  246
total optimization, 257, 258
Toyota Production System (TPS), 81,
  257
TP management, 154
traditional budgetary control system,
  77
transaction under common
  governance, 10, 11
transfer price, 90, 110
transfer pricing, 49
treasury stocks, 30
two-part structure of management
  control, 66, 70

uniting of interests, 5–7
US accounting standard, 28
useful life of lease appliance, 25

valuation of goodwill, 8
valuation of the business, 57
value chain, 241
Value Creation, 21, 42
value engineering, 120
value proposal, 114
value-based management, 103
values of the transferred asset, 52
variable cost, 131
virtual integration, 245

weighted average cost of capital, 23
Whinston, 167
working times, 200

Yokota (1998), 85

About the Volume Editors

Yasuhiro Monden
Professor and Dean of Faculty of Business Administration, Mejiro University, Tokyo, Japan
Professor-Emeritus of Tsukuba University, Tsukuba-shi, Japan
President, Monden Institute of Management (http://mondeninst.hp.infoseek.co.jp/)
Majoring in Operations Management, Managerial Accounting, and Corporate Finance
BA from Kwansei Gakuin University, MBA from Kobe University, Ph.D. from Tsukuba University

Main Publications
Toyota Production System, 1st edition, Industrial Engineering and Management Press 1983 (awarded Nikkei Prize in 1984).
Toyota Production System, 3rd edition, Industrial Engineering and Management Press 1998.
Japanese Management Accounting, Productivity Press 1989.
Cost Reduction System: Target Costing and Kaizen Costing, Productivity Press 1996.
Japanese Cost Management, Imperial College Press 2000.

Masanobu Kosuga
Professor, School of Business Administration, Kwansei Gakuin University, Japan
Majoring in Cost and Management Accounting
BA, MBA and Ph.D. from Kwansei Gakuin University

Main Publications
Behavioral Theory of Budgeting, 2nd edition, Tokyo: Chuou-Keizai-Sha 1997 (in Japanese).

Fundamentals of Cost Accounting, Tokyo: Chuou-Keizai-Sha 1999 (in Japanese).
An Introduction to Cost Accounting, Tokyo: Chuou-Keizai-Sha 2007 (in Japanese).
"Management Accounting in Japanese Multinational Corporations: Lessons from Matsushita and Sanyo," in Monden, Y. *et al.*, eds., *Value-Based Management of the Rising Sun*, World Scientific Pub. Co. 2006, Chapter 14 (Coauthored with K. Miyamoto).

Yoshiyuki Nagasaka
Professor of Faculty of Business Administration, Konan University, Kobe-city, Japan
Majoring in Managerial Accounting and Management Information
Bachelor of Engineering, Master of Engineering, and Doctor of Engineering from Osaka University

Main publications
"IT and Process Innovation in Japanese Enterprise," in Monden, Y. *et al.*, eds., *Value-Based Management of the Rising Sun*, World Scientific Pub. Co. 2006, Chapter 30.
Strategic Process Management (Research Project Series No. 4), Japanese Association of Management Accounting 2006 (in Japanese).
"Knowledge Management System for Manufacturing Design," A10, *Proc. of IPMM2003* 2003.
"Cost Reduction Approach to Manufacturing Administrative Departments in a Japanese Industry Machinery Manufacturer," in Monden, Y., ed., *Japanese Cost Management*, Imperial College Press 2000, Chapter 15.

Shufuku Hiraoka
Professor of Faculty of Business Administration, Soka University, Tokyo, Japan
Majoring in Managerial Accounting and Financial Statement Analysis
BA from Soka University, Master of Economics from Tsukuba University

Main publications
"Boundary between EVA and Other Economic Profit Measurements in Japan," *The Journal of Management Analysis Research* (Japan Management Analysis Association), Vol. 18, 2002, pp. 24–32 (in Japanese).
"Valuation and Goal Growth Rate of Business Segments: The Case Study of Matsushita Electric Works Ltd," in Monden, Y., ed., *Organization*

Design for Corporate Value Improvement and Management Accounting, Zeimukeirikyokai 2005, pp. 89–99 (in Japanese).
Contemporary Accounting and Financial Statements Analysis, Sou-sei-sya 2005 (in Japanese).
"Valuation of Business Based on EVA-Type Metrics in Japanese Companies," in Monden, Y. *et al.*, eds., *Value-Based Management of the Rising Sun*, World Scientific Pub. Co. 2006, Chapter 6.

Noriko Hoshi
Associate Professor of Faculty of Business Administration, Hakuoh University, Tochigi, Japan
Majoring in Managerial Accounting
BA from Hakuoh University, MBA and Ph.D. from Tsukuba University

Main publications
"Management of Franchise Chains and Multi-Divisional Organization: A Comparative Study on Royalty and Corporate Cost," in Monden, Y. *et al.*, eds., *Value-Based Management of the Rising Sun*, World Scientific Pub. Co. 2006, Chapter 8.
"Effect of Using Capital Efficiency Measures on Financial Performance," in Monden, Y., ed., *Organization Design for Corporate Value Improvement and Management Accounting*, Zeimukeirikyokai 2005, pp. 199–206 (in Japanese).
"Effects of Outsourcing in Manufacturing Companies on Consolidated Financial Performance," in Monden, Y., ed., *Corporate Design and Management Accounting*, Zeimukeirikyokai 2003, pp. 159–173 (in Japanese).
"Profit Evaluation Measure for the Division Managers in Japanese Decentralized Company: Focusing on Controllable and Corporate Costs," in Monden, Y., ed., *Japanese Cost Management*, Imperial College Press 2000, Chapter 20.